# HOLY QUR'AN

## AN INTIMATE PORTRAIT

John Herlihy

Holy Quran:
An Intimate Portrait

Ansar Books
Miami, Florida USA

ISBN: 0692260013
ISBN-13:9780692260012

# TABLE OF CONTENTS

-- Other Books --

by John Herlihy

_____

*In Search of the Truth*

*The Seeker and the Way*

*Veils and Keys*

*Modern Man at the Crossroads*

*Near and Distant Horizons*

*Borderlands of the Spirit*

*Wisdom's Journey*

*Journeys with Soul*

*Wisdom of the Senses*

*Islam For Our Time*

*The Essential René Guénon (ed.)*

Prologue

# A Book's Journey into Light

Everybody loves a good story, particularly if it involves some kind of travel, whether it be the account of such classic journeys as the trip of Livingston in search of the source of the Nile, the expedition of Lewis and Clark for the North West frontier passage through the Rockies to the Western shores of the American continent, or the voyages of Marco Polo along the Silk Route into the far-distant Orient. Some people have their own reasons for wanting to read books. My father, who loved reading all his life, added his own condition to what made a good story. He would read it only if it were true.

The story of the Qur'an, however, is like no other account that has ever existed and it is truer than anything my father ever read. The descent of the Qur'an from the Mind of the Supreme Being into the depths of the human mind in the sacred words of the Arabic language is a story whose earthly journey begins in the darkness of a cave in Makkah and ends in the light of the human heart where knowledge takes root and the human virtues flourish in a life well lived. It is a journey taken that will lead to an unexpected destination and a story told that will shape the future course of humanity as a rational and reflective being worthy of its gifts and attributes.

I am surprised by the number of people who are genuinely interested in the Holy Book of the Muslims and ask me probing questions about the Qur'an's origin and true nature. As a result, I decided not long ago to write down some thoughts that might address the kinds of questions that often arise from people with a sincere interest in better understanding its purpose and meaning, ranging from when and how the book came to be in the hands of the Muslims, to why they still treasure its sacred verses as knowledge and guidance in giving shape to the course of their daily lives. Many detailed and scholarly books have been written about the Qur'an in recent years—and down through the ages for that matter—with in-depth commentaries and analytical interpretations of its multi-layered meaning, but few books seek to uncover the secret that lies behind the sustained and devotional interest that Muslims the world over have preserved in their hearts when it comes to their reverence and love of God's inspiring revelation to humanity.

The Bible is well-known among Western readership familiar with the Christian tradition and its verses are easily identifiable by a broad segment of humanity across the globe. The Buddhist *Dhammapada* is the most widely read collection of sayings in verse form of the Buddha. Its opening verse is well familiar and oft-quoted by many people across the globe: "We are what we think." Nor do we intend to forget the writings of the Tao by Lao Tzu, a mysterious scribe, monk, mystic—the historical record is not sure how to describe him—a man of wisdom no doubt who disappeared into the mountain mist only to remain in the minds and hearts of millions of people who continue to read his pithy sayings about the "eternally nameless" that were originally written on bamboo stalks in the late 4$^{th}$ century BC. The Qur'an, however, is another matter altogether and continues to remain a mystery in many ways to many people—misunderstood, misread, and mistrusted—even though it contains the actual words of God eternally preserved, according to the Qur'an, on a "guarded tablet" (*lawh mahfouz, 85:22*) in Heaven.

The individual verses of the Qur'an were first delivered by the Archangel Gabriel over several decades as a recitation to the mind and heart of the Prophet Muhammad (PBUH)[1]; the Qur'an was later systematically codified as a formal book for the benefit of future generations. Its story has had a long and varied history that began its literal, historical journey in a cave outside of Makkah in the 7th century AD. Its luminous, symbolic journey, however, begins at the very borderland of time and eternity—the cosmic horizon we could call it—during the season of first creation when universal principles were born and

---

[1] An acronym PBUH used through this work stands for "peace be upon him", an epithet the traditions (*hadith*) encourage the Muslims to use when the name of the Prophet is invoked, out of respect and love for his memory. A spoken reference is made in Arabic; for simplicity's sake while remaining faithful to the traditional convention, the acronym will be used throughout this work.

cast into celestial laws that will never die.

Its remarkable journey from the darkness of a cave to light the world begins in the spirit of Truth which says that God exists as a single unifying principle that has created, sustains and guides the universe and all that lies within that vast field of dreams and awakenings. The writing of this book documents a journey that extends back in time beyond the 14 centuries of its literal inception on a journey from the outer fringes of time into the very heart of eternity in order to better understand why the Muslims continue to love and cherish their Holy Book. Even in this present era of secularism, materialism, and avowed insensitivity to the world of spirituality and the universal life of the spirit, the spirit of the book lives and the journey continues. The majority of Muslims around the globe continue to perpetuate the idea of the one God and its related principle of unity (*tawhid*) through their act of surrender (*islam*), giving Islam its name, and through their way of life (*din*) that gives practical meaning to their religion.

Ever since the descent of a revelatory scripture from Heaven and the coming of the Religion of Islam in the 7th century AD, tens of thousands—if not hundreds of thousands of books (*kutub*) and commentaries (*tafsir*)—have been written over the centuries about the Holy Qur'an from Islamic academics, scholars, and sheikhs, not to forget the Western orientalists, all of whom have poured over its meaning and analyzed its scope, parsed its nouns and verbs, dissected the elements of its grammar and style, established statistics concerning the number of chapters, verses, words and even letters,[2] and finally written esoteric commentaries down through the ages on the diversity of its meanings and the levels of its spirituality, in order to better understand the sacred text.

Arguments have arisen down through the centuries concerning the mystery of its origins, and people the world over have disputed its claim to be a revelatory scripture that represents the very words of the Divinity, identified in the Qur'an itself with the name of Allah, together with ninety-nine sacred names, "the best of names" (*al-asmaa' al-husna*), that distinguish His qualities and attributes. Critics have questioned its benevolence as a final dispensation from the Divine to the human,[3] and scrutinized the metaphoric descent of all knowledge and blessing that need be made available to humanity in order for

---

[2] The Abjad numbers are a decimal numeral system in which the 28 letters of the Arabic alphabet were assigned numeral value and have been used in the Arab world as a kind of mystic numerology since the coming of Islam in the 7th century.

[3] The Qur'an clearly identifies the Prophet as the "seal of the prophets" (*al-khatim al-anbiya*) and says outright that it is the last of a long line of revelations that have come to humanity over the ages.

people the world over to come to terms with the human condition.

Many Muslims themselves spend a lifetime becoming more and more familiar with the inner layers of knowledge and blessing their holy book contains. They recite whenever possible the sacred words and verses as a form of worship as well as a source of beatitude and blessing in order to fill their lives with its message of fulfillment of self and salvation of soul. Its epithets and verses are on their lips, in their language and in their hearts as remembrance of all they hold dear. The Qur'an as companion and friend accompanies individual Muslims wherever they go either literally (on their smart phones) or figuratively as a permanent guide in guiding them through life. On the other hand, many non-Muslims have no idea why the Qur'an plays such a major role in the lives of the Muslims, and why it virtually forms the cornerstone of their religion and the very heart stone of their lives.

The Jews have their scriptural testament preserved in the Torah, the Christians have the timeless Bible as their sacred scripture, with the life and times of Jesus Christ narrated in the four gospels of the New Testament (al-injīl in the Qur'an) as a source of inspiration for modern-day Christians. The Hindus find the source material of their spirituality in the Bhagavad-Gita, and Buddhist monks still chant the ancient sutras in Himalayan monasteries on the shelf of the world as the basis and springboard of their spirituality. It can be affirmed that no true world religion has touched the hearts of the people without an accompanying revelatory scripture of some sort to provide the essential guidance people need in life and to show them the way back to Heaven. However, most practitioners from these other great world religions have no idea of the role and significance the Qur'an plays in the lives of everyday Muslims. They have no idea why the Muslims revere and love the Holy Qur'an at whatever level of spirituality they may be, from the simple peasant farmer plowing his fields to the Emirs and Sheikhs of the middle crescent who roam the corridors of power in their palaces, but are obliged to abide by the injunctions written on the parchment of the sacred book unless they dare run the risk of losing their souls, if not their kingdoms.

The Muslims turn to the Qur'an for knowledge of themselves and the world, for guidance in living their lives, for inspiration when making decisions, and for support in times of trial and hardship. Its verses are whispered into the ear of the newly born at birth, becoming the first thing a Muslim infant hears in this world, and whenever possible, Qur'anic verses are whispered into the ear of the dying supplicant, becoming also the last thing a Muslim hears in this world. Worshippers and mystics whisper the sacred epithets of the Qur'an using their prayer beads and the opening chapter of the Qur'an forms the liturgical content in performing the Islamic prayer ritual five times a day. Even the mystics and Sufis who take part in silent and oral meditation (*dhikr*) are using the names of the Divinity identified within the verses of the Holy Book as the focus of their concentration and remembrance.

As we shall relate further on in subsequent chapters, Muslim children from many countries around the world, whether they speak Arabic as a native tongue or some other language such as Urdu, Turkish or Malay (referred to as Islamic languages), begin learning the strict pronunciation of the letters and vowels of the Arabic script at an early age in an unfailingly rigorous form of discipline in meeting the demands of the linguistic form of the book. By the time they are about ten years old, they have usually completed at least one full reading of the entire book and are adept at Qur'an reading, including all the rules and regulations that form the core of the science of *tajwīd* that distinguishes Qur'an recitation. When taken to heart, its sacred rhythms and harmonies overlay everything the Muslims think and do, at least in principle if not always in fact, and provide the backdrop and coloration of their minds and personalities when they incorporate into their lives the outwardly stated, as well as inwardly hidden, messages that abound within the sacred text.

For true Muslims, the recitation of the Qur'an never goes stale and never runs dry; there are levels of meaning to be uncovered and depths that may never be reached without sincere effort and constant probing as to the true meaning of the verses, and not just mindless mouthing of text to prove some theoretical point or to fulfill some ritual incantation. Some Muslims read the Qur'an daily, but at a minimum, most of the faithful try to read through all the verses of the Qur'an in the totality of its 30 equal parts[4] during the holy month of Ramadhan, thus completing the recitation of the book, oftentimes orally, at least once a year within the span of the holy month of Ramadhan. Many of the Qur'anic phrases and epithets are incorporated into their speech as a form of sacred remembrance virtually giving sacred color to the linguistic variances of a person's oral communication. Such phrases as God willing (*in sha'-Lah*) and praise to God (*al-hamdu-lil-Lah*) are common enough expression in speech, whether the language be Arabic, English or some other language such as Urdu or Turkish. The book holds a revered place in every Muslim home and is immediately reached for and taken in hand during times of both great happiness and great sorrow. In short, the Qur'an provides the response to the aura of mystery that engulfs the human condition here on earth with its

---

[4] Most notably, if not miraculously, the Qur'an is divided into thirty parts each of equal length and this greatly facilitates full Qur'an reading during the course of a month. Incidentally, it is also divided into seven equal parts, for those who wish to read the book within the context of one week.

haunting questions and inscrutable challenges.

The mystery of the Unseen (*al-ghaib*) that the Qur'an frequently mentions continues to haunt the sophisticated individual of today who lives in a rational, anti-spiritual world of materialism and secularism that denies outright any possibility of a reality beyond the physical reality that we can experience with the five senses, and that offers no goal or objective except the singular pursuit of pleasure and satisfaction of the human ego as an end in itself in this world. The concept of the Unseen substantiates the human impulse to have faith in something that transcends the world of sights and smells and sounds that verify for us so convincingly the true nature of this world. It lies hidden within every blade of grass and every flower petal. It rides the wings of butterflies and awakens the luminosity of the firefly. The wind bends the sacred oak tree in prostration and stirs the waves of the ocean to magisterial heights. Within every physical object, whether animate or inanimate, lies the unfathomable premonition of knowledge that lies beyond the realm of the physical world. It is a mystery that keeps humanity guessing and will never give up its secret until death knocks on our door and the light of "this world" is extinguished. Then, as a Qur'anic verse pointedly states: "The veil will be lifted from their eyes, and thy sight is keen." (50:22)

The main reason for writing this personal profile of the Qur'an is to attempt to explain to interested non-Muslims why the Muslims both love and cherish the Holy Qur'an as an extension of themselves, of the world, and of the great universe that has been created by God as a Living Presence as well as the Supreme Reality. By way of extension, the Muslim themselves may be interested in learning what their beloved book means to a person such as myself, who came to Islam as an outsider, who took up the Qur'an for the first time, wondering what Allah has chosen to say through the words and verses, a book like none other, full of revelations and secrets and mysteries, not to mention answers to questions that could not otherwise be known.

Without question, the holy Qur'an still plays a primary role in the lives of the Muslims. It has become imbedded within their language, has become a part of their household, forms the oral basis of the prayer ritual, serves as a form of worship through Qur'anic recitation, epitomizes both the visual and sonoral arts in the form of Islamic calligraphy and Qur'anic psalmody, lies on the tongue and within the heart of the Muslims as the source knowledge of their worldview, and finally forms the bottom line of their being and the very foundation and ground of their spiritual life. To the Muslims, the Qur'an contains the actual words of God transmitted through the vehicle of the Arabic language. As such, they have a divine vibration and rhythm, in addition to containing all the knowledge a person needs to know in order to fulfill themselves and find salvation. It is a revelation that articulates through letters, verses, and chapters what no human had heard before.

I am not an academician or scholar and distance myself from the Western orientalists, but the fact of my conversation to Islam 40 years ago perhaps gives me the possibility of seeing the Qur'an through fresh eyes, unfiltered as it were by cultural orientation or the habitual forces at work when one is born into a given belief system. I remember that when I was on the threshold of becoming Muslim, I felt fascinated by the possibility that there was a book full of guidance and light, a communication from the Divine to the human, preserved for humanity *in situ* in its original form. When I embraced Islam and formally became a Muslim nearly four decades ago, I read the Qur'an for the first time (in translation of course; familiarity with the original Arabic text would come later) at a time when the mind and heart are most susceptible to spiritual influence and could see things firsthand by virtue of free choice, without the encumbrances of history, culture, habit, accident of birth, and other forms of excess baggage that may inhibit the natural flow of understanding and faith from the human to the Divine.

To accomplish our objective in writing this tribute of the Holy Qur'an, the reader will find that we have divided the work into two equal parts, with nine discrete chapters in each part on a selected topic. In Part One, we have laid out and clarified the historical context in which the Qur'an was delivered, the circumstances around which the descent of the revelation was made known to humanity, how the initial recitation of the revelation by the Archangel Gabriel to the Prophet Muhammad (PBUH) came to be compiled and codified into a single book for future generations, and finally the influence the Qur'an had in the development of Islamic culture and science across the early centuries of Islam's growing stature as a global force. Many people today know of the existence of the Qur'an as the holy book of the Muslims, no doubt because the verses are often quoted by media pundits and terrorists alike to prove some obscure point that has nothing to do with the universal truths of the revelation, but they have very little idea of the historical narrative that brought the Islamic scripture to humanity in the first place or the context in which it was delivered.

In Part Two, we explore more deeply the spiritual life of the book which becomes the spiritual life of the Muslims who read and recite its verses. The Religion of Islam after all actually began with the descent of the first initial verses through the Archangel Gabriel to the mind of the Prophet Muhammad (PBUH). It is virtually the heart and soul of the religion. In fact, without the sacred revelatory verses of the Qur'an, it is safe to say there would be no Religion of Islam. We have sub-titled the book "An Intimate Portrait", because in unveiling its very heart as a living presence for the Muslims, we hope to reveal the source and origin of all the emotions and higher sentiments that have descended to humanity and will ascend back to God by making life's journey a personal journey with the Holy Book in hand and in heart. In addition to several chapters that identify the Qur'an as a book of knowledge and a book of blessing, I have included a practical first-hand account of how the Muslims, whether they are young children, natural born Muslims, non-Arabic speaking Muslims, or Muslim converts such as myself, learn to come to terms with the correct recitation of the verses in Arabic, including a focused knowledge of the correct pronunciation of the letters and complete awareness of the rules contained within the science of *tajwid* that govern the sonorous chanting of the sacred words and verses.

As we shall soon relate, the Qur'an is a companion and friend to the Muslims wherever they may be and whatever stage of life they may find themselves. It serves as lantern in the darkness, beacon on the shores of this world, and light in the form of knowledge and blessing with the power to shape the human heart into a unified whole in reflection of the universal principle of unity that the one God represents. It illuminates the soul of God's believing servants, all those who resolve the mystery of life and the secret of the human condition by surrendering themselves to the principle of the one God who unifies the multiplicity of the universe into a single, unified Whole. This is the first and final meaning of *tawhīd*, the principle of unity that the Religion of Islam has come to proclaim, a principle that lies at the heart of the Qur'an as well as at the crystalline core of all the great religions of the world. The overwhelming challenge for the Muslims is to integrate the spirit of the Book into the spirit of their lives to become a living revelation, so that the light of the book shines forth as their own light, a book's journey of light into the heart of the Muslims as they make their own journey back to God. As the Qur'an aptly states: "We come from God and to Him will we return." (2:156)

Let us examine more closely what the book has to offer, how it came into being, what it means to the Muslims, and why they love and cherish the sacred verses like nothing else on earth. Let us uncover the hidden treasures that lie in waiting as celestial offerings from the Divine to the human. Let us experience its compelling mystique that makes itself known as an instrument of rhythmic and sacred sound with which no melody can compare in this world. Let us set aside all arrogance and ignorance and let the heart quicken to the meaning of the sacred verses. Let us open the book to lay claim to an ancient wisdom that has journeyed through time from the darkness of a cave in the heart of Arabia to the light of the human heart, a beacon of knowledge and blessing that has survived the onslaught of time for past, present, and future generations of humanity and will continue to do so until the end of time.

# PART ONE

# HISTORICAL REVELATION

## Chapter One

## Inside Revelation

---

"Say: The (Qur'an) was sent down by Him Who knows the mystery in the heavens and the earth; He is Oft-Forgiving, Most Merciful." (25: 6).

Before embarking on a course that will take us through the intricacies of the Qur'an's historical context, its traditional injunctions, and its mystical lure, we need to clarify for today's interested readership the true significance of "revelation" and its relationship within the framework and meaning of the term religion itself. The individual religions are earthly manifestations as part of the historical record in the descent of knowledge from the Divine Source to the mind/heart of the human recipient. The concept of religion finds its origin and sustained relevance in the descent of a revelation from the Divine Being to the human creation. The actual form of the religion, and its entire structural framework, is born of divine revelation, a Word or *Logos*, in which the Supreme Being identifies Himself as the true reality and the only reality worthy of our worship and praise.

Every religious form builds its supporting tradition—social, cultural or spiritual—from the bedrock of a revelatory scripture that lays out in detail the essential knowledge of God and all that relates to the required human response to that knowledge. This revelatory knowledge speaks directly to the human faculties and senses. Then these inner faculties and the five senses process this knowledge and set the scene within the mind and heart for the development of the virtuous life through the pursuit of human excellence (*ihsan*) over the course of a lifetime. As knowledge from the Divine Realm, universal revelation substantiates each of the individual religious forms with its knowledge of universal origins and the metaphysical principles that underlie all of existence. As such, the main significance of revelation lies in the fact of its "Word-of-God" quality, taking part as it does in the character of absoluteness and universality transcending all forms of limitation characteristic of "this world", from sacred laws, to rites and rituals, to the importance of sacred symbols and myths and to the efficacy of the spiritual disciplines, all of which contain blessing (*barakah*) for Muslims, as well as knowledge that is absolute and beyond human argument.

In the Islamic context, the Holy Qur'an is the primary source of all knowledge *par excellence* within the Islamic tradition and both a sacred and intimate communication from the Mind of God to the mind of humanity, offering mankind divine, sacred verses in which God speaks directly to individuals in the words of the Arabic language. It is the direct descent of the essential knowledge from the Divine Being to the human being through Sacred Speech. The Religion of Islam began as a spiritual force with the first descent of the revelation to the Prophet Muhammad (PBUH) and with the arrival of the final verses came the completion and fulfillment of the religion as a spiritual force on earth for all future generations. "This day have I perfected your religion for you, completed My favor upon you, and have chosen for you Islam as your religion." (5:3)

The meaning of the word "religion", in the Islamic context, goes beyond the concept of revelation as the descent of knowledge from the Divine to the human as point of departure and source of the religion. The English word "religion", in Arabic, Qur'anic phrasing *al-dīn*, does little justice to the full significance of the word's meaning in Arabic, because the concept of *al-dīn* in Islam is less formal and more practical than the meaning understood within the English context of the word "religion". In addition to being the literal translation of the Arabic word, the term *dīn* signifies a way of life that adheres to a sacred norm in which the entire life is molded to become a way of being and not just isolated components of one's life style. It is a way of knowledge that commences with the descent of the Qur'an and the inscription of the pen on the heart of the Muslims, echoing the very first verse, in the form of a direct command, that descended into the mind and heart of the Prophet in the cave of Mt. Hira in the hills outside of Makkah: "Read (recite) in the name of thy

Lord Who created . . . . " (96:1)

To that end, what the Muslims call the Sunnah comprises not only the verses, laws, and guidance of the Holy Qur'an; but also the sayings of the Prophet, compiled a century or more after his death, that perpetuate his attitudes, his behavior and virtually his way of life down to the most arcane detail in which nothing escapes the scrutiny of the principle of unity that draws all earthly matters together into a single unifying principle. The Prophet himself represents the supreme example of an individual person who was the human receptacle and instrument of the sacred verses, the very words and harmonious energy of the Holy Spirit brought down into the practices of daily life.

Before we actually pick up the book and examine the verses and chapters of the Holy Qur'an in order to better understand its ancient mystique, its compelling attraction for the Muslims, and why Muslims love and cherish the book as an extension of themselves, we need a better understanding of the concept and nature of "revelation" itself, what it is and what it hopes to achieve as an instrument of communication for the Supreme Being. The concept of revelation needs to be addressed and understood since in today's world, the notion that there is a descent of universal divine knowledge in the form of sacred words to be recited or written on the page and preserved as a treasure is alien indeed to the mentality of modern individuals. People want to know who, what, when, where, why, responding to questions that run wild in the doubting mind that such a thing is possible, much less desirable.

Nothing challenges the secular, rationalist and earth-bound mind of modern individuals more than does the traditional, indeed the perennial, concept of revelation that embraces all religions. That the eternal word of a Divinity can cut through the fabric of the space-time continuum of "this world" with the knife blade of a knowledge of the reality seems incredible to the modern mind fully steeped in the believability of matter. This mentality is totally dependent upon the power of human reason to lead the way through the dark mystery and paradox of life. It requires people to accept as a matter of principle that there is a descent of a universal Logos, representing the Mind of God through a Divine Discourse that can shatter the illusions of "this world" by its very entrance into the world of multiplicity and then re-constitute and unify the pieces back together into a single and unified tapestry of truth. The idea itself requires an openness of mind and a willingness of heart to seek knowledge anywhere that the modern, scientific person is unwilling to extend, draped as we are in the rough folds of a physical, secular and materialistic philosophy that promises us freedom and happiness, not to forget a steady evolution to higher states of being whatever that may entail, but that actually

3

gives us only further uncertainty and doubt about who we really are and what we need to accomplish in life before death closes the window of consciousness on the individual soul.

The reality of a descent of knowledge in the form of revelation simply will not go away, however, in spite of the skeptical denial of modern scientists and contemporary sophisticates the world over, who reject outright all higher forms of spiritual experience and other levels of reality by insisting upon the doctrine of matter over mind and reason over the universal instincts of the human intellect in the pursuit and understanding of knowledge of the true reality. Revelation continues to remain the "key" to the perennial mysteries[5] of creation, life-genesis, and the origin of man precisely because the revealed word of the Divinity serves humanity viscerally, intellectually, psychologically and spiritually as the principal source of knowledge with primordial origins, because it traces the origin of the creation and the genesis of life forms back to the Divine Being as Creator of all life forms, and because it identifies once and for all the true nature of Reality within the framework of First Cause and Ultimate Source of all creation.

What haunts the existential worldview portrayed by the modern scientific establishment is the fact that human reason, together with the provability of matter as the basis of the scientific method and the cornerstone of the worldview resulting from it, is not surprisingly a credible source of universal knowledge. Instead, human reason is a human faculty, a sophisticated instrument if you will, for dealing with the demands of all primary sources of knowledge. In and of itself, human reason has no substance; for example, the faculty of reason will not tell you anything that it has not already been told from elsewhere, through revelation, through intuition, through the thinking process, and even—perhaps especially—through the perception of the outer senses. Its knowledge is borrowed in the same way that the light of the moon is borrowed from the sun. Yet, reason and the provability of matter through the observation of the senses, particularly the sense of sight (seeing is believing), constitute the basic sources of knowledge within the scientific framework, giving birth to the secular philosophy of rationalism as the polar opposite—and answer—to the mysterious descent of revelation of seemingly divine origin.

Rationalism continues to retain a deep-seated conviction that the physical senses are the true means of providing information that is certain and

---

[5] "Whether we like it or not, we live surrounded by mysteries, which logically and existentially lead us towards transcendence." Frithjof Schuon, *From the Divine to the Human*, Bloomington, Ind: World Wisdom Books, 1981, p. 141.

unquestionable, thus attesting to the objectivity of matter, a conviction that persists in the popular imagination in spite of the fact that quantum mechanics has virtually demolished the concept of 'solid matter' as a valid working hypothesis in the structural framework of the modern scientific worldview. Frithjof Schuon turns the tables on those who accuse religious-minded people of believing without seeing: "Scientists condemn themselves to seeing only what they believe; logic for them is their desire not to see what they do not want to believe."[6] Seeing may be believing for the modern establishment; but more importantly and worse still, not seeing is active disbelieving.

Schuon has further characterized the anti-spiritual ambiance of our time with the following words: "One of the greatest successes of the devil was to create around man surroundings in which God and immortality appear unbelievable."[7] During our modern era, if there is anything more difficult for the secular and scientific mind to accept as a working hypothesis than belief in the idea of God as Supreme Being, it is undoubtedly the traditional belief that revelation represents the absolute word of God, a belief still adhered to by over a billion Muslims the world over who revere the sacred text by considering the book a universe unto itself in which they place the very structure and framework of their lives. If a particular mentality refuses to believe in the idea of God, much less God Himself, then the concept of God "speaking" to humanity through the words of revelation will equally fall into the realm of a fantasy that modern sophisticates refuse to indulge themselves.

Similarly, if a person believes in God as a matter of spiritual instinct, if not as a result of proven scientific observation such as the proof that matter exists as the sole believable reality,[8] simple logic demands that the Divinity convey the essential knowledge of the reality to humanity in some comprehensible manner. What better way is there for people to come to know "in advance" and "eternally" the essential knowledge they need to know in order to fulfill their human vocation than through the Voice, the Word, indeed the very Mind and Consciousness of God, amounting to the ultimate act of benevolence and mercy[9] from the Divine Being to the human being. For millennia within many

---

[6] Frithjof Schuon, *From the Divine to the Human* (Bloomington, In: World Wisdom Books, 1981), p. 141.

[7] *Ibid.*, p. 148.

[8] Or does it? Physicists will now tell you otherwise in keeping with the indeterminate theory. The question of what is "real" and what is "illusory" is as controversial today as it has ever been through history.

[9] In the Islamic perspective, Allah is above all a benevolent Deity. Inscribed on the throne (*al-arsh*) of God are the words: "My Mercy precedes My Wrath."

traditional cultures[10], sacred scripture has breached the chasm that exists between the knowledge of the Divine and the ignorance of the human and will continue to do so, as long as there are people who can recognize the truth when they are confronted by its clear, open face. "Wherever you turn, there is the Face of God." (2:115)

Part of the contemporary prejudice that exists against the possibility of the descent of revelation in the form of a divine communication from God to humanity lies in the fact that the modern mentality, in its surface approach to the mysteries of life and because of its literalist and matter-based bias in its search for the knowledge of origins and final ends, makes a certain amount of simplistic assumptions about the important implications of a divine descent of knowledge without contemplating the full range, significance, and consequences of such an approach. They reject the concept of revelation, not through the logic of an intellectual argument and not through any mode of experimentation that examines the experience of billions of people over thousands of years. They reject it simply because it doesn't conform to their belief in the provability and thus the objectivity of matter and the supremacy of the human mind to reason its way through the labyrinthine mysteries of life based on the laws of mathematics and the rational experience of the physical senses.

Modern science—and the proponents of its secular philosophy—set out to explore, explain, and catalogue the vast and infinite complexity of the Real on its own, without the aid of the first—indeed the principial—science of the traditional world, namely metaphysics. It relies on the world of physics rather than metaphysics and it pursues the science of the relative rather than knowledge of the Absolute. In fact, it is partly because revelation identifies itself as the absolute word of God that modern science rejects it outright; Scientists today actually bristle at the definitive finality of the word "absolute". In the modern scientific worldview, human reason, inanimate matter and the physical senses establish the norm, set the standard and constitute the primary sources of knowledge concerning the true nature of reality.

There remains, however, one major existential conditional. What if, and admittedly it is a colossal **IF**, the principal mysteries confronting humanity were never to be disclosed? What if, for example, there were no hope of ever realizing, through the strictly scientific process of inquiry, the essential knowledge that lies behind the face of the great and universal secrets that

---

[10] According to the Qur'an: *Every nation has been sent a messenger* (10: 47), thus attesting to both the universality and the particularity of revealed scripture for every time and place.

season our lives with their unrelenting inscrutability and their unnerving power of attraction. After all, traditional history has amply proven that the Divinity has no special desire to reveal all and everything for no good reason, and even the revelation itself is articulated in such a way that it is a key for the open-hearted and a veil to the hard-hearted, summarily protecting itself from disbelieving souls with a shield of impenetrability. The Divine Reality does not limit itself to revealing the multiple aspects of its Being; on the contrary, it conceals as much as it reveals, the ample proof of this being that God continues to conceal the knowledge of origins and final ends totally from purely rational, mathematical minds precisely because the revelation is as much a veil as it is a key. Perhaps that is why people living in more traditional times have always answered the existential mysteries with the human affirmation of faith; perhaps that is why the modern, scientific establishment continues to attempt to answer the great metaphysical questions in the spirit of their own limited inquiry that casts away any possibility of accepting a truth that cannot be verified through its own well-identified, well-established—and narrowing—terms of reference.

♠ ♠ ♠

When we consider revelation as a manifestation from the spirit world, we must also think of religion as such in its conceptual and original form, as opposed to the specificity and particular aura of the individual religions that come to humanity in different eras of time for a specific civilization and mentality. In fact, the two concepts of religion and revelation are inseparable; one cannot exist without the other. There was a time when religion was one, just as God is the expression of a singular unity and just as there was one, original primordial revelation, revealed as guidance for Adam and Even when they exited and descended from the paradise. "Then Adam received (certain) words from his Lord. And He turned towards him (mercifully)." (2:37) In that sense, religion itself is one tree that grew during the primordial era and subsequently separated into different branches or manifestations in keeping with different time periods and different mentalities that required special guidance particular to their era and mental frame with a particular civilization with their own unique needs.

In its essential meaning, religion offers mankind the definitive argument on behalf of the Supreme Being, an argument that fully clarifies the mystery of man's origin, the meaning of his existence, and the nature of his final end. As such, the argument for a higher reality identifies a hierarchy of being and other levels of reality that include an evolution of soul through the various stages of life toward the perfection of the soul and promise of eternal life. This theme has taken different forms down through history including a *Logos*, a Word, a Person, and a Book. In short, religion relies on some form of revelation that amounts to a divine communication from God to man, the bridge between Heaven and earth, the sacred speech from the Superior Intelligence. The Creator has communicated with His thinking creatures that have the intelligence to comprehend the knowledge of God and the free will to meet the existing moment with the eternal moment of truth. The definitive proof of God lies within the knowledge of God's revelation by virtue of what it contains and within humans by virtue of the self-revelation they are in principle.

Paradoxically, contemporary individuals have developed a mentality that permits the pursuit of a science that replaces the simplicity and clarity of the divine argument with a theoretical reasoning that is complex, obscure, and thoroughly inaccessible in its implications to the mass population. For example, traditional people once implicitly accepted the myth of the creation of Adam *ex nihilo* and thereby displayed a willingness to overlook the apparent naiveté of the simple myth for the sake of the profound truth contained within that myth. The myth was a simple instrument of conveyance, a symbolic narrative story, to convey a profound truth that might otherwise be inexpressible and thus inaccessible to the human mentality. Contemporary individuals, on the other hand, do not see through the transparency of the myth with their rigid and literal mindset that sees everything in terms of the external form, often at the expense of the truth that lies beyond the physical form. In return, people today have the outer form of a truth, namely a cold fact—such as the blind forces of a physical evolution—that brings with it no subtlety, no imagination, no hope and ultimately no real foundation in truth's composite truth.

Secondly, religion—every religion—requires a spiritual discipline of its adherents and provides the framework for this spiritual discipline through its duties, rites, rituals and obligations. For example, the Islamic tradition speaks of the battle of the soul (*jihad al-nafs*) which is identified as the overwhelming necessity of all people to transcend their weaknesses and limitations according to their human nature. The religion also provides the five earthly duties, often referred to as pillars (*arkan*) including prayer and fasting, so that this inner *jihad* and this concerted effort can be contained within clear and self-contained parameters. The beauty of the spiritual disciplines is not only that they call for effort on the part of the believer, but also that they serve as a vehicle for the shower of divine blessing (*barakah*) that must accompany every spiritual struggle of the inwardly striving soul.

Thirdly, religion contains veils as well as keys and is not simply an open door through which people can pass into the mysteries of the unseen (*al-*

*ghaib*). The religion itself contains certain veils that protect the true extent of its knowledge and substance from the profane mentality, such as those who would abuse the knowledge contained in the religion. In other words, sufficient knowledge is made available to all people so they may save themselves, but the entire body of knowledge is not made available to everyone *carte blanche*. Behind the veil of the exoteric (formal) religion there lies the esoteric (mystical) dimension that hides and protects knowledge and understanding of the higher realities and the spiritual possibilities that are available to humans, provided that they have reached a certain level of spirituality. The esoteric knowledge is protected behind veils and is made accessible only to those people who have earned the right of access to that knowledge and have already proven themselves through the spiritual disciplines to be worthy receptacles of that knowledge.

A spiritual veil in the form of symbols and myths must exist to contain the various levels of knowledge within the context of the religion. Behind their implicit veil, these symbols and myths contain the capacity to withhold or divulge layers of meaning in order to instruct and guide the multi-levelled mentalities that the religious perspective must address and satisfy. If there were not a veil, or a number of veils, separating the human mentality from the knowledge of the Unseen (*al-ghaib*), then everything would be fully apparent at a glance and the mystery and spiritual challenge at the heart of the human condition would be forever neutralized. Rather, the religions contain levels of knowledge separated from the strictly worldly mentality by veils and protect as much as they reveal the divine mystery. Much of the knowledge contained in the religions remains protected behind a veil, but the possibility exists for lifting the veil through aspiration and spiritual effort that are the by-product of the spiritual disciplines.

Finally, religion provides people with a key that not only gives them access to the knowledge of God through intelligence, but also allows the possibility of an experience that amounts to a spiritual consciousness of the reality of God in all His wondrous beatitude. The concept of the term "religion" can be summed up with the two words "knowledge" and "action", for knowledge and action are reflected within the religions as doctrine and spiritual practices respectively, and are in turn reflected within the human being as intelligence and will since intelligence implies knowledge and free will leads to practical action based on a person's desires.

Knowledge, of course, always refers to knowledge of the Divine Being and this is necessarily veiled from the direct perception of humanity, thus the need for revelation in the form of words and verses, a person, or a book. Action, on the other hand, refers to the inner person in movement, expressing one's intelligence and will through spiritual experience manifested in this world, a sense of the sacred presence of God, and an open consciousness of the Divine Being. A truly spiritual man or women is a "person in movement" from the outer world of direct and concrete experience to the inner world of direct and synthetic experience. Because of human intelligence, the spiritual seeker recognizes the profound distance that exists between oneself and God. Because of the faculty of free will that can choose God over the world, the spiritual seeker has the proximity and presence of the Divine Being as one's innermost heart's desire.

The modern-day challenge for people everywhere both young and old is to put into practice what we profess to believe in, to combine the knowledge of God with the spiritual life as prescribed in a particular religion of choice, such as the Religion of Islam, in pursuit of higher consciousness and spiritual awakening of the individual soul. The importance of the interaction between knowledge and implementation through real-life experience is the key to understanding the entire approach to this vital study. It is intended, above all, to be a practical and personal account of what it means to take part in revelation as a form of guidance, not only to the sacred and revealed knowledge that Islam has made available to humanity since the descent of the Qur'an over 14 centuries ago to a Bedouin in the heart of Arabia, but also as a means of internalizing that knowledge within the mind and heart, thus inculcating within our thoughts and emotions a sense of the sacred that becomes a part of the practical side of life in today's busy and modern world.

This combination of knowledge and action must be applied to the everyday situations that life has to offer, and it must be internalized within the mind and heart, so that our actions shine with the light of virtue (*ihsan*). There is a well known *hadith* that summarizes very well the true nature of the dilemma concerning how to internalize the knowledge of the Unseen with the practical applications in life. We are told in a well-known *hadith* that human excellence in the form of virtue, in Qur'anic Arabic *ihsan*, can be achieved if we "worship Allah as if you actually saw Him; for even if you do not see Him, nevertheless, He sees you." In other words, the perennial challenge of all Muslims is to lift the veil that separates them from the direct experience of the unknown and unseen mystery (*sirr*) in life, by "worshipping Allah" through this great earthly conditional "as if", opening in compensation the inner eye of the heart in order to see and experience that which cannot be seen with the naked eye.

There can be no denying the fact that it is not easy to live a life of spirituality in today's anti-spiritual world. Everything that surrounds us, from the manner in which people eat and dress to the attitudes people have regarding their own origins and final end, are shaped by the prevailing secular and scientific worldview that dominates modern life with its insistence on human reason and the five senses as the sole instruments of observation, with matter itself as the *material prima* of a reality that does not extend beyond the physical plane of existence. When the body dies, according to the modern scientific worldview and nearly universally accepted by the psyche of the modern mentality, the spirit, such as it is within the modern framework, dies with it. That is what the modern scientific worldview tells us about the true extent of human life.

Needless to say, this notion runs counter to the spiritual culture of Islam that claims a knowledge that falls off the edge of matter and reaches beyond the physical horizon to reveal an integrated and unified Reality that lies beyond the purely physical manifestation of the world. As Muslims living in the modern world, we also need to actively make a choice, and in choosing pass through a door and take up residence in the heart, in order to discover and experience firsthand what has been revealed to us by the Supreme Being and Creator of the universe. This is the message of the primordial revelation that Islam has come to remember and emulate. The Religion of Islam is the modern-day religion of surrender, the primordial *islam* re-awakened and the primordial religion re-confirmed for present and future generations in today's struggling and bewildered world.

## Chapter Two

The Islamic Worldview

Before embarking on a personal and intimate journey into the heart of the Qur'anic experience; before endeavoring to recreate and explain the process of Qur'anic recitation as a form of worship in Islam; before identifying the significance of living within the enlightened presence of the holy book and profiting by its treasure of guidance and knowledge, we need to go back briefly in time to the very edge of eternity, when the individual soul of humanity accepted the sacred trust between the Divine and the human mentioned in the Qur'an, in which Allah asked the human soul the simple question: "Am I not your Lord," and the human soul responded with a simple answer: "Yes, we witness you!" (7:172) The sacred trust, momentous as it is as the initiator of the unique relationship between the Divine and the human, implies many things, not the least being that God would provide humanity with the essential knowledge of universal reality in the form of a primordial revelation when Adam received "verses from his Lord" (2:37) and was given "the names of things" (2:33).

In fulfillment of the sacred trust, human souls would respond with their own heart-felt ascent through the perpetual spark of faith, the intimacy of prayer and the life-changing modes of worship of the Divinity through sound thinking and good works (the oft-mentioned *salihan* in Qur'anic terminology). This marriage of knowledge and action forms the human—as well as universal—principle of the primordial worldview that acknowledges a Supreme Being who "knows what is in the heart and breast of mankind" (67:13), a Divine Being in communication with human beings who worship and praise God with the same devotion as the rest of nature, by being true to its true human nature and faithful to the sacred trust. "The seven heavens and the earth and all they contain glorify Him, and there is not a thing (in this world) but extols His glory; but you do not understand how they glorify Him." (17:44)

In this way, at the dawn of the human narrative, the primordial worldview gave shape, coloration, and substance to the way humanity understood and responded to the particular context they found themselves in here on earth. Many millennia later, during the life of our own time, humanity still relies on the support of a worldview to put into perspective how they understand the world and their place in that world. In today's world, however, there are the two great, modern-day worldviews that people must actively choose between. Like two great ships on a vast ocean, the traditional and modern scientific worldviews float through the waters of our time with the expressed purpose of taking us to the ultimate destination of the human destiny within a universal framework that not only makes sense, but that supposedly is in keeping with the true nature of reality. Regrettably, they are on a collision course with each other that could have devastating consequences for humanity if their present course goes unchecked.

Since the 17th century, the advance of modern science has proclaimed a universe whose laws are open to discovery through human reason and an emerging scientific methodology that plots reality through a precise study of the physical world of matter. The new science of that time sought, in the uncompromising words of one of its earliest exponent, Francis Bacon, "not to imagine or suppose, but to *discover* what nature does or may be made to do."[11] Similar to the traditional point of view, the modern, scientific mind is concerned with the imponderable mysteries of existence, and has sought to equip present and future generations with a long list of provable, objective, and thus convincing facts that may well serve humanity in the interest of factual truths whose physical presence are substantiated through the scientific method through reason and the observation of the senses. What modern science discovers, however, must not be at the expense of the reality that lies at the heart of all existence, as well as the heart of humanity, a perennial truth

---

[11] Loren Eiseley, *The Unexpected Universe* (New York: Harcourt Brace Jovanorich, Inc., 1969), p. 27.

that is proclaimed by all the great world traditions and accepted by countless billions of people down through the millennia.

The grand divide between modern science and traditional knowledge is everywhere apparent from their methods of study and in their angle of approach to the pursuit of knowledge of the Reality (al-Haqq) as a fundamental goal of humanity. The method of scientific research is outwardly directed, while the pursuit of traditional knowledge is directed inwardly. Modern science proves its theoretical principles through precise observations and deductions of sense data, together with the theories and facts that emerge from the pursuit of the scientific method, using the faculty of reason and the five senses as the primary instruments of verification of a reality identified as "objective" because it is "physical" and can be seen as a "fact".

Religion, on the other hand, finds its source of knowledge and inspiration in revelation and the human ability to understand the truth through the higher faculty of the intellect which then discriminates between truth and error through the use of intelligence and its brother reason, followed by realization and internalization of that truth through direct spiritual experience. The focus of science is on the physical manifestations within nature, while the focus of religion and its supporting traditions is on the human nature (fitrah) of humanity and the unique faculties of perception that humans enjoy as their birthright, permitting them to strive to understand the workings of their inner nature and attempting to grow beyond the limiting horizon of the earthly condition by putting into practice what they profess to believe, thus positioning individuals for a greater awakening than they could ever achieve on their own. Science is knowledge and its application within the physical world; religion is knowledge and transcendence of self within the "meta"-physical world.

These two worldviews clearly present two kinds of knowledge that have emerged down through history to the present moment, namely a traditional knowledge that finds its origin and source within the great world religions that ultimately trace their source and origin back to the primordial knowledge given to Adam, and the scientific knowledge that has evolved since the Renaissance with its well specified reliance on human reason and empirical methods of investigation based on reasoning and the pinpoint observation of facts and data. What makes traditional knowledge based on revelation the basis of a complete world order is the fact that far beyond its actuality lays its divine source that substantiates it and gives it meaning and a living vitality. What makes traditional knowledge unique is the fact that, because of its source within the Divinity, everything within the body of the tradition must already be there from the very beginning, in its essence. The latter developments of the tradition and its full articulation within a culture, the shades and colors of the traditional knowledge, and the diversity of its scope down through the ages of civilizations only serve to make it more explicit, without adding new elements from another, arbitrary—in fact merely human— source. According to Islamic doctrine, there is only one first origin and source, namely the knowledge of Unity (*tawhīd*) and the knowledge of the One (*al-Ahad*).

We wish to highlight the fact that traditional knowledge generally is shaped by the nature of its origins and we wish to emphasize the importance of identifying the first principles that form the coloration and ambiance of its enduring truth. The recognition of truth, the pursuit of knowledge, and the wisdom of life find their impetus and source within a realm that transcends the temporal and the earthly. It is the sacred realm of universals, of first principles, of first knowledge and first origins that live now and forever as they exist in the eternal day of eternity. It is a realm, needless to say, that has been identified through the revelation with the names of God representing His qualities and attributes. He is the First (*al-Awwal*) and the Last (*al-Akhir*), the Outer (*az-Zahir*) and the Inner (*al-Batin*). All that we know and the entire basis of our lives and unique destiny come from He who is the Knowing (*al-Alīm*), the Living (*al-Hayy*) and the Eternal (*al-Samad*). The 99 names of God are a great comfort to the Muslims. Each name identifies a unique quality that every Muslim would like to seal within themselves as a living tribute to their humanity viewed through the unique filter of the divine qualities and attributes.

The question of the source and authenticity of knowledge that serves as a paradigm of self-knowledge and as a worldview to explain the true nature of the cosmic reality strikes at the heart of the modern mentality's understanding of the word *knowledge* and the modern scientific approach to its acquisition. The question of source is fundamental to the entire endeavor in the search for knowledge and will ultimately define the contours, color and shape of any framework of knowledge that calls itself a worldview, whether it is metaphysical, traditional, rational or scientific knowledge. The question of the truth of a given framework of knowledge highlights, perhaps more than we would like to admit, the modern-day approach to the search for a unified theory of knowledge that serves as the purpose of the scientific enterprise. A comprehensive worldview seeks to project into the consciousness of the world its objectivity, its persuasiveness, and its validity to the extent that it is accessible and believable to mass populations at its source, is convincing at simple levels of expression, and is profound in its truth.

While no one would deny that a comprehensive knowledge of the reality is of vital interest and importance to humanity and always has been, during these times the modern-day approach and understanding of existential and ultimately essential knowledge has been two-edged, while the search for a complete knowledge runs forward on dual tracks. On the one hand, we have the traditional knowledge that has come down to us through the millennia and is followed instinctively by billions of people. For ages, the traditional worldview has embodied higher knowledge, spiritual knowledge, essential knowledge, traditional knowledge and metaphysical knowledge that ultimately reflects the instinctive and universal inclination of people in every time and place to resolve their doubts, have faith and believe in the existence of a Supreme, Divine Being. On the other hand, the defining worldview of the 21st century is a "scientific knowledge" that marks the parameters of the contemporary worldview within the limited framework of mind and matter as the *de facto* arbiter of what is real and what is not. Alternatively, this knowledge has been referred to as speculative knowledge, rational knowledge, secular knowledge, empirical knowledge, and of course scientific knowledge, but it ultimately reflects a self-proclaimed knowledge in the objectivity of physical matter, rational thinking and mathematical formulation that dominates today's intellectual horizon as a sign of our time.

What people yearn for unconsciously, however, is definitive knowledge, principial knowledge, and first knowledge that has the power to resolve the perennial mystery that lies at the heart of existence, as well as within the heart of humanity. What we are faced with first and foremost as the primary challenge of our lives is mystery rather than knowledge, and what we need to resolve before all else is to know the true origin of existence and have available the true sources of knowledge gathered together into the comprehensive form of a worldview that can be drawn from our pocket at will and relied on to provide the guidance that the demands of life call upon us. At face value, we do not know "on our own" what constitutes the true nature of the human reality in terms of first origin and final end, nor do we know what empowers and governs the reality of phenomenal nature that extends within our depths and beyond us into the metacosmic depths of the night sky. At the heart of all existential knowledge on earth lies a divine mystery that declines to give up its secrets and refuses to resolve the enigmatic challenges of life during this or any other time.

In the Islamic worldview, God is the ultimate source of all existent things in their multi-faceted manifestations and forms. God, as "unseen mystery" (*al-ghaib*) as well as "hidden secret" (*as-sirr*), is the Originator and the Source of all that exists. He is, therefore, the Originator of a time in the beginning, now and ever shall be *in illo tempore*, and He is the Creator (*al-khaliq*) and Giver of Life (*al-Muhyi*) of all that exists as created and manifested form, whether it be animate or inanimate. Out of the headwaters of the Source flow all primordial forms, all archetypes, all embryos, all seeds, germs, buds, eggs, rootlets, and sprigs. According to Ibn al-'Arabi, buds are possibilities that have not yet "smelled the perfume of existence". In the Source, all things are eternally present, just as in the bud the flower is forever present, just as in the silence of the bell lies the promise of its ringing. Nothing can appear on the plane of physical manifestation without having its transcendent cause and the primary root of its being well placed in the soil of the Primordial Source. Similarly, all existent things both contain and preserve the integrity of the bud, sprig, embryo, seed and source that begot it.

The notion of origin refers to a Supreme Being that is before us, behind us, below us and above us, both now, in the past and in the future, transcending terrestrial time as measured by the seasons and the earth's orbit around the sun out of deference to the eternal moment that never blinks and is forever fresh. It is He who begins the process of creation, and He repeats it." (10: 4) The Name of Allah identifies an eternal Presence and a living Reality that is certainly not subject to the conventional notions of time and space. He does not have a beginning in time; instead, He represents the ever-present Origin, Source, Center and Final End. According to a Holy Tradition of the Prophet (hadīth) in Islam, we learn that "there was a time when God existed, and nothing else existed alongside Him."

♠ ♠ ♠

Do we know why the Divinity created the universe? As human beings, we might project anthropomorphic feelings of loneliness in the face of an eternal solitude, but God has revealed another reason for His divine beneficence as Creator and Sustainer of all life. We have come to know why God created the universe because a well-known *hadith qudsi*[12] has conveyed this rarefied knowledge to humanity. "David (peace be upon him) said, 'Oh Lord, why did You cause creation to come into being?' God replied, 'I was a hidden treasure and I wanted to be known, therefore I created the universe.'" We have here in the words of God a direct statement of divine motivation and purpose that is conveyed to humanity as a divine disclosure through the prophets, so that we may know once and for all time the reason for our existence and the purpose for which we live, namely to live our lives in the shadow-knowledge of the Divinity, and through the realization of this knowledge, to worship and praise Him in our thoughts, words and actions that span a lifetime. The miraculous faculty of consciousness implicit in this revealed knowledge is the counterpart

---

[12] This is one of the traditional Holy Sayings of the Prophet Muhammad (PBUH) that is said to be the direct speech of Allah.

and reflection of the magnificent beauty of the creation.

To have faith in a body of traditional knowledge and to live a traditional life of spirituality is to live within sight of the Origin every day of our lives. It is because of the origin of existence and the sources of knowledge that every moment of life can be lived at all, giving life its spiritual and transcendent character, leading every human being toward a living awakening with the power to transform human destiny into a journey beyond the stars. To deny this concept is to deny the living reality that exists within humanity. To live "as if Allah exists" is to live in the fullness of a living reality, for according to a well-know *hadith*, we are encouraged to "worship Allah as if He truly exists, for even if we do not see Him, nevertheless, He sees us."

If the Divinity is the Primal Origin and Original Source of all knowledge as embodied in the revelation, in nature and in humankind, then the revelation as a transcendent world, cosmic nature as a book of phenomenal existence and humanity as microcosm and world within a world represent the intermediary sources of knowledge in the form of a written book, as a theatre of nature reflecting through multiple mirrors the Face of the Beloved (*Wherever you turn, there is the Face of God* [2:115]), and as the human revelation in which humans themselves become a mirror reflection of the Reality of the Divine Being. The correspondence between humanity, nature as cosmos, and revelation is crucial in the religious understanding of Islam, partly because each element forms a contiguous part as the source material for the religion, and partly because the written wisdom, the natural wisdom and the human wisdom contained in the scripture, in nature and in humans all deliver the essential knowledge that bespeaks of the true nature of the one Reality.

As such with regard to revelation, nature and humanity, each exhibits signs that are direct reflections of the Divinity and these "signs" are intended to serve us as a means of lifting the veil that separates humanity from direct knowledge of the Divinity. The revealed words of the Qur'an descend from the Mind of Allah, pass through the mind of the Messenger of Islam and ultimately set down as a written book (*al-Qur'an al-Tadwīnī*) with verses that in Arabic are called *ayat* which when translated means "signs" or "verses", linking the verses of the Book with the well known Qur'anic verse "We will show them Our signs on the horizon and within themselves" (41:53). The cosmos itself, referred to in Arabic as the cosmic Qur'an (*al-Qur'an al-Takwīnī*) or the book of existence,[13]

---

[13] The 8th/14th century Sufi 'Aziz al-Din Nasafi has written the following concerning the book of nature: "Each day destiny and the passage of time set this book before you, *surah* for *surah*, verse for verse, letter for letter, and read it to you . . . like one who sets a real book before you and reads it to you line for line, letter for letter, that you may

represents a vast universal book in complement to the Islamic book of revelation, and like the revealed scripture, it also contains signs and symbols, verses if you will, that have the power to reveal as much as they conceal. They possess levels of meaning that can serve the needs of every mentality and that ultimately lead toward a complete understanding of the true nature of reality. Finally, the archetype human, man himself as a generic thinking species unique (and wise, *Homo sapiens*) among the animal kingdom, is a book of self-revelation whose story becomes a conscious human life and whose thoughts and actions become the signs and symbols of a tale well lived.

Therefore, the *ayat* or verses manifest themselves within the Holy Book, within the macrocosmic universe, and within the soul of humanity, in other words, as the Qur'an says, "on the distant horizon and within their own selves." The Qur'an and the great phenomena of nature are twin manifestations of the divine act of Self-revelation. For Islam, the natural world in its totality is "a vast fabric into which the 'signs' of the Creator are woven."[14] We as humans can understand ourselves to be a "sign" of God, the cosmos as a grand theophany and mirror of the Divine Qualities and Attributes, and the revealed book that contains all the verses and thus all the knowledge that a human being needs to know in order to come to terms with him or herself and the universe as the *vestigia Dei*, according to Christian terminology, the signs of God. Each element has its own form of metaphysics and its own mode of prayer, humans through living the tale, the cosmos through being the sanctuary and theatre wherein the Divinity can become known, and revelation by recreating for humanity knowledge from the mind of God through words.

According to the modern scientific worldview, the universe constitutes a single, unified reality; all speculation concerning intangible, spiritual, or in any sense other-worldly phenomena is dismissed as an expression of "unreality". The objective of modern science is to uncover a unified theory of knowledge that would bring all the known laws of nature into a single comprehensive framework. According to the traditional perspective, however, the universe partakes of levels of reality. The message of its very magnitude and breadth amply attests to that truth. Its billions and billions of galaxies swirling around a central core and its light-years upon light years, reflecting as they do both immense distance and time, would only numb the mind with their unreal and incomprehensible projection without the enlightening perspective of the

---

learn the content of these lines and their letters." Quoted in *Islamic Spirituality: Foundations*, Seyyed Hossein Nasr (ed.), New York: Crossroad, 1987, p. 355.

[14] Charles Le Gai Eaton, *Islam and the Destiny of Man*, Albany, NY: SUNY Press, 1985, p. 87.

Transcendent Center that unifies both man and the universe into a single "principle" of knowledge at source. As such, in addition to the Qur'an, the universe itself is a great book of knowledge that can teach us far more about ourselves and our world than we might have thought possible or imaginable.

To understand the vision of the world of humankind and the world of nature as being closely related to the world of the revelation is to live and experience ourselves and the world we live in as the sacred realities that they are intended to be. Without a sense of the sacred and without a feeling for the sublime articulation of the Whole—of man and nature and the cosmos that envelopes them both—we would simply remain the three-dimensional figures we now envision ourselves to be, on the road to self-destruction and ultimately the oblivion of death. We need to abandon a paradigm of thought that relies solely on facts and figures to determine our self-image and worldview. We need to see through the one-sided and narrow perspective of modern science whose vision does not extend beyond the human perception of self and that uses reason alone to interact with the "stuff" of matter that constitutes the physical world as the basis of our lives.

When we think of the universe, how do we picture it and therefore what does it mean to us as a practical experience? Do we recreate in our mind's eye, for example, the dark matter and black holes, the red hot suns and white dwarfs, the forbidding distances and the vast aeons of time required to allow the universe "to happen" and be a meaningful experience to us? Or do we recreate in our mind's eye the vision of a Supreme Being that lives eternally as a Transcendent Center; but that has created the primordial point that expanded into the grand manifestation of a living and organic universe, because this transcendent and eternal Center wanted "to be known" and therefore executed the miracle of cosmic and human consciousness? Do the laws that govern what we witness to be an ordered cosmos exist as the blind expression of random facts accumulated by scientists and tucked away into their little bag of tricks, or are they the evidence of a divine self-disclosure and the reflection of intelligence, the Supreme Intelligence if you will, that has created, governs and sustains the universe? When the spiritual traditions say that man is the microcosm and the universe is the macrocosm, implying that the universe exists within man just as man exists within the universe, what does that mean and does anyone really know? Whatever may be the true answer, one thing is clear: In whatever sense or in whatever way the universe can be reflected in what the Muslims call *insan* (humanity), can I claim to be the offspring of that "true and universal man"? Is the order and purpose reflected within nature a motivating force in my awareness of self? Finally, is the universe a conscious and living reality, just as I know myself to be?

We began this chapter by relying on the source material of a *hadith qudsi* representing the very words of the Divinity that suggests the ultimate rationale for the creation of both humankind and the universe. The modern, scientific scale of the universe is staggering, benumbing the mind with its vast time frames and incredible distances because it is outside of us and we are not a part of it in some qualitative manner. The ancient and traditional scale of the universe is equally awesome, but in an entirely different way. The modern scale of the universe exceeds all of our expectations of quantity by dwarfing us in size in relation to the vast physical perspective, and leaving us bereft of a purpose and a meaning that can be integrated into the Whole, thereby disassociating people today from the world of nature and the universe in which they must inevitably take part. In addition, the speculative theories of modern scientists concerning such things as dark matter, black holes and parallel universes have no symbolic value that conveys a message to the mass population that is meaningful to them as individuals. Their theoretical existence may intrigue the mind with technical virtuosity and imaginative flare. Who doesn't marvel at the thought of a seductive black hole or the fantasy of a parallel universe; but in terms of how these ideas may possibly relate to us and enhance our experience of the world, they mean nothing.

Once upon a time and forever after, the sources of traditional knowledge found in revelation will continue to inspire the minds and hearts of humanity into future generations. The night sky will always be the "city of God" and the vast cosmic universe will always be a magnificent universal book and a mirror reflection of the Divinity. The traditional scale of the universe fully establishes the value of the qualitative experience behind the cold face of brute quantity. It weaves an intricate web of purpose and a hierarchy of meaning that permits humanity to find their place in the universe precisely because the essential elements of the universe exist within the human being, namely knowledge, intelligence, existence, life, and consciousness. The mystery of cosmic genesis and the knowledge of a true beginning lie hidden within the mystery of a transcendent consciousness that has proclaimed as an eternal remembrance of true origins: "I was a hidden treasure and wanted to be known. Therefore, I created the universe."

## Chapter Three

First Revelation, First Man

In the previous chapter, we considered the term revelation as a generic concept that serves as the universal foundation for all the particular revelations that have descended from some otherworldly realm to humanity as particularized versions of the principle of revelation. In this chapter, some brief mention of the pre-historic record documented in the Qur'an itself should be made of the so-called primordial revelation, namely the first revelation that was given to Adam and Eve upon their departure from the Paradise, when they found themselves confronted with the earthly and the human condition in which they no longer saw God "directly" and they no longer walked and talked with the Supreme Being as they did in the Garden of Eden. The Qur'an tells us that Adam received some verses from his Lord and was given the names of things, in which he understood implicitly, through a unique name, the inner nature and value of things in their essence. The angels themselves were commanded by God to bow down and prostrate themselves before Adam in light of his knowledge of *the names of things*, thus attesting to the symbolic nature of language and the human ability to be aware, to reason, and to articulate their experience of a higher reality.

The Religion of Islam understands very well its place in time and is well positioned within the universal scheme of things to serve humanity well into the future. While it is very prescriptive with clear dogmas, specific laws, well identified rituals and spiritual disciplines that constitute its own angle of vision and particular approach in meeting the challenge of addressing the mystery of the Unseen, it also identifies its role within the universal application of religion and connects into a broader system of metaphysical principles that transcend the individual religious forms. According to the Qur'an, Islam understands itself, not only as the last religion of humanity that recalls and summarizes all that went before with Muhammad as the "seal" of all the Prophets through time, but also it considers itself as a direct reflection of the primordial religion (al-dīn al-hanīf), a perennial doctrine that all religions espouse because it is based on the unique doctrine of Unity that lies at the heart of the universe, as well as within the framework of the natural order. To complement what lies at the heart of the universe, humanity has been given a "human nature", a primordial nature (fitrah) in Qur'anic terminology, an original and pure human nature that separates all humans from the rest of the animal kingdom, a nature that makes them not only uniquely human, but also uniquely spiritual beings.

The sacred trust established between the Divine Spirit and the human soul in the pre-dawn of creation forms the heart of the cosmic drama of the human soul and the basis of the primordial religion. The first human cry of affirmation of the principle of the one God actually represented the first witnessing and surrender in which humanity, in the person of Adam as first man, accepted complete servitude, as a human principle as well as a practical attitude, in the face of the Divine Principle. This is the primordial islam of surrender and the primordial religion of return to God that the Religion of Islam remembers and reconfirms. It is the religion of pure truth, both simple and profound, the din al-hanif in Qur'anic terms, based on the doctrine of the unity and oneness of God that has always existed and lies within the nature of things.

The human soul accepted the responsibility of the sacred trust, and thus revealed at once the bravery of human nature and the nobility of the human soul. Thereafter, humans was given access to the vast field of human experience that could become spiritual insofar as it reflected the divine preference and as long as people remains faithful to the sacred trust that is the birthmark of the soul. In this way, the Islamic perspective recaptures the original concept of religion itself (al-din) as not just doctrines, dogmatic laws, and archaic rituals; but a way of living and consequently a way of being that originates at the time of Adam before the fall from the paradise and continues to distinguish the human being today. This was the time of the primordial religion in which early humankind—Adam and his progeny—were true to their own nature, had not yet betrayed the sacred trust, and had direct access to the essential knowledge of God. Life itself was a direct revelation during this era of beginnings. The religion of Islam, with its distinct and original scripture, remembers and reconfirms the primordial religion of Adam. This concept is needless to say alien to the present-day secular prejudice that exists toward the very idea of religion as such and the levels of spiritual experience that religion embodies.

Similarly, Islam is considered to be the last of the great world religions both in its form and in its character. The Prophet Muhammad (PBUH) is identified in the Qur'an as the "seal of the prophets" (khatim al-anbiyah), and this is emphasized at the end of his mission with the descent of the final verse of the Qur'an that states dramatically (and definitively): "Today, I have perfected your religion for you, completed My favor upon you, and have chosen for you surrender (islam) as your religion." (5:3) It is none other than the religion of surrender (islam) that is the cornerstone of the first, primordial religion, bringing to full circle, with its universal theme of unity, the entire progression of the formal religious experience back to the original primordial point of trust and surrender out of which the universe and the soul of humanity was born. Before Islam was a formalized religion with a capital "I", cast within the stone of a fixed and ritualized community of worshippers with a professed history and an accepted body of dogma and laws based on a revealed Book, it was a community of men and women whose minds had been captured by the essence of what would later become sealed by the details of the religion and its formal practice. That essence is none other than the great witnessing in Islam, the shahādah, that seized the minds and hearts of the Companions of the Prophet with its incisive knowledge of the One and the clear path of return to the Source in order to internalize this knowledge through surrender (islam) and worship (ibādah).

The concept of religion, its original source and reason for existence, finds its origin and validity in the descent of a revelation from the Divine Being to the human creature. The actual form of the religion, and its entire structure and framework, is born out of such a direct communication, a Word or Logos, in which the Supreme Being identifies Himself as the true reality and the only reality worthy of our worship and praise. Every religious form builds its supporting traditions—social, cultural or otherwise—from the bedrock of a direct revelation that lays out in detail the essential knowledge of God and all that relates to the human response to that knowledge. This revelatory knowledge speaks directly to the human faculties and senses. Then the inner faculties and five senses process this knowledge and set the scene within the mind and heart for the development of human excellence (*ihsan*) over the course of a lifetime. As knowledge from the Divine Realm, universal revelation substantiates each of the individual religious forms with its knowledge of universal existence and the metaphysical principles that underlie all of existence. As such, the main significance of revelation lies in the fact of its "Word of God" quality, taking part as it does in the character of absoluteness, from sacred laws, to rites and rituals, to the importance of sacred symbols and myths and to the efficacy of the spiritual disciplines, all of which contain blessing (*barakah*) for Muslims, as well as knowledge that is absolute and beyond human argument.

The meaning of the word "religion", in the Islamic context, goes beyond the concept of revelation as the descent of knowledge from the Divine to the human and as the point of departure and source of the religion. The English word "religion", in Arabic *al-dīn*, does little justice to the full significance of the word's meaning in Arabic, because the concept of *al-dīn* in Islam is less formal and more practical than can be found within the English context for the word "religion". The Arabic *dīn* signifies a way of life that adheres to a sacred norm in which the entire life is molded to become a way of being, in addition to being a way of knowledge that commences with the descent of the Book and the inscription of the pen on the heart of the Muslims, echoing the very first verse, in the form of a direct command, to descend into the mind and heart of the Prophet in the cave of Mt. Hira in the barren foothills outside of Makkah: "Read (recite) in the name of thy Lord Who created. . . ." (96:1) To that end, what the Muslims call the Sunnah comprises not only the verses and laws and entreaties of the Holy Qur'an; but also the sayings of the Prophet, compiled a century or more after his death, that perpetuate his attitudes, his behavior and virtually his way of life. The Prophet himself represents the supreme example of a human being who was the receptacle and instrument of the sacred verses, the very words and harmonious energy of the Holy Spirit.

Obviously, we need the individual form of a specific religion to make our way in this world. Indeed, a particular religion provides not only the destination in the form of fulfillment, salvation, and ultimately the peace of the Paradise; but also the way to arrive at that destination. What is the good of knowing where you want to go and profess to believe in a body of knowledge that promises blessing, happiness and peace, if we do not know how to arrive at that self-professed goal? Young people today do not need convincing about the importance of being on top of their game, of being clever and skilled at what they need to accomplish, particularly for what they want from "this world". There are enough examples in the professional and entertainment world in the form of Superman and Spiderman, Iron man or batman—in short a person with special powers—to impress upon young people nowadays the importance of having goals and the value of being powerful and successful. There are ample stories of entrepreneurs like Bill Gates, a high-tech nerd who dropped out of college to become one of the richest men in the world, to attest to the fact that people now know that they need to develop themselves, to nurture their powers and fully develop their skills, in order to raise their consciousness and will power so that they can transcend their own limitations and be successful in this life and in the next one.

♣  ♣  ♣

The primordial man in the mythical and revelatory persona of Adam—as the original, prototype human—pre-figures all of humanity as the human image of man in his initial perfection. "Indeed, We have created man (humanity) in the best forms." (95: 4) Because of his pure nature, his pristine form, and his singularity of soul, primordial man still remains the model of our true spiritual identity, for Muslims and non-Muslims alike. Everything about him, including the luminous state of his body, the free innocence of his nature, and the unique singularity of his soul, all refer back to the Absolute Being, whom he represented in both form and essence. The betrayal of the inner self was still an unknown experience to primordial man's consciousness, and the veils had yet to be drawn across the inner sanctum of his being, separating the conscious self from the inner self. He understood life as the fullest expression of his own truth and not the expression of a deception or the illusions that fallen man would come to experience. He observed the world in its truest dimension, from within, and he had no reason to doubt the accuracy of his perception. The 'eye' of his heart was fully still open to the interaction of inner and outer worlds, and he still enjoyed the direct faith that comes with the perception of the "eye of certainty". (102: 7)

Of course, none other than Adam is the primordial man, since the primordial being needs a name as well as an image and cannot forever be referred to *incognito*. In fact, we gather our understanding about this rarefied primordial being from the precise sketch given in revelation of the symbolic persona of Adam, who is the human form cast from the divine mold, the first fully formed human body and the first human. Between the lines of the Qur'anic narrative, we sense that Adam is innocent yet knowing, naked yet without shame, naive of the world yet intuitive of the Real. He was completely at ease with himself and he enjoyed direct contact, without any curtains or veils, with his own inner, spiritual dimension. We can suppose that he understood his world in all its substantive meaning, at home in the imminent presence of his Creator and at one with the unity (*al-tawhid*) of God that he observed everywhere.

The creation myth of Adam and Eve is not just a mythical tale of possible human origins suggestive of 'once upon a time' *in illo tempore,* at some remote time-event, 'in the beginning'. The remarkable myth of Adam portrays knowledge concerning what constitutes the very essence of the prototype man, including his body, his nature, his intellect, his instinct, his soul and ultimately his spirit. His body was perfection of form, his mind mirrored objectivity (not in the modern sense of the word, but in the traditional sense of truths that transcend physical forms), his intellect reflected the absolute, his soul constituted the 'ground' of his person and his spirit the very breath of his being. The mythological tale of Adam and Eve as the first couple is a narrative message of descent and return, descent from the primordial perfection and a return to the paradise lost. As such, the tale represents the traditional dogma of the fall and rise of humanity rather than the evolutionary dogma of the rise and fall of *Homo sapiens,* commencing with a common ancestor that scientists revealingly call Mitochondrial Eve, and ultimately terminating through the inevitability and finality of physical, earthly death.

The persona of Adam as first man was created not as a primitive and primate being giving rise to growth and development on the purely physical plane whose chemicals and neurons would one day constitute his mind, consciousness, and emotions, an entity subject to a brief interlude of earthly time between two eternities and then enjoy existence no more. The Adamic first man is a symbol of none other than the primordial man who existed as a creature of centrality, totality, objectivity and perfection as the defining and definitive qualities of his essence. These were aspects and qualities that virtually defined the primordial man by virtue of his being made 'in the image' (*imago Dei*) of a Divine Being that expressed the aspects of the Center, the Whole, the Objective, the Absolute, and the Perfect One Who created him 'in His image'. Adam is the prime symbol of man *in divinis,* human by nature but reflective of the Divine Qualities and Attributes that make him man in principle.

As the prototype and progenitor of all future generations, Adam had a body that reflected perfection, a soul that reflected centrality, a nature that reflected totality and completeness of mind that reflected consciousness and an objectivity that reflected the Absolute. Let us consider more closely these human elements of body, soul, human nature, and mind, for they are the defining elements of a unique human entity.

Adam, whose body was the manifested image of the Divine Prototype, possessed symmetry of form and luminescence of spirit that expressed a perfection of form that translated into a symbolic meaning, his luminescence shining forth from the inner substance and spirituality of his being as a complement to his already unique physical presence. His centrality transcended space by placing himself through his surrender to the knowledge of revelation at the center of the Universal Center. By having a center, he could conquer the physical limitations of the human mind with reference to both outer and inner space by placing himself in proximity to the Center of the Divinity, and this center served as the foundation of his entire being. Prior to the fall from Paradise, his human nature expressed totality and completeness, being nothing other than what it was intended to be. Nothing was missing from his range of experience; he could literally communicate with the animals; he could see things directly and understand the symbolic messages within nature, and he symbolically walked and talked with God. Finally, the mind of the primordial Adam expressed consciousness and wisdom, consciousness by virtue of his subjectivity and wisdom by virtue of his intuitive knowledge that could express itself on the practical level.

His perfect body, his complete nature, and the centrality of his soul made him a symbolic image of the Divine Being, while his mind made the primordial Adamic man a human man. God breathed His enlivening Spirit into the water and clay form of humanity and in doing so granted formal participation in the life of the Divine Spirit, lending Adam and all future generations aspects of objectivity and the absolute that must accompany that Spirit. The objectivity of his mind permitted him to step out of his own subjectivity. He could step out of himself and therefore see himself with the eye of a higher consciousness, a human self-consciousness, reflecting a transcendent awareness of the Highest Reality that is unique to the human species. In addition, the human capacity for objectivity endowed his mind with an intelligence that could see and understand things as they are 'in themselves' and not merely as the reflection of one's own subjective being, a will that was free to choose, complemented by higher emotions that transcended the limitations of pure self interest into the higher realms of charity, compassion and selfless love. "To say that man, and consequently the human body, is 'made in the image of God,' means *a priori* that it manifests something absolute and for that very reason something unlimited and perfect. What distinguishes above all the human form from animal forms is its direct reference to absoluteness, indicated by its vertical posture."[15] This was the primordial, the Adamic, the first man whose symbolic image portrays what constitutes the essence of the human being. By living in the shadow of the Absolute, he retains something of the absolute within him,

---

[15] Frithjof Schuon, *From the Divine to the Human*, Bloomington, Ind: World Wisdom Books, 1982, p. 87.

and this permits certain qualities that manifest throughout the course of life as beauty (perfection), consciousness (objectivity), wisdom (knowledge), and virtue (action).

The primordial man in traditional terminology has emerged within the modern context as *Homo sapiens*, a totally human being, while at the same time being a theophany and "sign" of God. Both represent first man, but not in the temporal sense of the word since his actual and literal existence has no intrinsic importance in and of itself. Traditional people with genuine spiritual mentalities have no interest in speculating on whether Adam actually existed in time. It is not the temporality of the person that is of interest here; at issue is his identity, his meaning, and ultimately his origin that is at stake. Admittedly, it is a uniquely modern-day dilemma, for traditional societies didn't question the fundamentality of man's spiritual origins as a thinking creature of the Divinity. Primordial man is first man in kind and quality, if not necessarily in literal time. He is principle and prototype, unique and exemplar. *Homo* becomes *sapiens* by virtue of his intellectual intuition which is rooted in the very substance of the human intellect, because man's intuition connects him knowingly with the knowledge and Spirit of God. When he was created and manifested as a human and terrestrial creature, man is said to have "descended" to the earth in various stages of development.[16] His return and final resurrection within the fold of the Divine Spirit trace the parameters of the "vertical" dimension that commenced with man's descent from the Garden of Eden and will come to fruition with his ascent and return to God.

The disappearance of the Adamic man from the spiritual, intellectual and emotional horizon of modern philosophy marks the abandonment and loss of the spiritual message that his symbolic image implied. The characteristics mentioned earlier of his centrality, his totality, his perfection and his objectivity no longer have the meaning that has traditionally been associated

---

[16] "The human form cannot be transcended, its sufficient reason being precisely to express the Absolute, hence the untranscendable; and this cuts short the metaphysically and physically aberrant imaginations of the evolutionists, according to whom this form would be the result of a prolonged elaboration starting from animal forms; an elaboration which is at once arbitrary and unlimited. In reality, the evolutionist hypothesis is unnecessary because the creationist concept is so as well; for the creature appears on earth, not by falling from heaven, but by progressively passing – starting from the archetype – from the subtle to the material world, materialization being brought about within a kind of visible aura quite comparable to the 'spheres of light' which, according to many accounts, introduce and terminate celestial apparitions." *Ibid.,* p. 88. Reference is made to certain examples of such "spheres of light" such as the chariot of fire that lifted up Elijah, and the "cloud" which veiled Christ during his Ascension to heaven.

with the Supreme Being. The existence of the supra-natural designations of the soul, the intuitive mind and human nature must be denied by modern individuals as we have come to understand these elements within the humanly spiritual context. To abandon the spiritual perspective is to give up the essence of what makes humanity human and not animal. To embrace the naturalist perspective that links man's ancestry definitively with the animal kingdom through some arcane process of compatibility and interrelatedness is to desire the animal in man to define the border of who the primordial man has been and still fundamentally is within existing humanity.

In this way, the ground of the human soul serves the totality of the human experience, together with conscious surrender to the reality of a Supreme Being, thus placing the soul-center within the Center of existence. Without soul or center, humans are relegated to the periphery of existence, occupying a mere word in the voluminous book of life or a leaf in the cosmic jungle. Without a human nature that is made *in divinis* and reflective of the qualities and attributes of God, humans lose their totality and break down into fragments, occupying pieces of a broken mirror that is shattered beyond repair. The perfection of the human body and its implicit message becomes fallen and flawed, reduced to a machine occupying space in time and unable to depart from the inner border of the mechanism that people imagine for themselves. Finally, without the objectivity that permits humans to withdraw from themselves and move toward the image of the Absolute, they becomes purely subjective beings in a purely relative world, rather than the objective, and in the words of Frithjof Schuon, the "relatively absolute" being Adam once was by virtue of the sacred trust he made with the Divinity to be himself as he was created and to affirm the Divine Principle in the human form.

Are we a dream, dreamed by ancient wisdoms and wise beings that place the human entity beyond the realm of purely physical worlds? Are we merely a process of physical nature and not a reality that transcends the illusions of this world? Are we to believe the dark message of our animality as the only message there is, and if so, what is this message, for we do not approximate the nobility of the animal who lives well placed within itself, who has the intelligence to fulfill its earthly function and follow its natural instincts, and who prays and praises God by being what it was created to be? Did we rise through successive generations of apes and hominids or did we descend through successive phases of materialization leading to the ultimate denial of our true origins?

For credible answers to these universal mysteries, the Muslims rely on the revelations contained within the verses of their Holy Book to provide them with the knowledge and guidance that will give coloration and context to the manner in which they go about their duties and live their lives. The sacred verses give meaning and perspective to otherwise inscrutable mysteries and pave a path forward on their journey from darkness to light, a journey clearly illuminated by the sacred words of the Qur'anic text.

# Chapter Four

The Era of Pre-Islamic Arabia

Before describing in detail the remarkable narrative of how the final revelation came to a desert nomad living in Western Arabia at the turn of the 6th and 7th centuries AD, it might be helpful to take note of the political and social trends of the era in order to better understand the context of the miraculous descent of the revelation in the Arabic language and the development of a new religion that would proclaim not only a reaffirmation of the primordial religion of Adam, but also affirm the validity of all the subsequent religions and revelations that came to humanity down through the ages. "Indeed, those who have believed (in the Prophet) and those (before him) who were Jews or Sabeans or Christians, those who believed in Allah and the last day and were righteous, there will be no fear concerning them, nor will they grieve." (5:69)

A glimpse of pre-Islamic history, and the Arabs who lived at that time in Central Arabia, is more than a snapshot of what went on before the time of the Prophet (PBUH), and more than just a brief footnote to the rise of a new religion that would not only sweep across Arabia, but also expand across the broad spread of the earth, as though the Hand of God had cast the brush stroke of a lunar crescent across the equator of the earth from North Africa to the Far East, creating a handprint of the Divinity on the earth that touched the soul of humanity that is reflected in the heavens. The facts of linear history are interesting to know about, like a photo that gives insights into the customs and fashions of another era. They sit on the pages of history books like gazelles grazing on the African savannah that with close scrutiny become subject to flight and might disappear. The facts may enter the mind and roam around the various faculties such as reason and the imagination, like animals in search of water; but they end up leaving behind their bleached bones, giving rise to an appreciation that comes from an understanding of the tendencies, moods and colorations of a civilization on the brink of an impending disaster, a civilization whose values and belief system no longer represented their own self interests, much less the truth that should serve as a foundation to their thinking, a civilization ripe for overturning and rejuvenation, like a tired soil in need of sun and water after the upheaval of the plow.

At the time when the Prophet of Islam was born (c. 570) in the late 6th century), the plague during the reign of the Emperor Justinian had spread across the Byzantine Empire, a pandemic commonly known as bubonic plague, that afflicted the whole of the Eastern Roman Empire and nearly took the life of the Emperor himself. It was later classified as one of the deadliest plagues in history, killing up to 10,000 people in Constantinople daily at its height, according to the Byzantine historian, Procopius, who lived through the era to witness the plague and document its deadly impact on the population. The early 7th century in Arabia, during the era commonly known as the "Dark Ages" in central Europe, witnessed the longest and most destructive period of the Byzantine-Sassanid Wars (602-628) during the time when the Prophet was receiving verses of revelation from the Archangel Gabriel and the Religion of Islam was beginning to take shape and develop into its final form. One historian has suggested that the unnecessarily prolonged Byzantine-Persian conflict opened the way for the eventual rapid spread of Islam.

Even with the coming of the plague, the Byzantine Emperor Justinian attempted to resurrect the might of the Roman Empire by expanding into the northern regions of Arabia then known as the Fertile Crescent, an area of lush vegetation, including such places as Israel, Jordan, Syria, Lebanon and the West Bank that had a strategic interest in helping the Emperor fund expansion plans into both Europe and North Africa. By the time the last Byzantine-Sassanid war came to an end in 628, Islam was already united under the power of a single religious-politico leader, namely the Prophet of Islam. The Muslims were then able to launch attacks against both the Persian and Byzantine empires which resulted in destruction of the Sassanids and overthrowing the Byzantium's territories in the Levant, the Caucasus, Egypt, Syria and North Africa. Over the following centuries, most of the Byzantine Empire and the entirety of the Sassanid Empire came under Muslim rule. Within the lifetime of some of the children who met Muhammad (PBUH) and sat on the Prophet's knees, Arab armies controlled the land mass that extended from the Pyrenees Mountains in Europe to the Indus River Valley in South Asia. In less than a century, Arabs had come to rule over an area that spanned five thousand miles.

In addition, it is important for a complete understanding of the time to scrutinize the cultural life in pre-Islamic Arabia. The people of that time had their own "worldview", such as it was among primitive nomadic peoples driven to carve a way of life out of the harsh, demanding conditions of the desert; but the superficial force of their worldview was quickly abandoned by those who instinctively responded to the new wave of knowledge that was descending upon them in the form of an alien, yet strangely attractive and compelling wisdom. Perhaps they were tired of the lifeless and shallow belief system that they were accustomed to living with, or recognized it for the ineffectual and useless way of life that did not address the issues that most affected them at deeper levels of the human experience. The new Muslim converts responded with such an inner burning of the mind and heart that nothing and no one could turn them away from their new-found beliefs. They were quite simply on fire with the revelation of the one God and the principle of unity that tied their universe up into a unified whole and made perfect sense in an otherwise mysterious world full of questions and contradictions about the true meaning of life in which they floated through life like sagebrush across desert sands.

A secret had come down "from the heavens above", a wonderful secret, no doubt today we would call it awesome, revealed to the townspeople and companions of Muhammad (PBUH), known as the Trustworthy (al-amīn) even as a young man, a person who had a reputation for being thoughtful and contemplative, interested in truths that all the wise men of the world were not able to discover and unravel into a comprehensive vision. The newly converted companions of the Prophet could see with the vision of a clear day that the ancient beliefs were as worthless as the clay idols housed in the Ka'aba that they worshipped. It was not just the tired old pagan rituals and useless clay idols that suddenly seemed shameful, if not downright silly, a kind of insult to a person's native intelligence; but paying tribute to these vestiges of a pagan culture and mentality represented a way of life and a state of being that was in stark contrast to the new wave of the religion of surrender and return that was about to overturn and wash away the residue of an old and tired way of thinking that no longer served the needs of the people. The Qur'an and the later development of Islam based on revealed, universal principles had come at a timely moment to address the needs of the people of that time.

35

In pre-Islamic Arabia, the nomadic and marauding desert Bedouin worshipped inanimate idols and images; but in truth they believed in nothing but their own desires and needs; they lived for the moment in this world, for nothing existed beyond the horizon of their minds but their immediate satisfactions and their fleeting whims. With no grounding in the bedrock of a higher vision, they ended up living for the moment, for this world, for their own desires and whims, nothing more. They lived the life of this world and brought the life of pre-Islamic Arabia into being with its characteristic profanities, ignorance and vulgarity, destined to lie stagnant on the pages of history as the footnote in the era of the Dark Ages that they deserve to be. This was an era of stagnant and lifeless history that turned out to be the stuff out of which visions of higher consciousness and enlightenment are born. The era of pre-Islamic history lies in shame before the great portal of the Islamic awakening in the dim corridors of time, with no future and no past, remaining only a signpost of destiny as a remembrance of what needed to be overturned within the world at that time and with the people who lived in the shadow of their personal desires and limited ambitions, without the benefit of a vision that reflected a higher level of spiritual experience.

Perhaps it is worth reviewing once again the true nature of the pre-Islamic times because the pitfalls that people fell victim to during that era are not that far removed from our own weaknesses and inclinations during this so-called modern era that enjoys a mystique of progress and development of the fast emerging mobile technologies unprecedented in history that lure us into thinking that we are happy and successful in our ability to communicate at the speed of light through the miracle of wireless technology, even though a knowing insecurity and uncertainty weighs heavy on our hearts that is difficult to relieve and almost impossible to ignore. We blame the people of pre-Islamic Arabia for worshipping little clay idols and we laugh at the silliness of their mentalities that they could invest meaning and hope into something so ridiculous as clay images with crude and bloated faces. These images and idols were not just play things to soothe weary minds or a psychological crutch to soothe weary souls. They took up residence in the very Ka'aba in Makkah, even then a traditional pilgrimage point down through the ages from the time of Abraham, who according to the traditions and the Qur'an itself, built this house of God on earth with his own hands. Adjacent to the cubic proto-structure of the Ka'aba, the station of Abraham still stands to this day.

Does this sound familiar? In fact, we are not that far removed from such attitudes, primitive though they may seem to our supposedly sophisticated and enlightened 21$^{st}$ century minds. What about our own idols that we worship during this era? Admittedly, these petty gods are not clay dolls stacked in rows on a shelf with enlarged eyes and crooked smiles, but the idols that we worship today seize our minds—and worse our imaginations—with the same pagan vengeance that they once seized these more primitive peoples of the desert. No one calls the pursuit of money, fame, success, and physical pleasure clay idols or minor gods, but that's what they are. Why aren't we laughing at ourselves as we laugh at primitive peoples; perhaps if we, did we would realize how ridiculous we can be sometimes in our pursuit of objects and power and money and possessions that ultimately will have no true hold over us as we leave them behind at the time of our death. They are not clay dolls; but they are every bit a form of idol worship as the primitive gods of those pre-Islamic times. At least those people didn't know any better, until the commencement of the mission of the Prophet and the beginning of the descent of the Qur'an. What exactly was the true nature of those times that resembles so much our own time? Let us open once again the archives of history to glimpse for a few moments the flickering lights of another era, before they return to the night out of which they have strayed.

The pre-Islamic era has been characterized by later Muslims as an era of idolatry and a time of ignorance known as the *Jāhiliyyah*. It was an age of moral depravity and religious discord with its worship of idols, the plurality of gods, the killing of daughters, and the low status of women generally among other evils, obscuring the belief in the one true God and plunging 6th century Arabia into the confusing turmoil of a polytheistic religious environment. The nomadic desert Arabs of that era had fallen into a kind of pagan, although complex, belief system[17] whose religious perspective embodied a pantheon of gods and idols in which each tribe had its own particular favorite, such as Lāt and 'Uzzah for the Quraysh Tribe. The intercession of these gods was sought for any number of reasons; but the ancient memory of one great God still lingered, by name *Allāh*, which was not a proper name as such, but a contraction of the word *al-ilāh* which literally means "the god". While Allah was considered a god above the others, the pre-Islamic Arabs still turned for the sake of expediency to the lesser, more accessible gods who acted as Allah's intercessors. There were over 360 idols housed in and around the Ka'aba during this pre-Islamic time, representing every god recognized in the Arabian Peninsula. No doubt these were troubled times; but there were also signs seen in the heavens and on earth that portended the coming of a great man, a

---

[17] The Latin root word *paganus* actually means "a rustic bore" and was used by Christians to refer to a person who followed any religion but Christianity, rather than the derogatory suggestion it now conveys to mean a person totally outside any formally recognized tradition with ritual practices based on the most primitive impulses.

prophet and messenger to the world.

In Makkah at that time, the Quraysh was a powerful and wealthy tribe that had settled in that area just inland off the Red Sea centuries earlier and whose members were known throughout the mountainous Hijāz region of present-day Saudi Arabia as *al-ahl Allah*, People of God and Wardens of the Sanctuary. They presided over a city nestled in the rugged and barren hills just off the coast of the Red Sea, a prime location on the main international trade route from Yemen in the south to Syria and Palestine in the north. To the south-east of Makkah lies the ancient city of Taif, known as the "garden of the Hijāz" because of its location atop an antediluvian escarpment that leads into the Hijāz mountain range and overlooks the desolate expanse of the Makkan plain below from the dramatic height of 2,000 meters.

To the north-west lies the city of Madinah, called Yathrib during the pre-Islamic era until the Prophet migrated to the city, whereupon it was renamed *Madīnah al-Munawarrah* (the radiant city). Ancient caravans making their way due north and north-west ultimately arrived at the sacred crossroads of Jerusalem, the holiest city of Judaism and venerated as the site of Golgotha, the Hill of Calvary in Christianity, which the New Testament describes as the place where Christ was crucified. In Islam, present-day Jerusalem marks the site of the Noble Sanctuary (*haram ash-sharif*), the Dome of the Rock,[18] visited by the Prophet before his ascent on a night journey through the seven heavens unto the Throne (*al-arsh*) of God. A virtual sacred geography entwines the three great monotheistic religions together with Jerusalem and Makkah as the *terra firma* and provenance of a universal sacred history.

The city of Makkah itself was endowed with a special aura by virtue of the Ka'aba, a simple cube of masonry considered an ancient sanctuary and place of pilgrimage even in pre-Islamic times by virtue of its status as proto-art with a spiritual dimension as a historic place of pilgrimage. The Ka'aba as a site of pilgrimage in turn enhanced the prestige of the Quraysh and made the city of Makkah at that time a mandatory stopping off point for reasons other than trade. As such, the entire surrounding area was transformed into sacred ground and created a neutral zone in which fighting was not permitted and weapons were not allowed. Traders passing through on their way to Jizān and Yemen to the south, or Palestine and Syria to the north, would stop for a perfunctory circumambulation around the Ka'aba, a universal shrine that housed the complete pantheon of all of the idols and gods of Arabia within a

---

[18] Originally built in 691 CE on the order of the Umayyad Caliph Abu al-Malik to commemorate the miraculous "night journey" through the seven heavens by the Prophet Muhammad (PBUH).

unique prototype, indeed pre-historic, sanctuary.

In the modern era throughout the entire year, pilgrims flock from all parts of the globe to make their way to Makkah, not in perfunctory tribute to an ancient ritual as did the Hijāz traders of pre-Islamic Arabia, but rather in fulfillment of a lifetime aspiration to perform the final earthly duty of Islam, the *hajj* (pilgrimage) that should be done once in a lifetime if one has the means. According to the Qur'an (2:127), the Ka'aba itself was built by Abraham and his son Is(h)mael, asking God to make this place a "city of peace" (*balad amānah*). Abraham originally came from Ur in Babylonia; but he eventually migrated westward to escape the atmosphere of idolatry and corruption that prevailed there at that time as well. He lies buried in the Cave of the Patriarchs in Hebron on the West Bank, a place revered by the followers of all three sister religions of Judaism, Christianity and Islam.

As one of the key rituals of the *hajj*, modern-day Muslims recreate the plight of Abraham's wife Hājar who ran between the hills of Safā and Marwah with her son Ismael in a desperate search for water to quench the baby's thirst in those desert climes. In entering the sacred territory of Makkah and Madinah, Muslims return both physically and symbolically to an ancient and primeval landscape of undulating sands and rugged black hills that provided the backdrop to the coming of a new world religion. The stark frontier is as ancient and primordial now as it was at the time of the Prophet, a sacred geography whose arid and pristine wilderness still mirrors even today the austere and pure spirituality that forms the basis of the Islamic spiritual experience.

Beyond the geographic location that marks the setting for the descent of the revelation, and in order to appreciate more fully the origins and initial development of the religious experience of Islam, it is important to understand the social and cultural milieu of the pre-Islamic Arabs. While the society of that time could be characterized as being steeped in idolatry and tribal rivalries, it was also a time of poetry, nobility and valor. The Arabic language is noted for both its poetic and rhetorical flourishes and the Arabs of that time had cultivated an appreciation for both poetry and the rhetorical style compatible with an oral society. Poets already had an important role to play in pre-Islamic society as bards, tribal historians, social commentators, foretellers of the future, dispensers of moral philosophy, and on occasion, administrators of justice. In keeping with the social and oral traditions of this nomadic society, they developed an enduring love of poetry that still exists today.

Similarly, the nomadic Arabs called Bedouin, who move from place to place seeking livelihood in the arid desert and have a legendary affinity with the harsh rhythms of nature, are well known for their character traits of fidelity in keeping one's word, neighborliness in defending one's neighbour as one would defend oneself, hospitality elevated to an exclusive virtue, and finally chivalry that includes both courage and courtesy. It has been said that a Bedouin would sacrifice his life to the utterance of a single word, or to escape hearing one. As such, it does not stretch the imagination to link Bedouin pride and Arab chivalry with the religious fervor required to become a part of a new and growing community of believers and to adopt the alternative spiritual worldview of a single, all-inclusive Reality that was the heart of the Islamic message. It appealed to the innermost sympathies of the Arab soul. "Muslims are brothers," the Prophet was fond of reminding his Companions according to a reliable *hadith*, adding that "all men were of Adam, and Adam himself was of the dust," a stark reminder and tribute to the temporary nature of the earthly condition.

Finally, the Byzantine, Assyrian and Sassanid empires were in proximity to the country of the Quraysh and other Arabian tribes. Islam was born in an era of grand empires and global conquests as much as it was a part of the continuous raids and repercussions that are endemic to tribal life, an era in which the Byzantines and Sassanids were locked in a permanent state of religious war for territorial expansion.[19] Zoroastrianism, Christianity, and Judaism intermingled in the region of the Near East, creating a pluralistic environment that was soon to become a breeding ground for bold new ideas and an unexpected religious fervor. It is precisely a moment such as this, when sacred and recorded history collided to create a new spiritual dispensation where the primordial tradition would come to life at the very place where the age-old mystery of the Abrahamic tradition had once flourished.

The Islamic message was an attempt to reform the existing religious beliefs and cultural practices of pre-Islamic Arabia in order to bring the one God of the Jews and Christians to the Arabs once again and ultimately the rest of the world with the coming of future generations. "[God] has established for you [the Arabs] the same religion enjoined on Noah, on Abraham, on Moses, and on Jesus." (42:13) The coming of the Qur'an with its clear and reoccurring message of unity in the one God brings a progressive and perennial continuity with the previous revelations and religions that have come down to humanity through the ages.

---

[19] The Persian Empire fell to the Arabs in 640 CE. The last Sassanid kind died a fugitive in 651.

## Chapter Five

The Descent of the Luminous

---

The sacred narrative describing the initial descent of the Qur'an through the Archangel Gabriel to Muhammad (PBUH), the Prophet of Islam, is foremost in the minds of the Muslims to the extent that every Muslim child is told its story multiple times until it becomes part of their second nature in knowing the origins of their belief system. However, many non-Muslims know very little about the origin and descent of the sacred verses of the Holy Qur'an that have come to shape and give coloration to the lives of the Muslims in today's world much as it did in previous times.

At best, many people around the world, especially Westerners from English-speaking countries, know of its seemingly harsh pronouncements and its strict dictates, not to mention its absolute quality in which not a word can be changed that would serve as a desecration of the original recitation as it was originally delivered to the Prophet himself and preserved down through the centuries until the present time. They may hear as sound-bites the quotation of verses out of context through mass media or on the profane lips of terrorists who invoke verses of the Qur'an in the service of their own diabolic end and not for what they were intended. Of its sacred, mystical, otherworldly origin and the supernatural circumstances under which the Book arrived in this world, very little is known, much less appreciated, for the miracle that it is.

The earliest sources of the Islamic tradition will help us examine the extraordinary circumstances in which the Qur'an made its descent into the world of 7th century Arabia, a vertical descent that cut through the fabric of "this world" with the knife-blade of a transcendent reality, illuminating the dark mind of humanity with an insight comparable to a flash of lightning that was destined to illuminate the entire world until the last believing Muslim leaves the earth. This miraculous occurrence pierced forever the world of appearances and left behind a religion and a way of life, the Islamic *dīn*, that made possible a new world of spiritual experience to resolve the uncertainties and contingencies of this world. In Islam, the Qur'an forms the absolute basis of the religion, including its knowledge, its doctrine, its spiritual practices, its rich symbolism and art, its sacred sentiments and holy ambiance all combined into a collective whole to provide humanity the certainty people need to know in order to resolve the fundamental mysteries that destabilize the confused soul with their shadowy enigmas. When the verses of the Qur'an began to descend from the Divine Mind into the human sensibility of the Messenger Muhammad (PBUH), the religion began to manifest itself and take form since the religion is first and foremost the Qur'an from the point of view of its origin and source.

Every Muslim both knows and holds in holy remembrance the story of the descent of the Qur'an from the Divine to the human, a descent of the luminous into this world of shadow and contingency. The story brings to light the descent of a criterion in the form of a book and a recitation—"the mother of all books" according to the Qur'an itself (43:3)—that allows existing and future generations the ability to discern right from wrong, truth from falsehood, and the real from the illusory. It is a story that bears repeating, because of its miraculous quality and its ability to fill people's hearts with a spiritual emotion that we seldom have access to in today's modern, secular world and that is hard to recreate in our daily lives "on our own". It is a story that is treasured by children and never forgotten by the Muslims who remember the historical narrative with loving remembrance and in commemoration of the historical event when the first verses of the revelation were recited to the Prophet Muhammad (PBUH) by the Archangel Gabriel.

A brief glimpse at what occurred in Central Arabia during the early 7th century AD, at a time when Europe was still engulfed in the Dark Ages, will highlight certain extraordinary events that took place at that time and may reveal to the modern mentality an unexpected insight that could change the way they understand the world. The Noble Qur'an and the Traditions of the Prophet of Islam are two main sources of knowledge about the religion (called the *Sunnah*), its doctrines and guidance. The traditions are commonly referred to in English as *hadīth* that represent the reliable and traditionally-accepted sayings and actions of the Prophet that have been communicated through listening and hearsay among the companions who lived during the time of the Prophet and preserved throughout history. Both of these sources recall the miraculous event that occurred when the Archangel Gabriel first appeared in a vision to a simple Arab trader of pure character from Makkah with the initial verses of what were to become, over a twenty-three year span of delivery, the full revelation of a Divine Being who identified Himself with the Supreme Name of Allah. This future messenger of Islam was unsuspecting of the great role that was being placed upon his shoulders and was initially unacquainted with the full significance of both revelation and faith. "And thus have We, by our command, sent inspiration to thee: Thou knewest not (before) what was Revelation and what was Faith, but We have made the (Qur'an) a Light, wherewith We guide such of our servants as We will; and indeed thou dost guide (men) to the straight path." (42:52) In this way, this incredible book's journey into light began in a dark cave in the foothills of Makkah.

Early biographical sources have recorded that the Prophet was about thirty-five years old, approximately five years before the first descent of the initial verses of the Qur'anic revelation, when he began to retire into a cave near Makkah, called the Hirā' cave, located within the *Jabal al-Nūr*, the Mountain of Light. Traditionally, the cave[20] has been considered as a symbol of sacred space down through the ages, and thus was the perfect environment for the inward practices of contemplation and inner inquiry for a contemplative mind such as that of the Prophet. People have been fascinated with caves for millennia and mystics and saints have traditionally retired to the isolation and safety of a natural cave because such places offered perfect seclusion and were inaccessible to both men and animals. The Prophet was merely following the example of earlier descendants of Ismael who would periodically make retreats in mountain caves for the purposes of purification and enlightenment. The early traditional sources[21] of the life of the Prophet record that he spoke of

---

[20] The Prophet was later to rely once again on a cave to evade with his companion Abū Bakr the pursuing Makkans during the *hijrah* or migration to Madinah, well-known in the prophetic traditions because of the spider that sealed the cave with his web in order to deceive the Makkans into thinking that no one had entered the cave. The following morning, they proceeded unharmed to Madinah to complete the migration and fulfill the destined mandate of history.

[21] Ibn Hishām, an Egyptian renown as a grammarian and student of language and history (d. 834), edited the biography of the Prophet written by Ibn Isḥāq whose original work has been lost and is now only known in the recension of Ibn Hishām.

"true visions" during these moments of retreat, visions that came to him clearly while he was at rest or asleep in the cave of Hirā', visions that were "like the breaking of the light of dawn."

While he was reclining in meditation in the cave during the last days of the holy month of Ramadhān[22], which was the traditional month of retreat even in pre-Islamic times, the Prophet saw something strange and unexpected in a seemingly miraculous vision during his meditations, a vision that ranged far beyond anything he had ever experienced before in his life. At first, he did not know what was happening, the shock of the experience was so raw and powerful. A Qur'anic verse has later documented and fully confirmed what occurred to the messenger at that time: "He was taught by one mighty in power, filled with wisdom, for he appeared (in stately form) while he was in the highest part of the horizon. Then he approached and came closer and was at a distance of but two bow-lengths or (even) nearer. So did (Allah) convey the inspiration to His Servant what He (meant) to convey." (53:5-10) Of course, God does not speak directly to human beings; but He does speak through His Word and archangelic agencies to His prophets as He did to the Prophet of Islam, through whom the Divine Word was revealed to the world in the form of the Qur'an. "It is not fitting for a man that God should speak to him except by inspiration, or from behind a veil, or by the sending of a messenger to reveal, by God's permission, what God wills; for He is most High, Most Wise." (42:51)

The abrupt and unexpected visitor who stood before him was none other than an archangel in the form of a man. He was carrying what appeared to be a written document, enfolded upon "magical brocade" according to the biographer of the Prophet, Ibn Hishām. The archangel said: "I am Gabriel. God has sent me to communicate to you His message." He then intoned with solemn majesty the first revealed verse of the Qur'an[23]: "Recite (or read) this", and the Prophet immediately replied: "I am not a reciter (I do not know how to read)."[24] In fact, the Prophet was *ummī*, meaning unlettered and unable to

---

[22] According to the traditions, the Qur'an began to descend during the holy month of Ramadhān on a night identified as the *Laylat al-Qadr*, the Night of Power. A Qur'anic verse asks the question: "What is the Night of Power? The following verse answers that it is a night that is "better than a thousand months." (97:3) On that night, the angels descend together with "the Spirit of God". To this day, many Muslims spend the entire night, on the 27th of Ramadhan in night vigils in commemoration of this holy night.

[23] However, it is not the first verse of the Qur'an as traditionally laid out in book form. That position is reserved for the famed 7 verses of al-Fatihah (the first chapter of the Qur'an entitled The Opening).

[24] Perhaps there lies providential ambiguity in the fact that the first word of revelation was alternatively understood as both Recite! And Read! – recalling the cry of the Prophet Isaiah (xl, 6) when he heard a being say: "Recite!" and he said the very words:

read. As such, he was a pure, uncorrupted vessel called upon to receive the sacred words and thus the perfect receptacle to receive the divine revelation. Three times the archangel exhorted him to "recite" and three times the Prophet replied that he was not able to recite. Finally, the first revelation passed through his heart and soul and out into the world: "Recite (*iqra'*) in the name of thy Lord who created, created man out of a blood clot. Recite and thy Lord is most bountiful, who has taught by the Pen, taught man what he knew not." (96:1-5) Indeed, the event must have been a heart-rending one, firstly by the sight of the archangel before him, and secondly by the searing message that reached his ears and were engraved on his heart. He had experienced what no man had witnessed or heard in quite the same manner before.

The Prophet came back to his ordinary consciousness, terrified by what he had experienced. Was this a devil, a spell, an angelic inspiration, a divine revelation? The simple Makkan merchant—known as 'the trustworthy' among the people of his tribe because of the sense of balance and justice that were evidenced in his character—did not know exactly what he had encountered. Yet the words he heard rang out like a bell resonating in his ears and later he was to say: "It was as though the words were written on my heart." He fled the cave and proceeded down the side of the mountain, in a state of confusion and doubt. But as he stumbled down the slope, he heard a voice saying "Oh, Muhammad, thou art the messenger of God and I am Gabriel!" The Qur'an itself records that the Prophet raised his eyes and saw the vision of Gabriel now in full persona as an archangel, an image that filled the breadth of the horizon in radiant magnificence. "Without a doubt he saw him in the clear horizon, neither doth he withhold grudgingly knowledge of the Unseen." (81:23-24) Again the archangel said: "Oh Muhammad, thou art the messenger of God and I am Gabriel!" The Prophet turned to descend down the slope once again. But in whatever direction he turned, whether to the north, south, east or west, he saw the dazzling archangel standing astride "the highest part of the horizon." The only thing equal to this angelic vision was the prophetic mission of this messenger of God soon to spread forth across the world.

After the Archangel Gabriel turned away and disappeared, the Prophet of Islam descended the slope of the mountain and went to his house trembling from this unexpected and intense experience in the cave that far exceeded any mystical experience he had had before. His wife Khadijah consoled him by saying: "Be of good cheer and comfort thyself! I swear by Him in whose hand the life of Khadijah is, that I hope thou wilt be the prophet of this nation." She

---

"What shall I recite?"

45

then left and sought the advice of Waraqa, a Christian cousin and the one person she thought might understand what had happened to her husband. She described to Waraqa what the Prophet had said to her and he exclaimed: "Holy! Holy! I swear to Him in whose hands the life of Waraqa is that the Law of Moses has been bestowed on him and he is the prophet of this nation. Tell him to stand firm."[25] With the coming of the second verse of the revelation, God relieved the Prophet of any lingering anxiety about his sanity. "By the grace of your Lord, you are not a madman. Yours will be an unending reward; for you are a man of noble character. Soon, you shall see, and they shall see, who the madman is." (68:1-5)

It was a brief and stunning moment for the unsuspecting merchant from Makkah when the Invisible had suddenly become visible and the inaudible Word of God had momentarily become audible to receptive human ears. The Prophet had experienced a moment in which he was able to witness the monumental unveiling of one of the unseen mysteries (*al-ghaib*) that perennially protects, as from behind a veil, all direct knowledge of the Divinity. However, this was no ordinary human being; he was the Prophet (*nabī*) of God and Messenger (*rasūl*) to the world. Indeed, at that moment, in the deserts of western Arabia, the unseen mystery had commenced to become a living knowledge for all of humanity, both at that time and for future generations until the end of time as we know it. A light in the form of Arabic words had come down into the world once again with essential knowledge whose prevailing significance was to enlighten the future generations of humanity with the knowledge of the one God, a body of knowledge that remembered and reconfirmed the primordial revelation at the dawn of time.

The descent of the first verses of the Qur'anic revelation through an angelic messenger marked once again and for all time the formal descent of a divine knowledge to be preserved and acted upon by people within the earthly environment as a sacred testament of the truth. As Divine Speech, it was an absolute and final[26] communication of the Divine Being to humanity and all the generations to come until the end of time as we know it. After an initial appearance of the Aarchangel Gabriel and the delivery of the first verses of what came to be known as the Qur'an, a long interlude of silence took place that lasted for three years. Thereafter, the descent of the verses of the revelation continued to pass through the mind, heart, and soul of the

---

[25] Ibn Isḥāq's *The Life of Moḥammed*, A. Guillaume (tr.), New York: Oxford University Press, 2002, p. 37.

[26] Muhammad (PBUH) is identified in the Qur'an as "the seal of the prophets," which effectively closes the book on the plenary descent of knowledge in revelatory form.

messenger for twenty-three years until the final verses arrived just before the end of his life. During the moments of revelation, the Prophet had become a kind of human horizon over which the miraculous and blessed communication from the Divinity continued to emerge until all 6234 verses of the Qur'an had fully arrived within the human frame of reference and the revelation was brought to completion.

The messenger witnessed the initial descent of the Qur'anic revelation through the Archangel Gabriel, a luminous and virtually invisible 'being' made momentarily visible to the human eye by virtue of a special dispensation of nature. He heard the first sacred sound, the first word, and the first verse that would come to be known the world over as the sacred Speech of Allah. Throughout the course of the Prophet's ministry, the verses of the Qur'an entered upon his mind, his heart, his consciousness and in fact the whole of his being, and then passed through his heart and out into the collective consciousness of humanity both then and for all future generations. The love of the Prophet Muhammad (PBUH) continues to be a strong, living spiritual emotion among the faithful of Islam. One of the main reasons for this widespread love is the fact that through him the descent of the luminous in the form of the Noble Qur'an for the benefit of humanity was made possible.

Chapter Six

The Compilation of the Book

To this day, Arab culture is distinguished by being an oral culture as opposed to a written culture. Modern Arabs have a very sophisticated network of social communication that is efficient and far-reaching. I am not referring to the modern phenomenon of social networking which, while being characterized by the word "social", is actually a written and isolated form of communication in which individuals write down their thoughts and reflections, such as they are, through various social websites on their computers, sending messages out into the arbitrary mass population of the world without a true sense of audience that was an essential factor in more traditional social intercourse. To this day, many Arab houses in the Arabian Gulf have a *majlis*[27] nearby its entrance, a sitting area designed to accommodate visitors from outside the family who enter the *majlis* without entering the main part of the house. At any hour of the day or night, you are apt to find people gathered together talking with each other, exchanging news, thoughts, reflections, in short, passing their

---

[27] An Arabic word whose root means "to sit".

time in social intercourse. Arabs are seldom alone, preferring the company of others as a matter of instinct, and it is the odd exception that prefers to sit alone reading rather than sitting with friends and sharing their tales.

Small wonder, then, that the first verse of the Qur'an, the first injunction, and the first word delivered to the Prophet by the Archangel Gabriel was "Recite!" as opposed to "Read!" "Recite in the name of thy Lord who created, created humanity from a clot of blood." (96:1) In keeping with the true nature of the oral tradition of the time, the initial verses of the Qur'an were quickly transmitted orally among the companions of the Prophet and to anyone else who was inclined to listen to them. They were listened to, repeated over and over, recited to family and friends, and ultimately, having fallen in love with the spirit of the words and their true import, they engraved the words onto their memory and ultimately upon their heart, in commemoration of the Prophet himself who related that when he first heard the revelation, it was as thought they were "written upon his heart". Still, the Prophet realized that it would be necessary to write down the verses in order to preserve their accuracy and maintain their integrity without undue or spurious influence, corruption, or change for future generations. Thus, a process was set in motion once the Prophet died to compile an exact version of the book once the descent of the revelation was completed and the Prophet was no longer alive to definitively verify its contents.

The first verses of the Qur'an may have originally been shown to the Prophet on velvet brocade, according to the traditional literature, but the text itself as a written document was not compiled in book form during his lifetime. It was inscribed on his mind and engraved upon his heart, but the words that poured forth from his mouth were memorized at first by a small group of close companions, including Zayd bin Thābit, Abū Bakr and ʿAlī. Without doubt, verses of the Qur'an were also written down according to the traditions on such things as skins, camel bones and parchment leaves by Zayd and ʿAlī and perhaps others during the life of the Prophet, and the order of *sūrah and āyah* were made by him on Divine Command. Later, as the multitude of verses increased, a new class of scholars emerged, called *qurrāh* or readers, whom the Prophet personally instructed in the correct and accurate recitation of the sacred text. Eventually, large numbers of new Muslims committed the verses to memory because the Prophet said that there was implicit blessing in doing so. Those who could recite the Qur'an during the lifetime of the Prophet numbered in the thousands, while the number of Muslims at the time of his death exceeded 100,000. There can be no doubt that most of them had committed some, if not all, of the Qur'an to memory, a practice that continues to this day. These early believers were living torches of faith, on fire in devotion to the newly acquired faith and fully committed in surrender to God.

The first official compilation was made during the caliphate of Abū Bakr between 611 and 615 CE at the bidding of Umar. During the Battle of Yamāmah about ten years after the death of the Prophet, some 500 of the *qurrāh* or readers who knew the Qur'an by heart were killed, giving Umar, the second Caliph, the idea that the Qur'an should be formally collected in a book lest any of its parts be lost forever to future generations. He suggested this to Abū Bakr who appointed Zayd bin Thābit, the former secretary to the Prophet who was already known for his prodigious memory of the verses and who along with Alī had also written down many of the revealed verses during the lifetime of the Prophet. At first, Zayd refused to undertake the compilation of the Qur'an into book form on the grounds that the Prophet himself had never done so. "What right have I," said Zayd to Abū Bakr, "to gather in the form of a book what the Prophet has never intended to transmit to posterity by this channel? And since the Prophet never designed to give his message in this way, is it a lawful work that I am commanded to do?" Eventually, Abū Bakr convinced him to undertake the daunting task of collecting the text of the Qur'an in one volume and having it certified to be correct by others who knew it by heart as a heritage for future humanity. Thereafter, in addition to his own collection, Zayd gathered fragments of the Qur'an from every known quarter, including the ribs of palm branches, bits of leather, stone tablets and "from the hearts of men". He copied out what he had collected on sheets or leaves (*huhuf* in Arabic).[28] After the death of the Prophet, the *qurrāh* spread throughout the fast-growing community of Muslims as the authorized teachers of the Qur'an. A copy was given to Umar who bequeathed it to his daughter, one of the widows of the Prophet.

Ultimately, it was Uthmān, the third Caliph, who authorized the legendary prototype Qur'an as the universally definitive text about 650 CE. During his governance, Hudayfah ibn al-Yamānī, the commander-in-chief of the Muslim army in Central Asia, discovered that Muslims from other parts of the world recited the Qur'an in different ways. In addition, dialectical peculiarities had crept into the recitation because of the wide variety of Arab dialects existing at that time among the Arab tribes of the Arabian Peninsula. He turned once again to Zayd bin Thābit and entrusted the matter of the new compilation to him and three other leading Qurayshites. They borrowed from Hafsah the copy commissioned by Abū Bakr and brought together as many copies as they could lay their hands on, to prepare an edition which was to be considered the

---

[28] To this day, the Qur'an is still referred to as the *mushaf*, whose root meaning refers to the *huhuf* or leaves of the original hand-inscripted Qur'an.

canonical codex for all Muslims. To prevent any further disputes, they burned all the other codices except that of Hafsah, who had the original compilation developed years earlier that formed the basis for the new and final version of the Qur'an. Three copies were sent to the capitals of Damascus, Basrah, and Kufah, where they became metropolitan codices, while a fourth copy was retained at Madinah. All later manuscripts are derived from these four originals. Many early sources, especially Shi'ite sources but others also held the same opinion, believe that there was also a text of the Qur'an compiled by Alī, but later lost.

In the beginning, the verses came in intervals of months and in small segments. During the entire 23 year span that followed the initial descent in the cave of Hirā; they swelled into a continuous stream of revelatory knowledge, revealing the doctrines of the religion often through the many particular circumstances that occurred during the life of the Prophet, although all the Qur'anic verses have multiple layers of meaning and a universal significance that extend far beyond these specific circumstances that existed at the time of the Prophet. The early verses came when the Prophet was still in Makkah, while the later verses came after the *hirjah* to Madinah. Therefore, the Qur'an is divided into Makkak and Madinah verses and chapters according to where they were delivered. The arrangement of the verses was ultimately systematized in an order of descending length, according to the instructions of the Prophet himself, with the longer *sūrah* coming first and the shorter, more mystical *sūrah* coming at the end of the book. The traditions say that once a year, the Prophet collated together the verses that had thus far been revealed through the Archangel Gabriel.

♣ ♣ ♣

To this day, the Qur'an continues to be memorized in full by many devout Muslims, called *hāfiz al-Qur'an*, and every Muslim gives special attention to even the simplest reading to ensure that the sacred words are pronounced accurately and meticulously following the science of *tajwīd* with its strict rules of pronunciation and intonation, pacing and breathing. Western scholars have questioned the accuracy of the Qur'anic verses, citing the fact that the text itself was only compiled some years after the death of the Prophet. However, what they do not realize or accept is the true spirit of the verses as the absolute Word of God and how deeply the decisive words were etched on the memories of the first believers, who like other Arab and nomadic people had prodigious memories. As such, the verses have always been held in awe by the Muslims and the legacy memorization of the verses has been preserved until the present era. The accuracy of the verses as exact words of a true revelation never comes into question in the minds of the Muslims who in questioning the veracity of the Qur'an would be questioning the very ground upon which the religion is built.

Imagine, then, the intensity and fervor with which the immediate companions of the Prophet must have regarded the words of the Divine Speech coming from the lips of the Prophet himself, words and verses that had been delivered through the medium of an archangel standing in glory upon the horizon. What touched his heart with the fire of an emotional burning and the light of true knowledge must have seared the hearts of his Companions with a burning that is hard for us to imagine. The spoken words of the revelation rose up from the flames of a burning heart like smoke rising into the firmament as a calligraphic script of devotion and worship that was incomparable. However, in meeting the needs of future humanity, the sacred words of revelation needed to find a place to reside, thus preserving the letter as well as the spirit of the Divine Speech. It would be enough if they found permanent repose in the cavern of the heart of all peoples; but since that would not be the case for every Muslim in the future, these holy seed-words of the Divinity found themselves inscribed on leaves and bone and parchment, as well as within the breasts of men and women, to lend of their blessing, power and knowledge.

In this manner during the early history of Islam, the Qur'an came to be preserved for present and future generations of Muslims. To this day, most Muslims experience the Qur'an orally rather than through the written word, and by following the precepts and doctrines of the religion, they are able to internalize the very meaning of the revelation as it was intended to be. The sacred verses have been copied in meticulous splendor down through the ages in a variety of classical calligraphic styles. However, what decorates the manuscript of an individual life are not the *marginalia* or *illuminata* of an earthly scribe; what qualifies the narrative of a Muslim life with its own calligraphic splendor are the letters and words of a life story steeped in the mystery of the revelatory words of God, creating within one's life the simplicity and grandeur that characterize the revelation, and invoking a life of fidelity, love and action through the inspiration of the Noble Book.

Revelation brings a doctrine that conveys a meaning, a morality that establishes a purpose, and spiritual sensibilities that lead to a virtuous life, culminating in the perfection of the soul and a consciousness fully united with the knowledge of God. The depth and profundity of the knowledge of the Origin, the Real, the Truth, the Supreme Intelligence, and the One Reality, given its abundant luminescence and spiritual consequences for humanity, cannot be known and realized without the descent of a supernatural communication, whose divinely inspired text neutralizes all mystery and whose theurgic radiation suffuses the mind, heart and soul with its radiance (*al-nur*) and blessing (*al-baraka*). Muslims would feel abandoned and lost without the comforting presence of the book within their households and all of the knowledge and blessing the book contains within its sacred sympathies.

The Qur'an has alternatively been described as a recitation (*al-qur'an*), a discernment (*al-furqan*), the mother of all books (*umm al-kitab*), the essential guidance (*al-huda*), the perennial wisdom (*hikmah*), and the ultimate remembrance (*dhikr*). The name recitation (*al-qur'an*) recalls the manner in which it was delivered, the way it was received and remembered, and the means with which it is treasured and preserved, for the Qur'an is a reading and a recitation first and foremost, a compilation of verses and the word of God on the tongues of the faithful. As a criterion and discernment, it establishes once and for all time the true nature of the Real as opposed to the unreal, the light of truth overshadowing the darkness of falsehood and ignorance. The Qur'anic guidance shapes all personal and ethical conduct and gives definition and color to the actions of the believers, who would not always know otherwise how to behave in the light of their true desires; while its wisdom becomes an internalized knowledge within the heart and ultimately manifests itself back out into the world community as virtuous behavior that shines as light.

As Divine Remembrance, however, the Qur'an is the ultimate sacred psychology, leading the human soul back from the periphery to the Center and establishing the doctrinal knowledge and the sacred sentiments necessary for the soul's journey of return to the Divine Fold. The Qur'an is identified as the *dhikr Allah* which is also one of the names of the Prophet and remembers the Qur'anic verse: "Nothing is greater than the remembrance of God." (29: 45) Its living presence, as a kind of spiritual perfume in the mind, focuses the human consciousness on "the one thing needful" and recreates the ambiance of primordial beatitude that constituted the pure consciousness of Adam before the monumental fall from the Paradise, a consciousness that had direct perception of the Divinity without any shadows or veils, a consciousness that permitted Adam to actually see the Divinity in all the natural creations of Nature.

The interaction of human consciousness and Divine Remembrance is subtle and intricate. The very *raison d'etre* of the human consciousness is to realize within the individual self the knowledge of the Universal Self. Remembrance, then, whether it is through the Profession of Faith in the Islamic *shahadah*, in the repetition (*dhikr*) of the Name of God, or any one of the best of names (*al-asma' al-husna*) through the ceremony of prayer, or the remembrance of God through Qur'anic recitation, activates the human consciousness with the living presence of the Divinity. To fully enjoy a clear consciousness of the individual self without the possibility of connecting to the Supreme Self actually constitutes a desire to roam on the periphery rather than at the center, to live in an evanescent rather than a transcending world, and to recognize a fundamental mystery at the heart of existence, while denying its true origin and source.

The Qur'an, as Divine Discourse and Revelatory Word, remains the ultimate source of all essential knowledge, the well-spring of all morality and ethics, and the means of spiritual worship that permits the faithful to transcend their limitations and approach the true knowledge of the Reality as Truth and as Presence. Like the topographical features of the earth with its arctic and tropic regions, its seacoasts and plains, its mountain ranges and valleys, its deserts and savannas, its forests and woodlands, the Qur'an has a broad range of topical representations, including poetic heights and legalistic depths, dogmatic theology as well as mystic aphorisms, lists and litanies, prayers of supplication and modes of entreaty. Every letter, word, and verse is packed with layers of symbolic meaning that reach the human mind according to the receptiveness of the recipient. There is fresh meaning with every reading and the verses of the book are never stale or outdated. They remain a living testament to the inherent spirituality that lies at the heart of the created universe, a spirituality that we must activate within ourselves as a living reality, and can be done so through the recitation of the Holy Qur'an.

Whether recited from memory or read from the leaves of a palm tree, the words hover in the mind like dragonflies floating above the surface of a pond, with the force of a spirit whose fluttering wings create waves of inspiration across the surface of a human life to its very center within the human heart. From the man who initially protested that he could not read or recite there flowed the words of a luminous knowledge to be recited and revered by generations of devout Muslims until the end of time or until God Almighty brings their sounding to an unexpected close. When that happens, the silence will indeed be deafening. In reading or reciting the sacred text, the verses become God's voice on earth for those whose hearts burn with a godly flame, just as the Prophet himself, in becoming the human receptacle and transmitter of the sacred knowledge, became God's Messenger of return of His creation to the primordial truths embedded in the ancient wisdom of the universe.

As living legacy of a distant land from a remote era of the past, the Qur'an as Remembrance (*Dhikr*) and Guidance (*Hūda*) is the living embodiment of a voice that will never fade so long as human beings have faith in supernatural realities, have contact with the invisible, are willing to live life to its full spiritual potential, and preserve their ability to know things, not just as they are in their physical appearance, but to unveil their true nature through the language of a divine revelation. Every reading becomes a luminous echo of the Voice of God that hovers over the waters of creation with His abiding Spirit. Every intonation becomes an evocative memory of the voice of the archangel, majestically standing on the horizon with wings outstretched, robed in a mantle of light. Every utterance becomes once again the voice of an unlettered trader, in a secluded cave within the Mountain of Light, who listened and repeated in clear Arabic what no man had heard before, "Recite in the Name of thy Lord who created . . ."

# Chapter Seven

The Love of the Prophet

Muslims love the Prophet as a reflection of the love of the Prophet for Allah which in turn reflects the love Allah bestowed on His beloved Messenger who existed in principle according to reliable *hadith* before Adam was even born. There are, of course, mysteries and secrets that cannot be explored too deeply without shattering the quality of the mystique that surrounds them. In what follows in this chapter, we will attempt to convey a feeling of the spiritual emotion that emerges from deep within the soul and that expresses itself in this world as an enduring attachment and sense of longing and commitment that knows no equal among the other earthly emotions we usually experience.

Another mystery worth preserving as a hidden treasure that will never be fully disclosed is the place the Prophet holds within the grand scheme of prophethood, in the procession of Prophets that have come to nations with a divine revelation. As complement, the Prophet is also clearly identified in the Qur'an as the "seal of the prophets" and thus the seal of prophethood itself, implying that not only has the descent of knowledge in the form of prophecy come to completion, but that in a temporal sense, there will never be another prophet within this type cycle. The indelible seal of the Qur'an not only closed the cycle of prophethood, but also of prophecy as such, by a process in which a direct revelation containing the essential knowledge of the Divinity has come down to many different nations during the lifetime of humanity. The seal of prophecy shuts down not only the progression of knowledge down through the ages; but also reestablishes once again the primordial knowledge of unity (*tawhīd*) that initiated the universe to begin with.

In another work, I have attempted to describe the unique phenomenon that the Muslims refer to as the love of their Prophet.[29] Of course, love under any manifestation or guise is a difficult thing to explain, and perhaps rightly so it remains the exclusive prevue of experience within the human framework, but if the experience sheds any light on the spiritual emotion of love being described here, then it may be worth retelling. Like the facts of pre-Islamic Arabia, the details that outline the progression of the Prophet's life are well documented and have been studied and memorized by Muslims down through the ages until the present time. These facts also sit on the pages of the history books like clouds in the blue sky floating over the desert landscape, but what is the meaning of the shadows they cast down into the cave of our hearts, waiting for an explanation of their true import and significance in our lives and in the life of spirituality that we are attempting to pursue as true Muslims?

I found myself one blessed day making my way to the back of the great mosque of Madinah deep into the inner sanctum of the original mosque, which became the extension of the family quarters of the Prophet. It is here along the original southeasterly section of the mosque that the Prophet lies buried, together with his Companions and first Caliphs Abu Bakr al-Saddiq and Umar bin al-Khattaab. It is customary to visit the tomb of the Prophet and greet him with Salaams upon first entering the sacred enclosure of the mosque, which after the Ka'aba in Makkah is the second holiest place revered in Islam as a sacred sanctuary. I make my way slowly amid the multitude and savor every moment. The mosque is still jam packed with people of every race and nationality. Old and young intermingle; many are lying supine, others are gathered in groups or sitting in circles sharing their thoughts and impressions. People are moving about as I am, deferring to the space of others, careful to step over those who are resting supine on the floor without a care in the world.

As I move deeper into the mosque, I notice that the upper walls and ceiling are embellished with geometric forms, arabesques, Qur'anic calligraphy and mini domes hand-carved from wood in remembrance of the traditional era when the handcrafts represented a form of sacred art. Given the size and

---

[29] *Wisdom's Journey: Living the Spirit of Islam in the Modern World*, Bloomington, IND: World Wisdom Books, 2009.

dimensions of the mosque, it is quite a trek from front to back. Deep within the well of the enclosure, I come upon an inner open courtyard that gives rise to the heavens. It comes up unexpectedly and already the dawn light is bathing the inner courtyard in beams of early morning daylight. I take note, however, of a group of huge, light-colored sunshades that have been cleverly designed to open at the push of a remote controlled button and fan out overhead in perfect symmetry to protect the worshippers from the onslaught of the mid-day desert sun that promises to fill the courtyard that is open to the elements with its harsh light. I am told that the opening of these gigantic mechanical umbrellas is a sight to behold, like a double-decker Airbus 380 taking off into the heavens.

I know I am nearing the tomb of the Prophet through two pieces of evidence. Firstly, the architecture of the building has changed into a smaller and less grandiose aspect, and dates back many centuries to the time of the Prophet and the early Caliphate era. Secondly the density of the crowds has dramatically increased with people all vying for proximity to the final resting place of the Prophet. There is a section of the mosque cordoned off and positioned adjacent to the wall of the Prophet's tomb that is referred to and revered as the *al-riyadh al-jannah*, which roughly translates as a "garden" of the Paradise. The Prophet has referred to this part of the mosque by saying: "What is between my house and my *minbar* is a garden from the gardens of Paradise." It is an area that according to the traditions of the Prophet is actually a part of the Paradise that will rise upward and return to its original home on the Day of Judgment, which in Islam is alternatively referred to as the Day of Accounting and the Day of Religion. Whatever the truth may be, this *riyadh* is certainly a place to sojourn and rest before being confronted with the reality of the beloved Prophet's tomb.

As I sat in this "garden of Paradise", my mind took on wings and I began to fly through the peaks and valleys of my mind's inner eye. Call it auto suggestion of the tradition if you like, but a dream quality seemed to emerge like dawn mist over the waters of a lake. A strange, otherworldly scent began to raise my level of consciousness from the mundane to the sublime in some unconscious manner, and I felt I was entering another dimension virtually impossible to describe. Then without warning, I felt a surge of emotion well up inside me from depths I didn't know existed, an emotive feeling so strong and satiating that I could do nothing but surrender to the power of these sacred emotions and I began to sob a storm of hot tears for all I was worth. At first, I did not know why I was crying, except that I realized that the place, the moment, and the overall ambiance were powerful enough to evoke such an unexpected, powerful reaction. The outburst was not convulsive or hectic; it was sheer weeping without an obvious catalyst. It was not the kind of grief cause by the death of a loved one or the loss of a valued treasure; instead it was an emotive collapse without hill or valley, a release from the rigidity that holds us together in life, vast and inconsolable at first as a child's first confrontation with the unknown. The hot tears came as a soothing balm for the trials and tribulations of my life, the frustrations and the shattered hopes, the dreams gone wrong, the remorse filling my cup, the failures and perhaps even the successes taking their place in a long line of varied life experiences that I call my own. I sobbed for the person I had been and the person I might well become. The sobbing slowly died within me throb by throb until a wave as cool as spring water flowed across the shore of my being and an abiding peace streamed through my mind and body. I had received the gift of tears spoken of in the traditions of Islam in which the soul uses the mind and body to free itself of certain complexes of the psyche and psychological knots of the spirit as a form of liberation from the lower self and as a means of self purification.

The moment scaling such a height of spiritual emotion quickly passed because the section of the mosque called the *riyadh al-jannah* became a teaming caldron of wide-eyed humanity all in contest for a piece in this "paradise" on earth. I therefore joined the more sober, turgid throng making its way down the aisle that passes in front of the three tombs of the Prophet and his beloved companions, Abu Bakr and Umar. The energy surging through this area of the mosque was high and the atmosphere was electric. It was slow going indeed, and except for the occasional shove or elbow in the ribs, perhaps the slow pacing of worshippers was a good thing, because as we approached the ornate front doors of the tombs, with their silver-encrusted plating covered with Qur'anic verses, the realization suddenly dawns with an expectation brimming beyond belief that one is approaching the very presence of the Prophet. Here is where he lived, where he prayed and where he died. Here lies the man that Allah chose to receive His revelation and to deliver it as the Holy Qur'an to future generations of humanity. Through his mind passed the very words of God and from him, the word of the Qur'an passed out into the world of humanity down to the present time as an incomparable revelation, the final one to be delivered to humanity. Muslims spend a lifetime attempting to find ways to express their love of God, but their love of the Prophet comes naturally and spontaneously because he is the vehicle and the path through which the love of God is possible.

As I turn a corner and approach the aisle that passes in front of the sealed enclosures containing the various tombs, the dense but still orderly crowd thickens considerably. People, with cupped or extended hands in an attitude of prayerful supplication, are moving slowly forward at the slow pace of molasses and everyone proceeds deferentially, concerned for the comfort of their Muslim brothers and not wishing to create an undue stir. Then I am there in front of the tomb, and I send forth my salaams to the beloved Prophet Muhammad, upon him blessings and peace. Neither the hectic throng, nor the imposing and unexpected presence of military guards at the doors of the tombs, can disturb the surging feeling of humility and onrushing awe that begins in the pit of my stomach and rises to the tip of my cognitive consciousness, lifting me off my feet and beyond the gravity limits of this world. As I shuffle along with baby steps as one of a surging crowd of worshippers, I feel lost in the wave of a deep and abiding emotion and I think: We remember the Prophet Muhammad (PBUH) every day in our prayers and we invoke his name and sayings as a matter of course, but now I am here at his tomb, visiting his ancient home and place of earthly investiture. I have presented myself here in person to make my holy salaams to the memory of his sacred person and his exemplary life. Together with all Muslims, I feel a deep and overwhelming love for the Prophet to the extent that the evocation of his memory creates a feeling of melting in the heart and brings tears to the eyes. It is a powerful, indeed an overwhelming moment that will not easily takes it leave of me. In the presence of greatness, I utter my humble prayer as intercession to God through the Prophet, as I remember all those in need within the circle of my life, a dying brother on life support, my close friend suffering from advanced diabetes, and all those who asked me to intercede on their behalf. There is an unearthly quality to the moment, as thought a shaft of light were shining down upon my heart, filling me with a sacred and miraculous sense of wonder.

A moment whose quality will be remembered for years to come has passed me by, just as the slow-moving sea of humanity I am part of has passed by the tomb enclosure. Before I fully realize what has happened, the crowd has deposited me outside the mosque again like a piece of driftwood thrown ashore by the sea. I gaze distractedly and a little disoriented at the luminous glow on the eastern horizon as the sun announces its arrival and bathes the eastern face of the mosque with its harsh desert light, without any thought or mercy for the faithful.

♠ ♠ ♠

The love of the Prophet represents an extension of the love of God, just as the love of the Muslims within the *Ummah* of Islam reflects the love and respect one has for oneself as an individual soul yearning to be a reflection of the Spirit of God. The practice of *dhikr*, or invocation of the holy Name of Allah, is a spiritual discipline in the Islamic tradition that recalls the entreaties of both the

Qur'an and the Prophet to remember Allah as often as possible, since it is a spiritual means through which the Muslims can experience, internalize and ultimately realize the knowledge of God as a spiritually-felt reality. The remembrance of God (*dhikr Allah*) reaches deep within the practitioner to awaken the feelings of love and devotion to the Supreme Beloved that might otherwise lie dormant within the human heart. There is a wild and uncompromising spirit, unburdened by thought and book learning, waiting across the vast chasm that exists between the visible and the invisible, an ancient presence waiting to be approached that contains all the pasts and futures that anyone could ever want, a presence that only needs to be acknowledged in order to reveal the eternal moment within the present tense of our lives. To quote the beloved poet Wordsworth whose romanticism shares a border with high levels of spirituality: "I would stand, if the night blackened with a coming storm, beneath some rock, listening to notes that are the ghostly language of the ancient earth." (*The Prelude*) In return, there is the promise of a wild joy and a sense of otherworldly bliss awaiting those who bridge the gap between the known and the unknown, the seen and the unseen (*al-ghaib*).

I worked for a number of years in Alexandria, Egypt as a teacher at a local university. I was introduced to one of the Sufi sheikhs in the part of town where I lived and was made to feel welcome at his Thursday night gatherings.[30] The sheikh himself was well educated and had a magnetic personality that drew a person into the glow of his sanctified aura in the same way that the lodestone attracts metal. It wasn't surprising to learn that he had a huge following, many of whom would gather together with the sheikh for their Thursday night *dhikr* session that was the highpoint of the evening, after much socializing and conversation. There was never any fixed plan or program, no announcements and no encouragement to attend these gatherings. Given my Western upbringing, the sheikh made it clear that he wanted me to attend, if for no other reason than to make me feel welcome. In fact, between the sheikh and his beloved followers, they all made it clear that they extended every love and consideration to me while I was there in attendance at their gathering.

The love of the sheikh's companions and followers was spontaneous and given to me freely; my love for them was equally responsive and in reflection of their own heart-felt sentiments. Egyptians are very social people and they have great respect for foreigners of all sorts, at least in those days. This was

---

[30] The Islamic day begins at sunset, so technically speaking the gathering on Thursday evening had significance in that it was already Friday, the day of congregation when the Muslims gather en masse for the Friday noon prayer.

during the time of Sadat when there was great rapprochement between Egypt and the US in the wake of the Camp David agreement. Needless to say, every Egyptian's dream at that time was to find himself in America to take part in what they considered the great American dream which was in fact none other than the great Egyptian dream of the young *shabab* (young Arab males). Of course to them, I was a Muslim first and then an American as an added advantage, guaranteed to enter Paradise, they loved to tell me, by virtue of having converted to Islam of my own free will. "You are better than us," they loved to say, even though I knew otherwise and would shake my head firmly in protest.

The sheikh had a large apartment; but it is part of the domestic Islamic culture not to clutter rooms with excessive furniture, and certainly not to hang things such as pictures or Western artwork on the walls as decoration, the one exception being the occasional hanging of Qur'anic verses on the walls of a room or sacred Islamic art such as Qur'anic calligraphy, a form of art that embellishes phrases and verses of the Qur'an into masterpieces of artful script. At a signal from the sheikh, the large gathering of young, middle-aged, and elderly men dressed in Egyptian jallabiyahs[31] moved into a larger empty room but for an oriental carpet, and formed a grand circle with everyone holding hands, the sheikh taking up his central position within the group. For a few moments, there was a hushed silence, a kind of sacred anticipation if you will, in which all the negative energy of life seemed to drain away from the group, followed by a letting go as in a sigh, the noise and distraction of the world cast aside for this brief interlude of prayer and meditation. It felt like a collective pause, as if the group had taken a deep breath and had neglected to exhale, or perhaps purposefully held the spirit of the breath within themselves in anticipation of the sacred ritual that was about to commence. The sheikh began the ceremony by intoning certain sacred epithets from the Qur'an and these phrases were quickly taken up with rhythmic resonance by the large circle of initiates.

Immediately, the room became transformed into sacred space echoing in abundance the waves of sacred sound coming from the mouths of the worshippers. The circle of devotees held each other's hands and rhythmically began chanting the supreme Name of Allah while bending their knees and rocking their bodies back and forth, a revealing body language if there ever was one. I could see the white skull caps of the faithful as they bent their heads

---

[31] The Egyptian full length and flowing jallabiyah being a dead give-away that a person was from the nearby villages and were peasants or farmers, called *fallaheen* in Egyptian Arabic.

and the flowing multi-colored kaftans of the older sheikhs fluttered like banners in the turmoil of the wind created by the collective swaying back and forth of the group and the movement of the overhead fan that cooled the room with the cooling air of the Egyptian night. I felt at one with the multitude as we intoned the Name of Allah in a rising crescendo of sacred psalmody, my own body and mind at one with the bodies rocking back and forth in the darkness of the night. There was a rising tide of sound in the room that was impossible to countermand as the voices of what seemed like a thousand men uttered the name of God again and again in ritual repetition, forming a cadence and rhythm that was hypnotizing.

We in the West have completely forgotten the age-old tradition that repeating a divine name over and over in a mantra-like fashion is tantamount to identifying oneself with this name and consequently with God Himself.[32] It was as if the floor shook under our feet and my legs felt as weak as rubber. The sheikh himself worked the circle as though not wishing to neglect anyone and leaving no one alone, passing in front of each one of the devotees with his right hand raised in the air, pointing with his index finger in tribute to the great witnessing of the *shahadah* or sacred formula in Islam.[33] As he stood in front of me, I could feel his presence even though I had my eyes closed. The sheikh radiated a holy presence that seemed to sparkle and I could feel the power of his love enter my soul, mingling with my own heightened emotions as they rose back up to God, Who was in truth the Source of true desire for the multitude of worshippers in the room.

One hour, two hours, time went by as though in an instant, for the continuum of time has no true framework to contain this kind of experience. At times, I felt as though I was being lifted on high off the ground, the rhythm and resonance of the sacred name was so resounding and so powerful. It seemed as though a thousand echoes were making their way to some invisible shore on a tidal surge of sound; at other times it sounded like muted cloth that unfurled like banners in the wind, blowing in the direction of some distant horizon in search of fulfilment in the mythical realm of "beyond". Everything in my life that had once seemed beyond my reach, now seemed near at hand and accessible to the touch, to the mind, to the heart. I was one with God amid a multitude of voices, blending the humanity of our harmonic sympathies into the voice of the one true Reality.

---

[32] Ramahrishna has said: "God and His name are identical."). The Sufis have said: "God is present in His Name."

[33] After the bowing and prostrations of the prayer ritual, the Muslim silently intone the *shahadah* and at the same moment raise the index finger of the right hand as a visible symbolic gesture affirming faith in God.

There were those who faltered and lost their breath; one person fainted; several others fell to the floor, only to be helped back up by the ever vigilant sheikh who scrupulously watched over his flock and would let no one wander away and get lost either physically or mentally. The rhythm became breathless and the clarity of the sound united into some primitive, primal force that was indistinguishable from the ur-language of the Divinity. Eyes were shut and voices became hoarse; there were tears in the night. I do not know whether it was the collective emotion of the horde, or some secret door from within that had finally opened, but I felt a sudden rush of emotion and tears flooded my eyes and fell down my face in their salty pungency as I sank into a deep emotive well, feeling a lack of caring and an abandonment of all that I thought I loved, my friends, my job, my money, my books, my writing, my successes in life such as they were. It seemed like some great surge of love was being born out of the chrysalis of my former self as an exquisite butterfly, or as though a diamond-shaped crystal like the miracle of a snow flake, was beginning to emerge out of the lodestone of the heart. Something indefinable was being created approximating the feeling of limitless love that seemed to ride on the intonation of the sacred name as the Name of the Beloved. There was a feeling of intoxication to the experience that was undeniable, fused by the true spirit of the moment that brought the Infinite and the Eternal down into temporal time for one brief spellbound encounter with the holy Presence that was unmistakable because it was truly experienced.

Whether I had stepped across an invisible threshold or fallen off the edge of some symbolic horizon denoting the limits of "this world", there was an overwhelming sensation of having arrived at the open spaces of some expansive frontier whose horizon blended into the heavens in a seamless unity, heaven and earth together once again. A boundless spiritual freedom filled the room that was there for the taking and perpetuated by the swirling vortex of the sheikh, driving us forward with his compelling spiritual force—a vibrant, joyous freedom that rose up into the mind as in the vault of a vast cathedral, vaulted to the skies and reaching heavenward with its enveloping bliss. It was as though we were caught as a collective whole in a powerful embrace and were drowning in the wavelets of a universal sound that embodied the name of God and cleared the way to His Presence.

I remember thinking at one point: I am a ball of yarn unraveling, wondering what lie within the center of this disappearing universe, unraveling slowly but surely with every resonant sound. There was a distinct feeling of letting go and giving something up, something that once given up would set a person free. We sometimes have a similar sensation when we dream during the slumber of the night. Falling asleep is a letting go of sorts and a giving up of the active consciousness. There is the presumption of trust that in falling asleep, we will once again awaken. If we dream, there is the sense of a temporary freedom in the timelessness of the dream and provided it isn't a nightmare, the dream state can be extremely liberating. The *dhikr* or oral remembrance of God is a letting go of the self in search of union with the Supreme Self. In roaming through the inner world of darkness behind closed eyes, I began to see some inner world of light. A small point of illumination made its way through the darkness of my mind to become a swirling and multi-colored spiral, like a spinning sun with phosphorescent trails of light, undulating in the darkness like a living animal. I opened my eyes at one point, to replace the darkness behind my eyelids with the darkness of the room, but that spinning spiral of light continued to pulsate in the darkness of the room, turning into the vision of a million fire flies that was alarming to behold.

The profundity of the moment was so simple really; no one could deny the truth of the experience. You reach out through revelation and spiritual discipline; you engage the entire body in ritual movements that heighten the experience of the moment; you use the sound of your voice to call down the Spirit of God through invocation and remembrance that is witnessed by the angels, when behold, the very *sakinah* or supreme peace descends into the souls of the devotees. And nothing and no one could stand in the way of its holy presence.

Sometime later, the sheikh slowed down the rhythm of the multitude, brought the exclamations and shouts of the worshippers down to a whisper that soon drifted off into the night as the lights came back on in the empty darkened room. How long had we been entranced by the remembrance of the Sacred Name no one could tell or even cared to wonder. The sheikh's followers embraced and kiss one another with bright light on their faces and with gestures of deep fraternity that they felt for one another. I was, of course, included in the embrace of these bear hugs and felt at one with this rarefied community of friends. We sat down on the carpet and tea was served in miniature cups, clear, golden tea that tasted like the nectar of the paradise.

The tradition of the sheikh and his followers recalls the initial communal spirit of the Prophet and his first companions who came together in love and respect of one another as the first step in the remembrance of God.

# Chapter Eight

## Sources of Islamic Science

Before investigating the sources of Islamic science and its historic contribution to the body of scientific enrichment throughout history, a brief introductory clarification needs to be made regarding words and their meaning as they have evolved over time and within certain social and cultural contexts. When we write "Islamic sciences", what exactly does the word "Islamic" mean and what are the implications in today's world for the word "science", fully charged as this word is by its modern-day connotations?

When we think of "science" today or even hear the word, visions come to mind of black holes and event horizons, parallel universes and quantum mechanics, the Big Bang theory and the expanding universe. These modern mental constructions are not only examples of what modern science is capable of, they are also indicative of the kind of success and achievement that modern science symbolizes that casts a glow of wonder across the mind of modern humanity. We think to ourselves: this is what we humans are capable of in tracing our way back to the edge of time and down into the center of the nucleus of matter. If we can put a number to the birth and age of the universe and capture the singularity of the Big Bang on giant telescopes that float through the heavens with imperiousness, it leads to the notion that we are smokin', as the saying goes, and that nothing can stop us; we can do it on our own and without the aid of Heaven. The price we have to pay for this extravagant illusion, however, lies in the loss of our own souls and our ability through the Qur'anic revelation to lift the veil that separates us from the other side, the unseen side (*al-ghaib*), of the Reality.

Yet, the question remains to haunt us: What is the good of standing on the edge of time, if we have to give up the promise of eternity in return?

In the more traditional worlds of earlier eras that relied on scriptures and revealed knowledge such as we find—whether it be Hinduism, Buddhism or Christianity—in the word "science" used in its Sanskrit and Latinate contexts had a far different meaning than it does in today's world of modern scientific achievements. This is no more apparent than the meaning of the word "science" within the Islamic context in which the pursuit of knowledge, whether it be earthly or otherworldly, was brought to a height never before seen in the history of the world during the so-called Golden Age that lasted roughly 8 centuries from the first century after the death of the Prophet in the latter part of the 7th century to the end of the Medieval Era, or the beginning of the Renaissance in roughly the 16th century.

First of all, there was no distinctive word representing a unique and well defined concept of science as we have today with its aura of precision and technology, based on laws of mathematics and verified through reason and the scientific method. The Arabic word for knowledge, *al-'ilm*, embraced a far broader concept that was based on the metaphysical and universal principles laid down within the verses of the Qur'an. The starting point of this knowledge, its primordial point as it were, has been clearly identified in Islam as *tawhīd*, the principle of unity, that forms not only the pinnacle of all knowledge, but also the golden thread that sews together all the various elements of the creation and life into the fabric of a singular totality. From this starting point flows a structured hierarchy of knowledge—science if you will—that forms a grand procession of knowledge that leads into deeper and more formalized classifications of knowledge, together with the classification of the sciences, the levels of knowledge embedded within the verses of the Qur'an, the great chain of being that begins with God and passes through interconnecting links through angels, jinn, humans and lower forms of animals, and finally the varieties and levels of experience that represent the kind of knowledge we experience within life as truly human experience.

When the term science is invoked within the Islamic context, it is above all a traditional science or what can be called *sciencia sacra* (sacred science) that finds its roots in the Qur'an. It is traditional, and by correspondence sacred and universal, because it is based on principles that are unchanging and metaphysical, beyond the horizon of the physical world that reach into the world of the Unseen ('alam al-ghaib) for their nourishment and source. The true origin of all knowledge, no matter what its level of manifestation, is both sacred and original, sacred because it reflects something infinitely more than itself that it only gradually discloses, manifesting through a veil as it were, and original, not because it is first or new, but rather because it is a faithful image of the Origin and originates in the One Reality. "To Him is due the primal origin of the heavens and the earth." (6: 101) The point of departure of the traditional approach to understanding the true nature of the reality and the pursuit of knowledge is the same in all religious traditions, despite the wide diversity of the religious experience and the historical development of a variety of traditional civilizations. Knowledge, including the scientific knowledge of today's modern worldview, is understood in the traditional context as proceeding from a prime cause or first origin. This first cause is identified as the Transcendent with regard to the unveiling of the creation and the Center with regard to its presence within existence.

Modern science, on the other hand, has its starting point in what amounts to a revolution in human consciousness, a revolution that is an abrupt turning away from the traditional perception of a transcending knowledge that finds its origin and source in the Divine Principle. This impressive revolution of consciousness marks the revolt against Heaven and a turning inward toward humans, not through the intelligence of the heart and the emotions of a higher sensibility, but through the purely human faculty of reason, together with a rigid, earth-bound logic, that combined with the input of the senses forms the modus operandi of the scientific method. This approach limits rather than transcends the human perspective by denying a priori the authentic sources of knowledge and rejecting the powers of the higher faculties such as intuition, and the spiritual instincts such as faith and spiritual sentiment. As a consequence, the conceptions of modern science, relying as they do on the external world of raw sense-data and sense-impressions to establish what constitutes knowledge of the self and of reality, refers only to what is temporal and finite in the world, and reflects only the logical, mechanical, and "reasonable" criteria that conform to the five senses and to human reason.

The traditional sciences, on the other hand, operated within the framework of a traditional or sacred science based initially upon revelation that shaped not only the assumptions of Islamic scientists, but also provided the source material and principles that led to a complete understanding and philosophy of life. For example, through the pursuit of knowledge of the traditional sciences, the goal was never science in itself, nor was it the pursuit of a utilitarian knowledge that humanity could use only for its own benefit and control for its own questionable ends, without the guidance of God and His metaphysical principles. The lower domains that traditional science investigated were significant precisely because they were able to relate knowledge of the lower domain of reality to the higher plane of existence. In this way, the knowledge of physics, chemistry, and astronomy was placed within a context that led far beyond the individual facts of those individual sciences. The knowledge of these individual sciences was actually formal and mathematical expressions of a linear, physical reality that belongs to a higher metaphysical order. The physical manifestations here on earth revealed through the various sciences were not physical veils that blocked out all knowledge of higher levels of experience, rather they were symbolic expressions here on earth for a higher reality that is revealed when we lift the veil that separates the human mind from the higher, unseen realities.

Increasingly, it seems that we find ourselves in the uncharted territory of an exploratory and descriptive science, rather than the revealed and illuminating knowledge of the holy traditions, a knowledge that was the embodiment of a sacred science and a repository of meaning for the enigmatic mysteries of life. We roam today through the unknown territory of a frontier wilderness as wild and uncomprehending as anything encountered beyond the spiritual horizon of our time. Moreso now than ever before, there is a profound need for a comprehensive world-view concerning the nature of reality, such as Islam offers to the Muslim community, and there is a need for a perceptive approach to human origins and ends that can contextualize the identity of humanity within a framework of comprehensibility and true significance.

We have lost the knowledge of the Absolute, the Eternal and the Infinite, although this knowledge still lies embedded within the verses of the Holy Qur'an. We have lost the traditional message that was implicit in the symbolic image of the horizon, a message that spoke of the duality of humanity and the world, in which reality itself was shattered into two parts, the one above, the other below, with the horizon as the seam of the world that symbolically united once again the reality of this world into the seamless whole that mirrored the Transcendent Reality. We have lost the symbolic messages of Nature in which every divinely-created thing within the natural order expressed the unity of the Transcendent Reality. We have lost the ability to express the sacred sentiments of an inner spirituality that was once the human expression of higher emotions that reflected the knowledge and presence of the Divine Being. As a consequence, we have lost the *barakah* or channels of blessing and grace that flow through the arteries of the universe as a perennial dispensation from the Divinity to humanity to preserve the image of the Way.

Modern science risks developing a crisis of identity that is as objective and real as the findings that scientists have genuinely uncovered and have value in their own right. Modern science and her faithful scientists proclaim as a matter of pride to be objective, rationalistic, secularist, and empirical to the $n^{th}$ degree; yet in order to fill the incredible chasm that exists between traditional and perennial wisdom with speculative theory and hypothesis, scientists are trying to assess the metaphysical and/or human significance of their findings without the blessing (*barakah*) and benefit of true metaphysics and its corresponding spirituality.

We have the legitimate right to ask, therefore, what we are dealing with: science, philosophy, or a philosophy of science when it comes to the pursuit of scientific knowledge. Can science live with the prospect of routinely denying the existence of a "sacred science" while attempting to draw conclusions that are solely within the domain of the sacred? Can science pursue the discovery of facts and mathematical formulas without permitting itself the luxury of interpreting this knowledge within a cosmic framework of sacred philosophy and metaphysics, the very realm that modern science fundamental denies? What does modern science want to achieve? What is its purpose and goal within its self-proclaimed random, purposeless and chance environment, a point of principle that scientists so meticulously hold fast to like some kind of lifeline? Indeed, how does modern science identify itself, what does it stand for, and what is its mandate for a civilization that will share its fate?

The traditional sciences were never considered purely utilitarian in the modern sense, and "sacred science" was never the pursuit of knowledge purely for the sake of science. Traditional science always maintained a window to the sacred, to eternity. Through the use of the faculty of reason alone and without the aid of spiritual intelligence and the sacred intuition of things, which in the traditional perspective are actually faculties of objectification of the reality, modern society relies solely on the domain of the senses and rational mind, thus declaring the primacy of discursive thought and sheer intellectual prowess over spiritual intuition. Through a science of our own creation, we as modern individuals attempt to face nature directly, without any intermediaries or veils such as symbols or revelation, that were the traditional go-betweens of humanity and the supernatural.

When you withdraw the knowledge and the illumination of the Divine Principles outlined within the verses of the Qur'an from the intellect, the intelligence, and the faculty of reason, what remains is a human reason that must turn for information to the phenomenal world in which it will be preconditioned by its own accepted suppositions and assumptions. In its analysis and classification, it will take account only of those aspects that can be verified through some kind of measurable frame of reference. Thus, a purely scientific reason cannot avoid imposing its own limitations on the analysis and conclusions it arrives at. It is small wonder that the word knowledge, as it is now understood, consists mainly of human characteristics and is limited by the secular assumptions it has adopted. It is but a pale reflection of the "sacred science" and "illuminative knowledge" found within the traditional literature and the universal knowledge found within revelation. Without the benefit of this sacred and illuminative knowledge based on revelatory and immutable principles, we find ourselves back once again at our starting point in rationalism and empiricism, in the peripatetic world of mind and the enclosed world of matter without the vision of an alternative reality to substantiate the physical world within the mystic embrace of a higher reality.

♠ ♠ ♠

Islamic sciences must always be understood as being independent and clearly distinctive from the framework of Western science that has other sources of knowledge and maintains essentially secular philosophic approaches to an understanding of science and its broader philosophic and existential questions. Granted, the Islamic sciences were influenced initially by its predecessors of the sciences of antiquity, such as were found in Mesopotamia, Greece, Egypt, India, and China. In some ways, the Islamic sciences are a continuation of the groundwork of those sciences together with its own special Islamic flavor and coloration, aided as it was by the knowledge that came with the Qur'anic revelation. The Islamic sciences are a completely independent way of studying the phenomena of nature, the relationships between minerals and plants and animals, the meaning of the changes and developments that we observe within nature, and finally nature's true significance and final goal as a sacred sign of a higher Reality. As such, it is important to understand the Islamic sciences, not just from the point of view of their historical development in time, but as they are set within the totality of the Islamic spiritual, intellectual and cultural setting.

Within the Islamic intellectual and spiritual tradition, there were hierarchies or levels of knowledge and experience not only within the domain of religious faith and spirituality, but also within the domain of knowledge and all that it contains. Just as there is clearly identified levels of faith expressed within the Qur'an, so also there are levels of knowledge that are reflected within the natural world of phenomena, from the astronomical world of the cosmic universe to the quantum world of quarks and quasars, levels and planes of existence that are brought together within the Islamic framework by the spirit of *tawhīd* or unity that lies at the heart of the Islamic universe. The search and discovery of the key relationships between the various disciplines within the fields of the individual sciences was the goal of the leading Islamic intellectual and scientific figures of their time, from philosophers and historians to Sufi mystics. The principle of unity always lies at the heart of both the Qur'an as source knowledge for the Islamic scientific endeavor and this is what distinguishes the Islamic scientific and intellectual tradition.

The great chain or hierarchy of being begins first and foremost, of course, with Allah as the Supreme Being. He is the First (al-Awal) and the Last (al-Akhir) and "nothing compares to Him" as the Absolute Reality. Then there are the angelic orders, the intermediate imaginal world (the 'ālam al-khayāl), then the world of the jinn, the world of humanity and finally the world of the natural order of nature. The Qur'an continually refers to these levels of realities, and every Muslim takes this knowledge of levels of being and experience for granted as "second nature" to them as manifestations of the essential and absolute Reality of the Supreme Principle of Unity at the summit and pinnacle of all knowledge. The universe itself is comprised of "seven heavens" and the revelation continually refers to the "heavens and the earth and what lies between". (25:59)

In addition, there is a hierarchy within the human being representing levels of knowing and perception. The human being is not just the mind that processes knowledge and information as it comes to it; but rather humans enjoy a number of faculties that allow them to process a wide variety of knowledge in various ways, through the senses of course, but also through the faculty of the intellect that perceives God directly and unconditionally, through human reason that can be an instrument of the principle of unity as well as a reflection of the intellect, through the imagination and the higher emotions and through the heart which in Islam is actually the "seat" of the intelligence and what is often referred to in the Qur'an as the "eye of the heart" or the ayn al-kalb. In this way, the objective knowledge contained within the Qur'an and the subjective processes of knowing and perception with humanity come together into a unique harmony that once again reflects the principle of unity at work within the universe in which the modes of knowledge effectively interact with the modes of knowing.

Needless to say, this concept of the hierarchy of knowledge and levels of knowing and perception within humanity represents a unique philosophical approach to the classification of knowledge within the sciences, whether they be modern, traditional or ancient, to reach an understanding of the true nature of reality. It creates a unique and distinctively Islamic approach to the philosophy of science and clearly identifies the background and filter through which the natural sciences should be studied, a background that puts the natural and physical world within a greater context beyond the purely horizontal level of existence and a filter that fuses the physical creation with the Spirit of God. The philosophical approach of the modern sciences does not take into account either the great chain of being or the classification of knowledge, according to hierarchical manifestations of existence or levels of the creation. The Islamic perspective views as incredible the inability of modern science to put into perspective the knowledge of God, the angels, devils, and multiple forms of the animal kingdom, not to mention the kingdom of humankind, or even more incredibly, the knowledge that is based on the five senses and the faculty of reason in comparison with the knowledge directly derived from the faculty of the intellect and the "eye" of heart-knowledge.

Now, with regard to the classification of knowledge within the individual sciences, the natural sciences in the Islamic perspective are closely bound to the metaphysical, religious, and philosophical ideas that govern the entire Islamic civilization based as such on the revelations within the Holy Book. What is at stake here is less the facts themselves that are uncovered through investigation and experiment, facts that may be based on certain natural laws together with the formulations of mathematics that are irrefutable, and more about how these facts are interpreted and into what philosophical context they are placed and understood. It is one thing to know that something is true and quite another to give meaning and significance to those facts and their truth that go beyond their surface meaning through their application to the life experience. Consequently, the knowledge uncovered within the fully comprehensive Islamic vision of the universe, indeed the cosmos itself, provides not only a key to a true understanding of the individual sciences, but also the foundation and background to the study of all natural phenomena. To this extent, there is nothing stopping the Muslims from taking the discoveries and irrefutable facts of modern science and placing them within the context of the traditional Islamic vision of the world with its hierarchical approach to the classification of knowledge, so long as it conforms to the spirit of the revelation and the traditional Islamic worldview based on that revelation.

After the descent of the revelation in the form of the Qur'an and the completion of the ministry of the Prophet with his death, the first several centuries of the development of Islam as a growing religious phenomena were marked by the intensity of the religious and spiritual forces of the religion itself as a framework of a higher order of experience, with special focus on the solidification of the *hadīth*, on Arabic and Qur'anic grammar, and on sacred history. The second century then witnessed the sorting out of political conflicts together with the development of the schools of law and theology. During the 3$^{rd}$ century, the Islamic spirit began to crystallize into its permanent form, through the formation of the schools of law and the Sufi brotherhoods. The 4<sup>th</sup> and 5<sup>th</sup> (10<sup>th</sup> and 11<sup>th</sup> centuries AD) centuries witnessed the formation of the Islamic arts and sciences, and the beginning of the period in which the basis of the Islamic sciences was laid down as foundation to the Islamic understanding of knowledge. The fourth and fifth centuries are often referred to as the "Golden Age" of Islamic culture, when literature and the sciences expanded in many different directions, and there was a corresponding economic prosperity. In the sixth century, the political climate shifted away from this kind of intellectual development, and with the Mongol invasions of the seventh century, there began a general intellectual and religious decline. The Golden Age of the Islamic intellectual and scientific tradition became a part of the firmament within the progress of Islamic history, an age that was never to return.

What makes the Islamic sciences Islamic is not the fact that they were pursued and cultivated by Muslim scientists; they are Islamic because the pursuit of these sciences is based on the principles of Islam and the entire spiritual, cosmological and metaphysical framework revealed by God and set forth in the Qur'anic revelation. The original frame of reference is always God and His handiwork and not humanity and the desire of people to control the forces of the natural order. Within the Islamic sciences, the end of a particular science lies outside the immediate area of that science; in other words, the individual sciences are a means to an end, but do not define the end in and of itself, which within the Islamic perspective is the understanding of the true nature of reality as created and defined (and sustained) by God Almighty. The goal of the Islamic sciences, and its defining quality, is always the interrelatedness of all things that lie at the heart of Islam, namely the doctrine of unity (*tawhīd*).

Islamic science lays its roots in the concept of a Supreme Being who has created the natural universe, a science that reflects a systematic knowledge of nature in light of the principle of the Supreme Being, a science that classifies knowledge according to a grand plan of hierarchies and levels that reflect the levels of experience that extend beyond the physical world, and finally a science that understands all phenomena found within nature to be a sign and symbol of a higher reality that actually sing the praises of the one truth God and the principle of unity that He represents. Muslim scientists had the most rigorous standards of critical thought, while at the same time adhering closely to the principles they firmly believed in, thus maintaining their integrity as well as their vision of purpose. Let us now turn to the Qur'an to investigate and briefly summarize what it offers in terms of a scientific knowledge that transcends the limitations of "this world".

Chapter Nine

# The Science of the Qur'an

The Qur'an not only reminds us of the knowledge of first principles and thus represents a knowledge of a sacred science steeped in universal first principles, it also reminds us again and again that we are living in a sacred universe and that we ourselves are sacred individuals with human faculties such as intuition, intelligence and reason that open us to the sacred quality in life and offer us a sense of the sacred inspired by the holy presence of every created thing. One of the truths that shine clearly through the verses of the Qur'an is that both the world we live in and the universe that surrounds us are not just facts and objects to be discovered by modern scientific inquiry; but rather are symbols and mirrors of a greater and more universal truth that the Qur'an repeatedly identifies as the principle of unity (al-tawhīd) and the Oneness of Allah's omnipresence. Everything in the universe reflects and points toward this principle of unity to the extent that "Wherever you turn, there is the Face of God." (2:15) The Face of God lies embedded in every aspect of the manifested creation, a Supreme Being who originated everything in the creation "and to Him will you return."

Because of the unique status of the Qur'an as revelation and words of God that are still preserved as delivered down into the modern era, the very words and sounds of the Qur'an have inspired an elaborate system of esoteric sciences connected with the Arabic language and alphabet. As such, Arabic is considered a sacred language and every letter of the alphabet has symbolic value. According to Islam, there is an archetypal Qur'an that is unwritten and uncreated, called the 'cosmic Qur'an', in Arabic *al-Qur'ān al-Takwīnī*, and the Holy Book that was delivered to the Prophet Muhammad (PBUH) by the Archangel Gabriel, called in Arabic *al-Qur'ān al-Tadwīnī*. The cosmos itself is referred to in Arabic as the cosmic Qur'an or the book of existence,[34] representing a vast book in complement to the Islamic book of revelation, and like the revealed scripture, it also contains signs and symbols, verses (*ayat*) if you will, that have the power to reveal as much as they conceal and possess levels of meaning that can serve the needs of every mentality and that ultimately lead toward a complete understanding of the true nature of reality. The traditional sciences that developed over time were concerned with both the sounds and the alphabet of Arabic because they were virtually the keys, not only for understanding the verses of the Holy Book, but also the meaning and significance of the cosmos itself.

Therefore, the *ayat* manifest themselves within the Holy Book, within the macrocosmic universe, and within the soul of humanity, in other words "on the distant horizon and within their own selves" (41:53) as manifestations of the truth. "The Qur'an and the great phenomena of nature are twin manifestations of the divine act of self-revelation. For Islam, the natural world in its totality is a vast fabric into which the 'signs' of the Creator are woven."[35] Humans can understand their own being as a sign of God, the cosmos as a grand theophany and mirror reflection of the divine qualities and attributes, and the revealed book that contains all the verses and thus all the knowledge that a human being needs to know in order to come to terms with him/herself and the universe as the *vestigia Dei*, according to Christian terminology or *ayat Allah*, according to Islamic terminology. Each element has its own form of metaphysics and its own mode of prayer. Humans have the opportunity of living the human narrative in light of the divine revelation; the cosmos serves as the theater wherein the Divinity can become manifest.

---

[34] The 8th/14th century Sufi 'Aziz al-Din Nasafi has written the following concerning the book of nature: "Each day destiny and the passage of time set this book before you, *surah* for *surah*, verse for verse, letter for letter, and read it to you . . . like one who sets a real book before you and reads it to you line for line, letter for letter, that you may learn the content of these lines and their letters." Quoted in *Islamic Spirituality: Foundations*, Seyyed Hossein Nasr (ed.), New York: Crossroad, 1987, p. 355.
[35] Charles Le Gai Eaton, *Islam and the Destiny of Man*, Albany, NY: SUNY Press, 1985, p. 87.

Today's emphasis on human reason has overshadowed the fact that humanity enjoys another faculty that makes possible the reception of a knowledge "from above", namely the faculty of the intellect, which according to the traditional perspective is the faculty of direct perception and the human repository of the divine knowledge. Without the faculty of the intellect, humans would not have the means to either perceive or appreciate the direct knowledge contained within the Qur'an. Needless to say, modern science refuses to recognize the intellect of humanity as the receiving faculty of the essential knowledge of God and the filter through which people can perceive the higher truths, directly as it were, without any intermediary or veil. The human intellect knows in a direct manner, in principle and with an irrefutable certainty, the reality of God and the truths that govern the universe. It is a faculty of perception capable of receiving and reflecting the objective and raw knowledge of the Divine Intellect. The uncreated Qur'an—the Logos—is the Divine Intellect and this is what the religion means when it refers to the Mind of God being made manifest in the form of revelation, since the Divine Mind or Intellect has become crystalized in the form of an earthly revelation and provides to the subjective, human intellect the objective knowledge it instinctively yearns for.

According to a Holy Tradition,[36] God wrote with a Mystic Pen that symbolizes the Universal Intellect, the inner reality of all things preserved on the Guarded Tablet before the creation of the world. "The first of the things Allah created is the Pen (*Qalam*) which He created of Light (*Nur*), and which is made of white pearl; its length is equal to the distance between the sky and the earth. Then He created the Tablet (*Lawh*, or *Lawh al-mahfuz*, the 'guarded tablet'), and it is made of white pearl and its surfaces are of red rubies; its length is equal to the distance between the sky and the earth and its width stretches from the East to the West." The Supreme Pen (*al-Qalam al-a'la*) has traditionally been identified with the Universal Intellect, while the ink is the reflection of All-Possibility and results in the possibility of the manifestation of the creation, recalling the Qur'anic verse: And "if all the trees on earth were pens and the sea—with seven seas added—[were ink] yet the words of Allah could not be exhausted." (31:27) The Pen also symbolizes the Word, the Logos, in addition to the Universal Intellect, while the Tablet recalls the Universal Substance, so that it can be said that all things are created by the Word. These

---

[36] Another tradition, reported by Ibn Abbas, says that "Allah created the Pen before He created the Creation." Also, "the Pen burst open and the Ink flows from it until the Day of the Resurrection."

are the two instruments—symbolically speaking—that bring about and perpetuate the miracle of universal manifestation.

Under the circumstances of the descent of the revelation and the entire context in which the Holy Book of Islam is enwrapped, it is understandable that the validity and veracity of the Qur'an is never questioned by the Muslim Ummah. With the descent of the Qur'an, the religion of Islam came into being and with the descent of the final verse of the revelation, the religion itself was brought to completion and perfection as the Word of God on earth for the benefit and guidance of humanity. As such, it is taken for granted that the knowledge and more specifically the well specified facts and data contained with the Noble Book are accurate in every sense and do not come in conflict with emerging scientific data. While much of the Qur'an deals with the broader, more universal themes that relate to the cosmos and the sacred histories or ethical questions that relate to the human soul, there are many subjects in the Qur'an of a scientific nature that are of great interest to modern science.[37] In fact, none of the scientific facts referred to in the Qur'an can be contested within the modern scientific framework.

In addition to the grand cosmic questions that affect the soul of humanity, the Qur'an also makes repeated reference to natural phenomena on earth and within the universe. It will not be possible to give an extensive study of the verses that make reference to the phenomena of nature regarding the origin of the universe, of life, or man, etc. Those with a deeper interest to pursue these questions are welcome to explore the Qur'an directly in order to uncover its hidden treasures. For our limited purposes here, it will be enough to make the point that references to specific scientific data in the Qur'an do not contradict existing, known scientific facts that have been clearly proven beyond a shadow of a doubt. Let's look at a case in point. The Qur'an, like the Bible, says that "Your Lord is God Who created the heavens and the earth in six days." (54:7) In this instance, the question is less about the meaning of day and more about the meaning of the word in the original Arabic. The Arabic yawm and the plural ayam have the broader symbolic meaning of a (long) period of time in addition to the literal 24-hour concept that we understand in today's world. To further shed light on the subject of time, there are a number of verses in the Qur'an that actually emphasize the transient and relative nature of time, depending on the context in which it is invoked. First: "In a period of

---

[37] It needs to be clearly footnoted that we are referring here to absolute, fully verified facts that cannot be questioned. This rules out any number of explanatory working theories that may conflict with the Qur'anic account, such as the (in)famous theory of evolution, that are indeed in direct conflict with both the letter and the spirit of the Qur'anic verses.

time (*yawm*) whereof the measure is a thousand years of your reckoning," (32:5) and second: "in a period of time whereof the measure is 50,000 years." (74:4) The clear message here is that time is relative in our world rather than absolute, and not just a matter of "your reckoning" and the earth's orbital movements around the sun. To further complicate the issue, the word "day" in Arabic could also be understood to mean "events". Indeed, the concept that Allah created the universe "in six days" is simply not understood on its literal level by anyone, except perhaps Western scientists who take the verse literally to mean "six days" as a means of ridiculing the true significance of the Biblical and Qur'anic verses whose symbolic meaning touch the hearts of billions across the globe.

In addition to multiple verses that qualify the nature of the creation and how it was created, verses on astronomy also feature highly in the Qur'an; the Qur'an is full of reflections on the heavens and the true nature of the heavenly bodies and their orbits. There are over 50 verses of the Qur'an that provide information of one sort or another on astronomy that are surprisingly in keeping with the discoveries and known facts of modern science. Some examples are as follows:

**Seven Heavens**
"Say: Who is Lord of the seven heavens and Lord of the tremendous throne!" (23:86)

**The Heavens subjected to Divine Order**
"The Sun and moon (are subjected) to calculations." (55:5)
"(God) appointed the night for rest and the sun and the moon for reckoning." (6:96)
(For you (God) subjected the sun and the moon, both diligently pursuing their courses." (14:33)
"And for the moon We have appointed mansions till she returns like an old shriveled palm branch." (36:39)

**The Nature of the Heavenly Bodies**
"Blessed is He One Who placed the constellations in heaven and placed therein a lamp and a moon giving light." (26:61)
"Did you see how God created seven heavens one above another and made the moon a light therein and made the sun a lamp?" (71:15-16)

"We have built above you seven strong (heavens) and placed a blazing lamp."[38]

## The Planets
"We have indeed adorned the lowest heaven with an ornament, the planets." (37:6)

## The Orbits of the Sun and Moon
"(God is) the One Who created the night, the day, the sun and the moon. Each one is traveling in an orbit with its own motion." (21:33)
"The sun must not catch up the moon,[39] nor does the night outstrip the day. Each one is traveling in an orbit with its own motion." (36:40)

## The Evolution of the Heavens
A number of Qur'anic verses (13:2; 31:29; 35:13; 39:5) state that: "God subjected the sun and the moon: each one runs its course to an appointed term."
"The Sun runs its course to a settled place. This is the decree of the All Mighty, Full of Knowledge." (36:38)[40]

## The Expanding Universe
"The heavens, We have built it with power. Verily, We are expanding it." (41:47)[41]

Once again, it is not possible within this context to provide a comprehensive overview to the number of ideas and verses that contain interesting scientific information that was not only well ahead of its time, but also has later been given evidence and affirmed by modern science. For our limited purposes here within this context, and to make the point that there is a close correlation

---

[38] The moon is defined as a body that gives light (*munir* from the same root as *nur* or light). The sun, however, is compared to a torch (*siraj*) and a blazing lamp (*wahhāj*).

[39] Modern science has finally worked out the details of the sun's orbit around the center of its own galaxy. To complete the revolution on its own axis, the galaxy and the Sun take roughly 250 million years. The Sun travels at roughly 150 miles per second in the completion of this orbit. As with many other issues relating religion and science, the devil is in the details; but God lies within the first principles!

[40] Modern science verifies that the sun has "an appointed time" and will arrive at a final destination, called the Solar Apex. The solar system is evolving in space towards a point situated in the Constellation of Hercules (*alpha lyrae*) whose exact location is firmly established. The sun is moving at a speed in the region of 12 miles per second.

[41] Needless to say, the expanding universe is the most imposing discover of modern science.

between certain scientific facts laid out in the Qur'an that do not contradict the facts and discoveries of modern science, we will provide samples of verses in the Qur'an with interesting scientific data concerning the earth, the origin of life and the reproduction of the human being.

## The Earth
### Verses containing general statements
"Behold, In the creation of the heavens and the earth, in the disparity of night and day, in the ship which runs upon the sea for the profit of mankind, in the water which God sent down from the sky thereby reviving the earth after its death, in the beasts of all kinds He scatters therein, in the change of the winds and the subjected clouds between the sky and earth, Here are Signs for people who are wise." (2:164)

"The earth, We spread it out and set thereon mountains standing firm. We caused all kinds of things to grow therein in due balance. Therein We have provided you and those you do not supply with means of subsistence and there is not a thing but its stores are with Us. We do not send it down save in appointed measure." (15:19-21)

### The water cycle and the seas
"We sent down water from the sky in measure and lodged it in the ground." (23:18)

"We sent forth the winds that fecundate. We caused the water to descend from the sky. We provided you with the water; you could not be the guardians of its reserves." (15:22)

"God is the One Who sends forth the winds which raised up the clouds. We drive them to a dead land. Therewith We revive the ground after its death. So will be the Resurrection." 35:9)

### The seas
"(God) is the One Who subjected the sea, so that you eat fresh meat from it and you extract from it ornaments which you wear. Thou seest the ships plowing the waves, so that you seek of His Bounty." (16:14)

His are the ships erected upon the sea like tokens." (55:24)

"(God) is the One Who has let free the two seas, one is agreeable and sweet, the other salty and bitter. He placed a barrier between them, a partition that it is forbidden to pass." (25:53)[42]

### The formation of the Earth's relief
"For you God made the earth a carpet so that you travel along its roads and the paths of valleys." (71:19-20)

"The mountains, how they have been pitched (like a tent). The Earth how it was made even." (88:19-20)
"Have We not made the earth an expanse and the mountains as stakes." (78:6-7)

### The earth's atmosphere
"Those whom God wills to guide, He opens their breast to Islam. Those whom He wills lose their way. He makes their breast narrow and constricted, as if they were climbing in the sky." (125:6)[43]

### Electricity in the atmosphere
"Hast thou not seen that God makes the clouds move gently, then joins them together, then makes them a heap. And thou seest raindrops issuing from within it. He sends down from the sky mountains of hail, He strikes therewith whom He wills and He turns it away from whom He wills. The flashing of its lightning almost snatches away the sight." (24:43)[44]

### The origin of life
"Do not the Unbelievers see that the heavens and the earth were joined together, then We clove them sunder and We got every living thing out of the water. They they then not believe?" (21:30)[45]

"God created every animal from water." (24:46)

---

[42] This phenomenon is well known and often seen whereby the immediate mixing of salty seawater and fresh river water does not occur.
[43] Reference here is made to the levels of altitude and oxygen in the earth's atmosphere.
[44] Here we have the correlation between the formation of heavy rain clouds or clouds containing hail and the occurrence of lightning. The connection between the two phenomena is verified by present-day knowledge of electricity in the atmosphere.
[45] Scientific data tell us that life in fact is of aquatic origin and water is the major component of all living cells. Without water, life is not possible.

"There is no animal on earth, no bird which flies on wings, that (does not belong to) communities like you. We have not neglected anything in the Book." (6:38)[46]

"Have they not looked at the girds above them spreading their wings out and folding them? None can hold them up (in his power) except the Beneficent." (67:19)[47]

### Human Reproduction
### Fertilization is performed by a small volume of liquid[48]
"Was (man) not a small quantity of sperm which has been poured out?" (73:37)

"Then We placed (man) as a small quantity (of sperm) in a safe lodging firmly established." 23:13)

### The implementation of the egg
"We cause whom We will to rest in the womb for an appointed term." (22:5)

"We have fashioned the small quantity (of sperm) into something that clings." 23:14)

### Evolution of the Embryo inside the Uterus
"We fashioned the thing which clings into a chewed lump of flesh and We fashioned the chewed flesh into bones and We clothed the bones with intact flesh." 23:14)

"And (God) made of him a pair, the male and female." (75:39)

"God created you from dust, then from a sperm-drop, then He made you pairs (male and female)." (35:11)

---

[46] Animal behavior has been closely investigated in recent times, with the result that genuine animal communities have been shown to exist. The most studied and best known cases are of bees and ants.

[47] Modern data shows the degree of perfection in the migratory movement of certain species. Only a migratory program in the genetic code of these birds could account for the extremely long and complicated journeys which very young birds make, without any prior experience or guide, to accomplish this feat. There is the well-known case of the "mutton-bird" that lives in the Pacific, with its journey of over 15,500 miles in the shape of a figure 8. They are most definitely programmed, but who is the Programmer?

[48] Repeated 11 times throughout the Qur'an.

These examples form only a very brief selected summary of the many points of interest that were embedded within the Qur'an in the 7th century of the present era, data that were later to become identified as genuine scientific facts verified during the era of modern science. From the creation of the universe, the constitution of the universe, the nature of the earth and its atmosphere, the habits and communities of animals and finally the miracle of the inception and birth of the human being, all of these examples show the modern world that the verses of the Qur'an contain data and points of interest that are not only scientific in nature according to the modern use of the term, but that actually pre-dated their discovery in time through the development of the individual sciences. More than a thousand years before the current era of science and technology, the early Muslims had a knowledge contained within the Qur'an that provided statements that express simple truths of an essential importance to a fuller understanding of humans and the universe they inhabit, information that it took many centuries to discover and verify according to the laws of the physical universe.

# PART TWO

# LIVING REVELATION

# Chapter Ten

## Tribute to the Book

---

For now, we can put the historical perspective of the book back into the archives of the past and bring its journey from a cave outside Makkah through 14 centuries of history into the present era when Muslims the world over still love and cherish their noble book with a vigilance that is impressive in this sophisticated, enlightened age grounded in the findings of modern science and the all-pervasive influence of its secular worldview. To an outsider such as myself before I became Muslim, the attachment of the Muslims to their holy book was most impressive to my inquiring mind, but difficult to understand for those outside the community of believers with little knowledge of its historical context and little experience in what the recitation of the sacred words and verses means to the devout worshipper.

As a young Catholic growing up in the suburbs of Boston, I knew very little about the Bible, particularly the Old Testament. The family Bible sat on a bookshelf collecting dust; even the family milestones such as births, weddings and deaths lay undocumented and empty at the front of the book. In catechism lessons early each day in grade school, we learned about Eve's apple, Noah's ark, and the cutting of Samson's hair; but that was about the extent of it. As for the four Gospels, we learned the stories of Jesus in catechism class and during the priest's sermon when we attended Sunday

Mass, usually constructed around some verses from one of the Gospels, I listened attentively and felt inspired by the good words and noble needs of this holy man called by the unusual name Jesus. Bible studies were not an active endeavor in our household, although as devout Catholics, recitation of the rosary was compulsory when my five siblings and I were dragged back from the streets of our neighborhood on a summer's evening to sit with our mother and recite our beads together with the Archbishop of Boston that was broadcast at 7:00 at night on the radio.

As children, we didn't sit around the house reading the Bible as an act of worship. When I first became Muslim, I was personally intrigued to read the Qur'an with the understanding that this was, as the Muslims say, the very word of God. My own spiritual fantasy led me to wonder what God had said to the world at a time when the civilizations of Europe were experiencing the Dark Ages. It was not only a source of intrigue to have firsthand the knowledge of God in words that could be understood and/or translated if necessary, but also a source of wonder that such knowledge could survive intact until the present era without corruption or compromise. Of all the revelations and scriptures that have come down to humanity, this one was the only one still preserved in its original language and form. This was a journey of the timeless through time until the present era when the words and verses are still revered by those who believe in their true value and their efficacy on the mind, heart and soul of humanity.

I was scheduled to give a talk recently to a group of young university students about my experience as a Muslim convert living the traditional life that is set forth through the traditions designated by the Religion of Islam. In contrast to the traditional way of life that is the valued legacy of the millennia, I had grown up in the West, living much of my life in my adolescence and young adulthood as a wild, carefree, and seemingly independent youth, attempting to find myself and my own place within the riotous coming-of-age decades of the 60s and 70s, the so-called Hippie or Flower Child era, when hair became the icon of a generation and roses stuffed into the barrel of a gun symbolized the defiance of the decade. While it is true that I still believed in God and had not given away to obscurity, as many of my generation had, my commitment of faith in some kind of Supreme Being and Creator, I pursued mostly a personal God of my own fantasy, thinking that would save me from the uncertainty, turmoil and psychological complexes that life freely offers up to those without a comprehensive system of belief and without a clear path that will bring people to their chosen destination.

With traditional Arabic hyperbole, my host was introducing me to the student body in such glowing terms that I half expected a halo of golden light to appear as a circular orb hovering over my head in counterpoint to the humble rogue that I knew myself to be, full of all the faults and weaknesses that we have come to expect of ourselves, bound as we are in this age of shimmering mirages and endless horizons, with the illusions of greatness and absolute freedom that we wrap around ourselves during these times like ribbons and bangles. "He became Muslim after a careful study of the history, doctrine, and verses of the Qur'an," Dr. Abdullah proclaimed with a smile full of light before handing over the microphone to me, his face beaming with respect and anticipation.

All the facts of his introduction were true, that I was an American born in Boston of Irish descent at the very end of the Second World War, and that I had become Muslim nearly 40 years ago—not last week as many Muslims think when they are first introduced to me—while teaching academic writing in the English Department at Kuwait University, "before all of you were born," I quipped later on to the crowd of professors and students, much to their delight. However, his last statement about conducting a "careful study" of the doctrines and creeds of the religion before becoming Muslim was not true and I told the audience as much. "When I became Muslim many years ago," I confessed to the group of eager faces ready to savor my every word like honeyed candy, "I knew very little about the religion, its history, its doctrines, its demands as a rigorous way of life, requiring effort and commitment. And I knew nothing at all about the Qur'an," I quietly confessed to the group of surprised onlookers. "All I had going for me was a complete faith in God as the Supreme Being and a willingness to pursue that belief through the path laid out by the Prophet Muhammad (PBUH) that came to be identified as the Religion of Islam. My familiarity of the Qur'an as the holy book of Islam would come later, after careful study and systematic practice in reading its verses, first in English and then in Arabic, once I had "mastered the rigors of the Arabic alphabet," I confessed to the attentive audience.

Yes, it would take some years to become familiar with the vast historical, doctrinal, and spiritual record that supports the Islamic religion and its varied traditions that still comprise a virtually traditional way of life in today's modern world. Yes, it would take even more years to develop the skill and expertise to be able to effectively read the Quran in the original Arabic with accuracy and fluency. And yes, it will take a lifetime to not only learn and absorb the many levels of the essential knowledge that is made available in the Quran, but also to incorporate that knowledge into my life as virtue and light. What I had when I first became Muslim was the famed *shahadah* or testimony of faith in the one God with Mohammad (PBUH) as His messenger. As initial first step, that was all I needed, together with the burning fire in the heart that accompanies a person's conversion and newly found faith. The convert's experience of an Islamic spirituality would come later through struggle and effort in meeting one's destiny and coming to terms with life's challenges.

♠ ♠ ♠

At the time of my conversion, my only handle on the religion as a path of self discovery and heightened consciousness—not to mention the peace and salvation of soul that the religion promises—was the well-known *shahadah* of Islam, the well-known proclamation of faith that "there is no god but God Himself", that forms not only the first of the earthly duties, but that also constitutes the very foundation and ground of all spirituality within the context of the religion, with its combination of knowledge and practice, its first principles and universal knowledge, and its fundamental, enlightening message to humanity. The religion, indeed the Qur'an itself, begins and ends with the sacred testimony of faith in the one God; all the rest, including the Sharia, the worship, the historical development, and the individual precepts and doctrines of the religion constituting the framework and practical aspect of the religion, is summarized in one four-word phrase in Arabic that identifies the true nature of Reality once and for all time. The profound simplicity of these four words of the *shahadah* were like burning embers in my heart; with its simplest utterance as a kind of breath of the Spirit, I was on fire as in a bright, clear flame with the love of God and burning with the desire to fill my thoughts, my actions, indeed my consciousness and my entire life with the realization and experience of this new and unexpected truth.

Almost immediately after my conversion, I turned to the Qur'an which Muslims believe to be the sacred words of Allah. The Qur'an, as revelation, is the source of the religion as well as the source of all essential knowledge. "We have sent down the book with the expressed purpose of clarifying their differences and it is guidance and mercy for those who believe" (16: 64). Here is the final version, delivered the Messenger and Prophet Mohammed (PBUH), of the sacred book of knowledge, an illuminated scripture, preserved eternally on a tablet in Heaven, that offers humanity the ultimate understanding of themselves and the world as it is prefigured in its true reality. As such, it is a comfort and a healing during the course of the Muslim life. Here is the Explanation and the Criterion that every civilization must have in order to function effectively on the earthly plane. Indeed, the silence of Heaven would have been unbearable if Allah had not spoken directly and with words to mankind: The divine Speech is for those who have faith and whose hearts find a serene peacefulness and sense of calm in the remembrance of God. "Indeed, in the remembrance of God do hearts find serenity and peace" (13: 28).

Since the way of Islam promised to lead me to a higher and deeper consciousness of that Reality, I considered myself ready and committed to following this path to the end of the earth and beyond the known horizon. The details, the so-called "careful study" of the religion, would come later, when I had time to study the history and development of the religion and what it actually means to the millions of Muslims who are its practitioners, time to live within the great Islamic civilization with its collective outpouring of faith in a Supreme Being in the spirit of *tawhid* or unity that makes the Reality of God a unified and comprehensive totality as well as a complete universe, time to absorb the warmth and companionship of the true brotherhood of the *ummah*, or the Islamic community, that bespeaks of friendship and generosity, patience and tolerance, and a host of other qualities and attributes that are identified through the 99 names of God that serious Muslims emulate throughout the course of their lives.

When I first became Muslim nearly four decades ago, I had virtually no knowledge or understanding of the purpose and import of the Qur'an, much less what the Holy Book means in the spiritual life of the average Muslim. I had yet to fully understand the broad implications that resulted from the compilation of the book after the death of the Prophet, and I had yet to incorporate the sacred treasures of the book into my mind to guide me through the routine of my life through modes of worship and practical spirituality. My own experience with the Bible through my Catholic upbringing was with the four Gospels, identified in the Qur'an as the *injeel*, and much less with the chapters of the Old Testament. At best, I had read the account of Genesis, but not much more. As a child, we had all seen the story of Moses' parting of the Red Sea in the grand spectacle of the film "The Ten Commandments" staring Charlton Heston, nobly playing the part of Moses; but as for actually reading through the many books of the Old Testament, that clearly remained beyond the realm of my religious experience.

Interestingly enough, the Qur'an does refer to the practitioners of Judaism and Christianity as "People of the Book" (*Ahl al-Kitab*) and look upon them as kindred spirits, since many of the Biblical stories and other sources of inspiration overlap with the sacred history and precepts of the Qur'an. Unlike other world religions such as Hinduism and Buddhism, they are monotheistic religions and firmly believe in the concept of the one God. As for the Qur'an, prior to my arrival in Kuwait when I had my first contact with Islamic culture, I had never read a single verse of the Qur'an and had no contact at all with the Noble Book. In fact, I didn't even have a clear concept of the true meaning of revelation as a "divine descent" of knowledge to the human mind, and that the verses, as transmitted to the Prophet, were considered to be the actual words of God, a kind of Sacred Speech from the Divine to the human.

We know very little about the primordial first couple Adam and Eve, except what the spiritual traditions have related to us in scripture and through primal feelings empowered by our own spiritual instincts. Still, the symbol of the primordial couple remains within the depths of our being as an echo from some remote and distant past, a potential spark of purity and perfection that lies within us as a latent force of the spirit, and a premonition of future possibility for the human race, not as a purely physical evolution that witnesses the dull and deadened face of our animal ancestors the apes morph into the enlightened visage of reasoned, self-aware humans, but as a spiritual process that begins in the Golden Era of primordial time and leads humanity back to its origins at the hearth of the Supreme Being. Our inner world consists of a borderland that recalls the Qur'anic reference to the isthmus (*barzakh*) that separates the two seas, a borderland that provides ample room for us to maneuver in our exploration of self, and that bridges the gap between the external world we must deal with every day of our lives and the inner world of the spirit that animates our being and gives us our distinctive edge over the animals in the kingdom of this world.

The inner world of humanity is a spiritual wilderness of incredible possibility that we inhabit without the need for any formal borders. We move freely and easily between the two worlds that shape our existence according to the physical impulses and spiritual instincts that drive us forward in our pursuit of the undivided self. There are outer and inner world that complement each other, the one physical, tempting, beautiful; the other spiritual, revealing, awesome. It is within the borderland of the mind and spirit that we commence our search for the sounding cord of our being, a harmonious balance that has the power to return us to our primordial origins, recapture the perfection that we have lost, and become a "finished" person once again, complete and at one with God, unlike the unfinished entities we find ourselves to be here on earth with all our weaknesses and limitations.

All of the spiritual traditions allude to something that has become hidden or lost as part of the legacy of Adamic man within the primordial tradition. We recall the *soma* of the Hindus and the Persian *haoma*, which refers to the "draught of immortality" that confers on those who receive it the sense of eternity. The origin and purpose of the Sphinx, whose wisdom is summarized in its noble head and whose strength is contained within its leonine body crouched on the ground in mental repose, is enclosed within the folds of some distant epoch as an enduring mystery, a hint of something remote and a premonition of a secret that evanesces into thin air the moment we draw near. The Greeks recount the mythological tale of Jason in search of the Golden

Fleece, while in Christianity there is the quest for the Holy Grail, revered as the sacred chalice that contained the blood of Christ and thus the "draught of immortality." The Jews highlight the symbolism of the word in which the true pronunciation of the divine Name has been lost because it could never be uttered. In this respect, we could also refer to the "lost word" of the Masons that symbolizes the hidden secrets of true initiation or the lost word of many of the former revelations whose original texts have disappeared with the lost civilizations of ancient history.

No one from former, more traditional times could have predicted the lost world of the self that is clearly the modern human condition, a condition in which consciousness of a spiritual center has become weakened beyond recognition and the direct connection with the Supreme Center has been lost beyond our control. In today's world, in what we proudly refer to as the modern world, with all of its sophisticated achievements and technological wizardry, the central pin has been pulled from the axis of the cosmic universe. The vast world of the spirit that we cannot see, touch, or experience with the external senses is lost to us because we have closed the inner eye that once had the power, not to see the beauty of the world only physically, but to experience the metaphysical reality as an inner, human revelation beyond comparison with anything in this world.

The moral life of our time has disintegrated into the ashes of a spent fire and this in turn threatens with extinction the traditional virtues that we have come to rely upon to put order and clarity into our lives and to raise us above ourselves and our limitations. Our intellectual life has been narrowed by the abandonment of ancient customs and traditional beliefs that have well served humanity down through the millennia. The profound certainties of our inmost instincts have lost their edge; as a result, we are floundering in a sea of doubt and incertitude about who we are and what we need to accomplish as productive individuals in a flourishing society here on earth. We have no inner picture of ourselves that confirms to our true identity and sustains us through life as a true image of the self. Without the search for the Holy Grail and without the instinctive yearning for the "draught of immortality" that lies within us as a sacred remembrance, we are nobody and we are worth nothing. The physical being that we have come to glorify as an end in itself can be reduced to a single cell rendering us no more glamorous than a period on a page or a bundle of subatomic particles too small to behold, so that we can only see ourselves now "through a glass, darkly" as it were, without the aid of Heaven.

A brief survey of history reminds us that certain selected individuals made their search for that which was lost the stuff of myth and legends. They were in pursuit of that element or spark that would turn the world inside out and lead them into the freshness of an eternal day, in full view of an everlasting knowledge that would reflect the true nature of Reality, wrapped in dreams that had no wrinkles on their skin, because such dreams have no sense of time and no dust on their surfaces. They only survive as the promise they truly convey to humanity. Wise men have pursued the Philosopher's Stone in the magical form of a legendary substance that could change base metals, particularly lead, into gold. They risked grave dangers in the pursuit of the elixir of life, the "white drops of liquid gold" of legendary lore, sought after for its powers of rejuvenation and ultimately immortality. They crossed borders and submitted to rigorous rituals in order to uncover the Holy Grail, said to be used at the Last Supper and as such was considered to be an instrument with miraculous powers.

The legend has been linked to Joseph of Arimathea who according to the apocrypha was allegedly given the Grail by none other than the resurrected Christ, and eventually passed on to Percival who was a knight of King Arthur's round table. Jason and his band of Argonauts sought out the Golden Fleece, said to be the fleece of the gold-haired ram, in order to place Jason on the throne of Iolcus in Thessaly, understood to represent the search for the legitimacy of kingship. The story itself is of great antiquity and was a sacred myth current at the time of Homer. Whether it be the gold of King Solomon's mines or the treasures of the Sierra Madre, humanity has perennially been in search of the elusive ring or magic wand, mirage though they may seem, that will return them to the perfection, happiness and peace that is the legacy of the Golden Era and that still lies sequestered within us as a promise of a good and happy life. Sacred rings, invincible swords, and magic mirrors had the power to neutralize time and cut through the solidity of this world with the raw power of the spirit world.

That which speaks to us from within, the imagining that leads us beyond the limitations of the individual self, the intuitive knowledge that seizes the mind with its clear insight and its profound certainty, the higher sentiments that say this is the way of my heart, all that and more is lost to the modern sensibility with its focus on the material, the physical, and the merely practical side of life at the expense of the spiritual side. As products of the unique modernist vision, we reach deep down into the world of matter to examine the minutest particles of quantum physics and explore with high-tech space telescopes the vast reaches of the universe in search of a knowledge that will prove our theories right. We wait to be chosen and want to be called. Like children, we are expecting to hear the secrets of the universe without any active attempt to listen; we want to see a visionary world of truth and reality without any intuitive insight to substantiate such a sublime vision.

The call of the world and the call of the Spirit are the two halves of a single truth that cannot find their truest expression as isolated parts separated from the Whole. The open gate of the inner faculties, the feelings of hope and expectation, of a hidden inner voice, of promises to be fulfilled and hopes to be realized are all there, in a well-preserved niche within our consciousness, which we preserve as the expression of our inmost selves. It is our higher faculties that receive the essential knowledge of God and perceive the meaning of the one Reality in order to create an external life that reflects the inner person who lives it. The passing of days, the change of seasons, the success of people, the construction of all the churches, temples, and mosques across the earth, the accumulation of friends, money, and fame are one and the same within the context of the world. They happen, they have their place, and then they disappear and are forgotten.

Clearly, people living within the modern era still respond to those heart-felt instincts that continue to be symbolized within popular culture and the social media as the encoded map, the cloak of invisibility, or the book written with an encryption contains the secrets of the universe; all you need to do is crack the code in order to unleash the miraculous wonders of the universe, its hidden treasures, and its empowering knowledge. Wouldn't be love to cross a bridge or walk through a mirror into the enchanted land of our dreams.

What, then, of a book of revelation such as the Qur'an that contains the secrets of the universe within its pages? Don't we care enough to wonder? Do we risk ignoring a book that is already available to us and that lies within our reach; but that we pay no attention to as an antiquated tome from another era? Could we later justify to ourselves the fact that we have overlooked such a sacred treasure because of simple negligence, indifference, or worse prejudice for that which we know nothing about, embracing the closed door of our consciousness as an entry point to ignorance and loss? Do we prefer to pursue any number of books written today that spread half-truths across the page like phantoms of the night?

What would we think of a book of revelations whose words rise from the page and float through the hyper-sensitive silence of the surrounding air like the smoke of incense, conveying a secret message to the listener before the calligraphic tendrils of smoke disappear into the darkness of the night air. What would be you think of a book that has the power to hold us in its thrall, like a child in the arms of its mother? Do we dare to disregard its enlightening verses based on a prejudice against its humble origins? It would become a book that would never speak the beauty of its words again to the mind of humanity. The ensuing void would silence the aspirations of the heart.

Imagine a book that gives nothing freely away and lies in perpetual silence awaiting our discovery. The calligraphic script of the words is enveloped in darkness on the written parchment until we open its pages and the slow, thoughtful recitation can bring the words to life in the light of day. The noble book is wrapped in velvet in a remote corner of the house, a comforting presence waiting to be lifted from its resting place by some unsuspecting person in search of an insight or clue into the mysteries of the universe, or the intricacies of their soul, something that lies deep within them that they cannot put their finger on, but that lies between the letters and words of the page as silent sentinels of an ancient knowledge that when internalized in the mind and heart brings about the peace and sense of fulfillment that we humans instinctively yearn for.

Imagine a book that makes no sound and harbors no pretentions of being anything other than what it truly is, namely a sacred narrative that is older than time and nearer to us than the very breath that gives us life. If we knew its true value, we would seize the book and never let it out of our hands. We would carry it in our breast pocket to feel its cover against the beating of our hearts, or we would shove it into our trouser pocket along with the keys, wallet, and other essentials of our functioning lives as a talisman against evil and as an amulet to attract blessing. Its gold edging and calligraphic script beckon the expectant eye with its rare, visual allure, the Arabic lettering lifting off the page like tendrils of knowledge and smoke signals of ancient lore. A scarlet strip of cloth slips out from within its pages to serve as a bookmark of return to that place of peace and repose embedded within the script on the page from the turmoil and uncertainties of our daily lives.

Imagine a book that when opened sends forth penetrating beams of light full of knowledge and guidance into open receptacles of human eyes and ears and hearts, a book that contains a sacred history that precedes us by millennia, a book that preserves all the knowledge that we need to know as humans in order to understand our origins, our true significance, and our ultimate end, a knowledge of the essential truths that will lift the veil from our eyes and show us the true nature of reality. If only we had at our disposal a book that gives us a sense of true identity, a spiritual identity that draws upon our instinctive spiritual impulses to reach beyond our own limits to a higher unified reality in which we take part as conscious and thinking individuals and not as duped and deluded individuals in an the evolutionary profile of progression from monkey to ape to hominid to Neanderthal and finally to *Homo sapiens* that modern scientists would have us believe.

Imagine a book that identifies a true *Homo spiritualis* that has been created in principle with a human nature that is incomparable and unique of its kind, created as such and *in situ* as it were, human beings based on the divine model and created in the divine image, and not the random and chance development of mindless physical forces that somehow, magically, began to think and become self-aware, in a giant leap of mind of any known physical process that is as fantastical as it is illusory, like some grand mirage in the desert of the modern world.

Imagine a book that illuminates the darkness within the cave of the heart and sets it afire with desire and love, a book that throws us down into the depths of an earthly despair as we compare ourselves to the divine prototype, a book that lifts us on high with the wings of its presence and power, sending energy, rhythm and vibration into every cell and fiber of our bodies, a book that fills the mind and heart with a higher consciousness of its ancient mysteries and brings with it a clarity and certainty that relieves all doubt.

Imagine a book with secrets that would never be revealed, and admonitions that would never be listened to, and revelations that would never see the light of day if the book were not opened, recited and taken to heart by those who actively recite its verses. We bring the open book of our lives into the open book of the revelation, in order to bring together into a seamless whole the split identity of the human soul cast within the confines of a relative and temporal world.

Imagine a book that points to a place beyond conflict and war, anger and resentment, desire and regret, a place where our true identity is made clear, a place that unveils the object of our truest desires, a place where good works and art and sincere efforts and the true war against the limitations of the self lead to a better understanding of the inner self hovering on the threshold of eternity, a book whose verses give glimpses into how we should live our lives, a book that reveals the secret of a good death and offers premonitions of the future life of the soul. All anyone has to do is pick up the book, open its pages, and intone the words and verses in order to listen to and hear the very sound of the Divinity.

There is something inside the Qur'an that lures the Muslims back to its inner embrace; something mysterious and evocative of the promise of fulfillment, full of sound and light that beckons like a distant star in the darkness of the firmament with its pulsating mystery evocative of eternal time and infinite space. There is something inside every human being, as though written with invisible ink, something unknowable and mysterious, lurking in the spaces within which no one can touch, but that needs to be approached cautiously, something desperately obscure, but that needs to be cracked open and experienced come what may, to become known and make a difference, not just as a latent curiosity of the mind, but also something that opens into the spirit of humanity that must be revealed and make itself felt within the immediacy of the world.

The Qur'an enlightens our minds, breaks our hearts, and ultimately shatters our world in order to bring the pieces back together again in the spirit of unity that the holy book has come to proclaim, a sense of unity that once instilled within the hearts of the Muslims could change the destiny of the world, one by one, heart by heart.

## Chapter Eleven

## Seed Words of the Divinity

Every spiritual tradition and the corresponding religion that forms the cornerstone of that tradition, contains an initial spark—a miracle if you will—that becomes the smoldering ember at its heart whose perennial glow keeps the tradition alive as it finds its way into the hearts of its followers. Because this source of knowledge and illumination finds its way into this world from an otherworldly dimension that is "unseen," it is referred to as revelation and can take a variety of forms.

In principle and as the ultimate mode of communication from the Divine Being to the human being, revelation—in whatever form it reveals itself—dispels the fundamental predicament facing people who live under the spell of a "holy mystery" (*mysterium sacrum*), a spell that it cannot avoid and that has been laid on it since the beginning of time. It reveals the secret nature of both humanity and the universe and creates pathways through the perennial mystery that overlays the true nature of the universal experience. Revelation touches upon primordial memories within us that exist as the birthright of our true inner nature. Between the covers of revelation, time becomes eternal; space becomes infinite; light becomes a symbol that reminds us of the Light of God that illuminates our source and origin. The Qur'an states it explicitly so that there is no doubt: "God is the Light of the Heavens and Earth." (24:35)

While every spiritual tradition has its own unique character, the miracle of the Islamic tradition comes in the form of a book. Its initial descent as verses into the mind of the Prophet Muhammad (PBUH) marks the beginning of the Religion of Islam, while the final verse once delivered marked the completion and perfection of the religion as the ultimate and final message to mankind[49] and seals the mission of the prophets in the progression of prophethood for all time.[50] Through the words of revelation, the worshipper can send forth beyond earth's shadow and into infinite space words of a divine discourse that have a Divine Listener awaiting the echo of these entreating from the human domain.

The Religion of Islam is founded on the principles of revealed knowledge that originate with a Supreme Being Who is the First Cause (*al-Awwal*), the Final End (*al-Akhir*), the Truth (*al-Haqq*), and the One *(al-Ahad)* among other sublime attributes.[51] This revelatory knowledge forms the solid foundation of a science of knowing and perception that fully integrates the outer appearances of all natural phenomena, as well as their qualitative and numinous value, into a single unified reality, which is actually the holy grail of a single unified theory of knowledge that modern science aggressively seeks through the theory of relativity and quantum physics but hasn't yet found on the strictly human plane of existence. In Islam, there cannot be only a knowledge of the outward appearance of things—or what we usually call natural phenomena—without a knowledge of their inner reality; just as there cannot be a knowledge of this inner reality without a corresponding knowledge of the outer appearance of that reality within the context of this world.

Similarly with the Holy Qur'an that the Muslims rely on as the source of their inspiration and guidance, the integrality of the revelation cannot be

---

[49] The descent of the Qur'anic revelation began in the cave of Hira outside Makkah with the word *iqra'* which means "recite" or "read": "Recite in the name of thy Lord and Cherisher, who created, created man from the clot of blood" (96:102). Thus, God immediately identified Himself to the messenger Muhammad as the Lord and Creator of all mankind. His earthly ministry came to its final conclusion with the words of the last revealed verse: "This day have I perfected your religion for you, completed My favor upon you, and have chosen for you Islam as your religion" (5:3). It was not long after the revelation of this final verse that the messenger died.

[50] "Muhammad is not the father of any of your men, but (he is) the Messenger of Allah, and the Seal of the Prophets: and Allah has full knowledge of all things" (33:40).

[51] The Qur'an officially identifies 99 qualifying Names of God in addition to the reference of other attributes that are implicit in the Qur'anic text. Needless to say, these "Names" aid considerably the human mentality in coming to terms with the great unknown and unknowable quality—the factor of mystery—that hovers perennially around the idea of God.

understood simply from its letters and words, from its outward literal sense; it can be understood only when interpreted by the spiritual science[52] of its inner meaning through sacred symbolism. There is an absolute union that exists between the inner reality of a thing and its external appearance, and it requires both spiritual and natural science to define the true vision of the one Reality. This remains the modern-day challenge, namely to unite the vision of sacred science with the practical knowledge of modern science so that the future generations of humanity may enjoy a more truly enlightened worldview that combines the best of both worlds.

According to the Islamic worldview, a divine revelation is the vision of the Absolute from the viewpoint of the Absolute; a Self-Disclosure from God to His thinking, rational, human creation that recalls the primordial revelation[53] and sends forth knowledge into the world of humanity from the original, ultimate source of all knowledge. Revelation portrays the physical world as the consequence of actions initiated by the Creator and it offers the study of nature as a science of signs and symbols whose intricacy and deeper levels of meaning reflect the design and intelligence of the Supreme Being and not the random encounters that physical matter may opportune by way of accident.

The traditional worldview understands human beings to be thinking beings made as the human reflection of the Divine Being, with a consciousness that mirrors the Supreme Consciousness, beings that enjoy a variety of higher faculties that can connect them directly with this higher order of Reality. Thus, the Truth has been made known to the human mentality in an absolute and unequivocal manner. Because of free will, human beings are at liberty to accept, turn to, and surrender their minds and hearts to this Supreme Intelligence and this Omniscient Being. Human intelligence, supported by both intellect at its upper range and reason at its lower range, can form its own judgments. The way people live their lives and meet their destiny as it unfolds to them like a banner in the winds of time becomes sufficient evidence of the

---

[52] We use this term, deliberately running the risk of accusations of misappropriation. The term "science" itself was once understood within a sacred, revelatory, and philosophical context as a true knowledge, a first knowledge of the reality. The term 'science' as knowledge of an earth-bound, secular, and strictly rational as opposed to metaphysical worldview is a relatively recent phenomenon.

[53] The typical point of origin of any well-developed traditional culture was an external revelation whether it be in the form of a man or a book, such as Moses for Judaism, Lao-Tzu for Taoism, the Buddha for Buddhism, Jesus for Christianity. Each of these revelations, which contained multiple meanings *ab initio*, both remembered the Primordial Tradition in its essential form and resulted in creating an established "religion" that could relate to the aspirations and needs of a humanity that would otherwise be "groping in the dark."

validity of their choice of purpose and direction.

The traditional view in Islam is that there are two Qur'ans, the one metacosmic and uncreated and the other an earthly document, created in an auditory and ultimately written form suited to the demands of this world and the human mentalities that rely on its knowledge and power to enlighten their minds and awaken their higher spiritual emotions. The celestial Qur'an is referred to in the Islamic traditions as *al-Qur'an al-Takwini* and the terrestrial Qur'an is called *al-Qur'an al-Tadwini* whose mode of expression is determined by certain human contingencies so that the Muslims can actually hold the Book in their hands[54] and partake of its knowledge and blessing. For the Muslims, the written book that rests on the uppermost shelves of their homes partakes of a different dimension than any ordinary book we have ever known or will ever know, partly because its substance is not of this world and partly because its inner reality lies far beyond the contingencies of this world.

The question could be asked why Muslims treasure and love what they sometimes refer to as the Noble Qur'an. The answer must lie in many different factors, not the least of which is that it is an expression of their love of both the Prophet and their love of God. For one thing, the Qur'an addresses itself directly to the human soul rather than to the human mind, possessing an inner dimension that no literal, philological, or literary analysis can set forth and explain away as a purely human document. As such, it has powers and properties that reflect its celestial origin, and when read or recited, its influence moves into the innermost core of the human entity to give shape and coloration to the fundamental instincts that emanate out of the soul in search of their fullest expression and fulfillment. Through vibration, through sound, through letters, words and phrases that constitute the holy Book, the divine discourse enters the mind, heart and soul of the believing Muslim as a profound remembrance (*dhikr*) of the Divine Being and knowledge of the one Reality.

Moreover, it is said that the Book addresses the soul directly because it overwhelms the profane and the earthly environment that we understand all too well with a sense of the sacred and otherworldly, because it casts the absolute and objective quality of the Real upon the relative and subjective aspects of the temporal world, because it responds to the human yearning for the Beyond with the plenitude of the Divine Self-disclosure, and because it brings the presence of the Source and Center into the world of diffusion and periphery. This yearning of the mind and heart for the absolute, definitive

---

[54] After the ritual purification, while non-Muslims read translations that have no particular liturgical value and require no special precaution.

knowledge of God is fundamental to the human soul and lies at the very heart of our ambition to transcend the broad range of human limitations through the aid and benevolence of a Supreme Intelligence Who ultimately provides the means for the transcendence of the human condition.

In return for the beatitude of the Divine Disclosure, the soul responds naturally to the Object of its innermost desire. What is it that the soul desires most and reflects within the mind and heart as the fundamental human aspiration? The answer must lie somewhere within the intricate weave of human nature and the aspiration of the human soul to transcend its fragmented and lonely state of being here on earth, cut off as it is both from the knowledge and the experience of the unity that lies at the heart of creation. As everyone knows through direct experience, the human soul as we understand it, is fragile and weak, prone to waywardness and suffering, and divided by the temptations of this world and the glories of the world beyond physical forms. The great themes of the Qur'an address the broad expanse of all human endeavors and enlighten humanity on the mysteries of the human condition. The profound doctrinal themes, the great ethical questions, and the sacred sentiments all reflect the fundamental elements that constitute the framework of spirituality that takes into account the human ability of thought, free will and practical action.

The trials and insecurity of life are counterbalanced by the serenity and peace that is the promise of a person's *islam* (surrender). The uncertainty reflected in the perennial mystery of life is counterbalanced by the absolute quality and the certainty that is the cornerstone of the Word of God. The imbalance and disequilibrium of the human soul is counterbalanced by the balance and equilibrium implicit in the knowledge of the one Reality. The chronic forgetfulness of our true self-identity is counterbalanced by the consciousness of the Supreme Identity associated with the Name of God. The density of the earthly and the mundane is offset by the ethereal quality of the mystic and the spiritual with its liberating quality and overwhelming joy. The linear quality of the strictly horizontal perception with its perennial uncertainty and doubt is seared through like a knife and revitalized by the incisive quality of the vertical disclosure. Finally, the endless diversity and multiplicity of "this world" is counterbalanced—indeed resolved—by the unity and oneness of the Transcendent Center that exists at the heart of the metacosmic vortex of the universe. All these grand themes lead toward the development within the soul of that unity implicit in the human world, the Qur'anic world and the cosmic world.

The Holy Qur'an is a terrestrial (written in formal, classical Arabic words and grammar) as well as celestial (echoed through timeless eternity through sound vibration) book, capable of being contained in the heart as well as held in the hand of the Muslims. Its exclusive quality lies in the manner in which it has become audible and visible, and therefore those who come in contact with it without prejudice, and with a traditional sensibility for the majestic and the sacred, are ready to be the human instrument that is played upon by the divine sound and the visual symbols of the Arabic letters. The Qur'an is a sonorous and visual universe that enters the mind and heart as forms of audible and visual forms of sacred and revelatory art that have the power to transform the human body into a living reed, a human calamus and flute. Psalmody is the first art of Islam, while its second sacred art is stylized through calligraphy,[55] constituting the letters and words of the Noble Book and reflecting on the earthly plane the writing on the Guarded Tablet (al-lawh al-mahfouz) that is preserved in Heaven. Psalmody moderates the sound and modulation of the verses, while calligraphy is a sacred art that humans carry within themselves from the delivery of the first revelation since the Qur'an states that "He taught man with the Pen, taught man what he knew not." (96:4-5)

♠ ♠ ♠

If you make a survey of the monotheistic religions, you will discover that Judaism came within an era that represented the young soul of humanity, a collective soul that needed to be reminded of the universal principle of the one God and the unity that lies at the heart of the cosmic reality. It was a religion of strict laws and professed obedience to the Grand Patriarch of the Lord God, a religion that created the Jewish nation within the framework of a sacred history that saw these people led out of the bondage they experienced in Egypt, a way of exile that eventually brought them to the edge of the Promise Land.

Christianity, on the other hand, was born out of the historical life of Jesus of Nazareth who became the living revelation that embodied within the incarnation of a man the knowledge and spirit of the Divinity. In fact, in the Qur'anic view, Jesus was a prophet to humanity: "He (Jesus) said: Indeed, I am a servant of Allah; He hath given me revelation and made me a prophet." (19:30) Christianity came to be known as the religion of love precisely because it was the love that Jesus expressed to others that formed the ground and overarching spirit of the religion.

---

[55] "Calligraphy is the basic art of creation of points and lines in an endless variety of forms and rhythms which never cease to bring about recollection (tidhkar or dhikr) of the Primordial Act of the Divine Pen for those who are capable of contemplating in forms the trace of the Formless" (S. H. Nasr, Islamic Art and Spirituality [Albany, NY: SUNY Press, 1987], p. 19).

Then, in the 7<sup>th</sup> century in central Arabic, the Religion of Islam came to fruition with the descent of the Qur'an, the most recent revelation bestowed upon humanity as a living document of the Word of God. Islam distinguishes itself as a way of life that remembers the primordial religion of the Golden Era of Eden, the *din al-hanif*, when the first human couple, Adam and Eve, walked and talked with God, a religion that also puts the "seal of the prophets" upon the entire process of revelation, and brings the concept of religion to completion and perfection as the last of the revelations from the Divine to the human.

As we wrote earlier but that bears repeating, the descent of the first verses of the Qur'anic revelation through the Archangel Messenger, Gabriel, marked the formal descent of a divine knowledge to be preserved and acted upon by people within the earthly environment. As Divine Speech, it was an absolute and final[56] communication of the Divine Being to present humanity. After an initial interlude of silence that lasted for three years, the descent of the verses of the revelation continued to pass through the heart, soul, and mind of the messenger for twenty-three years until just before the end of his life. During the moments of revelation, the Prophet had become a kind of human horizon over which the miraculous and blessed communication from the Divinity continued to emerge until all 6234 verses of the Qur'an had fully arrived within the human frame of reference and the revelation was complete.

The messenger witnessed the initial descent of the Qur'anic revelation through the Archangel Gabriel, a luminous and virtually invisible 'being' made momentarily visible to the human eye. He heard the first sacred sound, the first word and the first verse that would come to be known the world over as the sacred Speech of Allah. Throughout the course of the Prophet's ministry, the verses of the Qur'an entered upon his mind, his heart, his consciousness and in fact the whole of his being, and then passed through his heart and out into the collective consciousness of humanity both then and for all future generations. The love of the Prophet Muhammad (PBUH) continues to be a strong and living spiritual emotion among the faithful of Islam, and one of the main reasons is the fact that through him the descent of the luminous in the form of the Noble Qur'an was made possible.

The meaning of religion in the Islamic context goes beyond the concept of revelation as the descent of knowledge from the Divine to the human as point of departure and source of the religion. The Arabic word *din*, usually translated into English as "religion", does little justice to the full significance of the word's

---

[56] Muhammad is identified in the Qur'an as "the seal of the prophets," which effectively closes the book on the plenary descent of knowledge in revelatory form.

meaning in Arabic, because the concept of *din* in Islam is less formal and more practical than you find within the English context. It consists in being a way of life that adheres to a sacred norm in which the entire life is molded to become a way of being, in addition to being a way of knowledge that commences with the descent of the Book and the inscription of the pen on the heart of the Muslims, echoing the very first verse, in the form of a direct command, to descend into the mind and heart of the Prophet in the cave of Mt. Hira: "Read (recite) in the name of thy Lord Who created. . . " (96:1) To that end, what the Muslims call the Sunnah comprises not only the verses and laws and entreaties of the Holy Qur'an; but also the sayings of the Prophet, compiled a century or more after his death, that perpetuate his attitudes, his behavior and virtually his way of life. The Prophet himself represents the supreme example of a human being who was the receptacle and instrument of the sacred verses, the very words and vibration of the Holy Spirit.

The question is how can these fundamental insights that are self-evident to all be accomplished not only in this life but within the context of a greater, inner journey into the soul and spirit of ourselves and the universe? We cannot just run through fields with our shoes off or desire to float upon clouds and expect to arrive at the true destination that is built into the human condition. The great gift of Islam is that it provides the Muslims with the means to achieve transcendence within the human condition. This transcendence means an escape from their own weaknesses and limitations through the inner *jihad al-nafs*, or battle of the mind, heart, and soul, and the ability to rise above themselves to higher level of consciousness through the remembrance of God every moment of their lives and to achieve a high level of virtue through application of the principles of the religion in their actions and in their lives. The great *shahadah*, or testament of faith in Islam, is not just a one-time recitation, but an inner truth that shapes and colors every moment of a Muslim life.

It is not so much what we believe as Muslims, but rather how we can give meaning to the form of the religion through our actions and lives. It is not the ritual acts of prayer and fasting and the other duties that make Muslims what they are. These are just the artifacts of a ritual foundation to the religion that attempts to remember and uphold the truths of the religion through a scaffolding of rites and rituals. We should not say that I am Muslim because I pray and fast and have made the *hajj*. These things are between you and God whose effectiveness depends on their level of sincerity and commitment, especially the fast, for who knows but God whether a person has truly abstained from food and drink during the daylight hours.

If being a Muslim means being a member of a club whose clubhouse contains all the tomes of literature that describe the knowledge of God, then we can close the door of this house and confine ourselves within some small box. But that is not what the great sheikhs and walis and spiritual poets of the past have left behind as a legacy of the spiritual life. What they have left behind to emulate is the manner of being Muslim, the "how" and not the "what" of a Muslim life, through actions that contain their own truth, through intentions that have the backing of the divine will, through surrender that meets the moment of the divine command and through virtue that contains its own light and that shines from the human face to light the way.

This is the true meaning of the Islamic *din*. As one of the family of the great and revealed world religious, Islam adds its own particular perspective to the history of formal religious unfolding by highlighting once again the supreme principle of unity (*tawhīd*) expressed in the first of the two statements of the *shahadah* that there is "no god but God". Secondly, Islam emphasizes the importance of commitment to the singular Islamic path in the second of the two statement of the *shahadah*, namely that "Mohamed is His Messenger". As such, Islam's unique angle of vision rests with the polarity "knowledge and action", or alternatively "faith and surrender", or yet again "law and path".

As Muslims, young people need to understand the unique position that Islam now plays as a religion both worthy of the world's attention and capable of leading people into the future of themselves and the world. It identifies itself with the primordial religion that always was since the symbolic time of Adam and the Golden Era, and as the final religion and "seal" of all religion-hood, it recognizes and accepts the chain of prophets and religions that have preceded it. It could be called the "natural religion" insofar as it is the religion of proto-nature (*al-din al-fitrah*), that is to say that this religion is in the nature of things and identifies the true nature of both man and the natural order. The Oneness of the Absolute is revealed in the natural order and in the heart of humanity as the "primordial message" that lies within the very heart of the universe. This is the true meaning and significance of Islam as a religion within the broader concept of religion "as such", as a principle of unfolding spiritual life in the knowledge of God that is expressed and realized within the *Ummah* (community) of Islam as a living tradition.

Any betrayal in preserving a way of life that reflects the very spirit of *din* as understood in the Islamic worldview as an elaborate and well specified way of life of precepts, dogmas, and modes of action runs the risk of a self-betrayal in the way Muslims understand themselves and their place in the world. As bearers of the banner of Islam, they set the example that needs to be upheld like a flag in the wind of a way of living and of being that reflects the traditional knowledge and the universal truth, the individual religion and the universal prototype of religion coming together in the silhouette of man against the distant horizon. Islam has bestowed a powerful gift upon the Muslims; a gift that they themselves can become in their encounter with the Spirit of God within this world.

# Chapter Twelve

# Journey of the Book

The religion of Islam carries the tradition of the mantra and the Jesus prayer to its logical conclusion with the availability of a sacred formula with the capacity to transform the individual into a beacon of higher consciousness. Its formal substance in primordial sound and divinely revealed words strike a holy cord of sacred vibration within the body of the individual and whose inner content of knowledge and wisdom provides in a phrase all that a person needs to know in order to get to Heaven. The witnessing, commonly referred to as the testimony of faith, in Arabic the *shahadah*, represents the perfect marriage of wisdom and method, to use the phraseology of the Tibetan Buddhists. Its knowledge reflects the ultimate statement of principle, while its method arises out of the bold affirmation of the truth that is implicit in its repetition and in the actions that are conducted in its spirit. It is the union of wisdom and method, thus representing the meeting of pure wisdom and pure method on the plane of practicality and human experience.

Within the method and wisdom of every act of worship lie both an implicit doctrine and an explicit activity in the form of a spiritual discipline. Prayer, meditation, fasting, pilgrimages, good works, and invocation of the Divine Name are all spiritual forms that convey not only a blessing to the faithful, but also a knowledge and a meaning that can guide the Muslims in their daily lives and enhance their spirits. The *shahadah*,[57] which is the quintessential spiritual formula in Islam and the spearhead of Islamic faith, does just the opposite. It proclaims an explicit doctrine that reflects an implicit activity on the mind and heart of the Muslim believer with its clear knowledge, its active means of discernment, and its dynamic power to move forward, change and ultimately perfect the Muslims in both their inner and external worlds. The *shahadah* proclaims in a phrase that God is the one reality and that Muhammad is His earthly messenger. It is the sacred formula of Islam that summarizes in four words and formalizes in speech the entire substance of the Qur'an and thus of the religion. In order to resolve the enigmatic mystery that confronts people in their daily lives here on earth, the Muslims have the benefit of a formal synthesis that is both concise in its expression and rich in its possibilities. The *shahadah* serves this purpose in Islam. For the Muslims, it is a means of spiritual identification, in which they assert what they know to be the essence of a truth that recalls in a phrase the entire substance of the religion.

The *shahadah* summarizes an essential knowledge that draws on the very source of knowledge itself, and its inward (or outward) recitation becomes the formal vehicle through which to approach and draw near to the Presence of God. It is not only knowledge, it is a sacred emotion; it is not only a theology, it is also a sacred psychology. As the ultimate source of knowledge, the *shahadah* states the truth of the one God and the need for a particular messenger to convey that truth to humanity. If nothing more than the *shahadah* were written in the believer's heart, there would not be need for anything more. As the perfect means of worship and thus of expressing their profound devotion to God, the testimony of faith that slips off the tongue has the capacity to expand the heart immeasurably. Repeated recitation of the sacred formula brings the Muslim into immediate contact with the truth, physically, emotionally, psychically and spiritually. Through repetition of the formula of the sacred words, faith becomes strengthened until it reaches toward the highest levels of spirituality that are available through the use of the sacred formula. The witnessing is a bold summary of the entire religion, the ultimate motivation, and the absolute foundation of the spiritual life of all

---

[57] "This formula consists of two parts: the two first words, which constitute the *nafy* (the 'negation'), and the last two words, which constitute the *ithbat* (the 'affirmation')." F. Schuon, *Dimensions of Islam*, p. 147. Also worth noting is the fact that the *shahadah* is the first sound that the newly born Muslim child hears whispered into the ear, and hopefully the last phrase to part the lips at the moment of death, to accompany the soul on its sacred journey across the divide that separates this world from the next.

Muslims. The Muslim convert becomes Muslim when he or she makes a formal (official) proclamation; the words of the *shahadah* are the first words whispered into the ears of a newly born infant.

Through revelation, God has always proclaimed himself "to exist and be", and has even characterized Himself as the "Hidden Treasure ", even if today His existence has been cast into doubt to the extent that people no longer believe in the possibility of a superior Being. Tracing a spiritual line back to one of the earliest religious traditions, we find a similar sacred formula in the scriptures of the Vedanta in which God also identified Himself as the only reality worth knowing: "Brahman is real, the world is an appearance," thereby establishing once and for all the nature of Reality as well as the true nature of this world as a dream and a mere appearance. Speaking to Moses from the burning bush, God has described Himself in the Bible with these words: "I am that I am" (*Eheyeh asher eheyeh* [Exodus III. 14]). Moses of course did not see the face of God, but he heard God's words, just as humanity has heard the words of revelation down through the millennia, words that have identified God as the Lord and Master of all the creation, including mankind ( the Islamic *insan*). Christianity manifests itself clearly through the personality and life of Christ. Nevertheless, it still contains in the Gospels the same essential key with this saying of Jesus in the Gospel: "There is none good but one, that is, God" (*nemo bonus nisi unus Deus*, St. Mark X, 18).

The Qur'an has come not only to proclaim, but also to reconfirm the truth of the one Reality (*al-Haqq*) and the reality of the One (*al-Ahad*). As the final revelation whose messenger seals all prophethood, the Qur'an makes no pretence of saying something that has never been said before. On the contrary," for every nation there has been a messenger" (*al-khatim al-anbiya*) that served as the vehicle of the message of truth, and who communicated a universal and perennial truth to satisfy the needs of the people of his time and place. As the final source of the essential knowledge for humanity, the Qur'an also highlights the identity of the Supreme Being with the phrase "I am Allah, there is no god but I", and the unity of all existence as *the* central doctrine of the entire religion – He is Allah in the heavens and on the earth" (6:3). As such, the sacred formula of the *shahadah* is a summary statement of all that the religion contains.

♠ ♠ ♠

The yearning of the mind and heart for an absolute and definitive knowledge is fundamental to the human condition and lies at the very heart of the earthly ambition of humanity to transcend themselves and their limitations. This is no truer than at the present time, with contemporary people everywhere still in search of that archetype of the human being represented in the person of the primordial Adam and still in search of knowledge of the reality through the pursuit of the knowledge of modern science and technology. Modern and contemporary scientists have come far and achieved much, yet all their accomplishments have a vague air of "unreality" about them because they are missing the one thing essential: namely, the message of the *shahadah*, which is the essential knowledge of the One and the one thing worth knowing when stacked up against all the knowledge of "this world".

When I first became Muslim, I had no idea of the possible intimacy that could be developed in one's relationship with a book. I nurtured a love of the classics, had read the Russian and British 19th century classic novels, studied the famous essayists from Charles Lamb to Ralph Waldo Emerson and treasured not only the beauty and style of the language that I hoped to emulate as a writer myself, but also recognized the extraordinary benefit that I have taken from these great works of literature in terms of their ethics, their higher sentiments, and the deep abiding life-values these works convey to the attentive reader. Nothing, however, could have adequately prepared my receptive mind for the encounter with the Qur'an in terms of the depth, the intimacy, and the close companionship that would result from reading its chapters and verses word for word as the actual words of God, not as a one-off reading from cover to cover, but as an in-depth and enduring lifetime study.

Not long after formally embracing Islam as my religion of choice as opposed to the religion into which I was born, I set myself the task of getting to know the Holy Book in the deepest manner possible as a life journey in quest of mystery and revelation. I held a deep fascination for what the book may contain once I embraced the Religion of Islam and accepted in principle its doctrines and precepts. If God had chosen to speak formally to humanity in words, what, then, would He reveal to them as His thinking, talking, human creation? We profess to believe in God. We believe that there has been a descent of knowledge in the form of revelation with letters, words and verses that actually constitute the actual sacred speech of the Divinity.

We call the book the Noble Book and the Holy Book. We wrapped the actual book in velvet cloth, and it holds a position of prominence in the house. Before touching or opening the book's pages to proceed with a Qur'anic recitation, a Muslim is obliged to perform the so-called ablution, or *wudhu* as it is referred to in Arabic, in the same manner as when one prepares to perform the Islamic prayer ritual five times a day, as a symbolic as well as literal gesture of purification. Before recitation, Muslims may kiss the book, touch it to their foreheads and hearts in ritual gestures of reverence and love, then place it on a Qur'anic reading holder often made of hand-carved wood. The book is always there in the background of a Muslim life. It is read in stages on a weekly if not daily basis. Muslims traditionally read the entire Qur'an during the holy month of Ramadhan in commemoration of its first descent on the Night of Power identified in the Qur'an as the Laylat al-Qadr, a night that is "better than a thousand months", when time stands still, when the angels and the Spirit of God descend to witness its first recitation.

Before I came to know of and experience the blessed Qur'anic recitation in its true form after I became Muslim, with its precise knowledge, its sense of sacred history, its mysterious presence, clear guidance, and comforting sense of tranquility and peace, I had no idea that such a book existed, a book of universal principles with the power to raise spiritual consciousness and thereby transform lives. I had wandered through life thinking I could make my simple way through life on my own. I enjoyed vague premonitions of God; I didn't disbelieve; but instead I had a simple faith in a Supreme Being who created the universe and everything in it; but I had no idea how to relate to this idea and no experience that could be characterized as truly spiritual, otherworldly, or inspirational. I wanted to be a good person; but had no idea how to go about being good, knowing full well my own limitations and weaknesses, my fears and psychological complexes that prey upon the immature mind, and the overwhelming uncertainties that plague our daily lives with their inscrutable mystery. What mysterious force would cradle me in its arms and lift me out of myself, well beyond earth's gravity and the evil tendencies of the lower soul?

It seemed to me that for all my life prior to becoming Muslim, the desire to have what could be called genuine spiritual experience always existed; but the experience itself had never made its presence known in any convincing way. I wanted to feel the holy presence of something that lingers inside as some mysterious secret waiting to be revealed that would enrich my life and give me the direction I sought in fulfilling my destiny. I wanted to raise my consciousness beyond the mundane world in order to uncover the extraordinary potential that seems to lie all around us in the natural world. Why shouldn't that potential exist within myself as well?

I had taken note, for example, of the instinctive intelligence of the animals, the symmetry of the natural laws of gravity and regeneration, the harmony implicit in the phases of the moon and the changing of the seasons that find their source in their earthly orbit around the glorious sun which itself is not stationary but moves majestically around a higher nexus within the galaxy, but the messages of the natural order had remained asleep within me and never stirred beyond vague aspirations to be good, to refine my character, to develop my personality, and ultimately to find my true self. Nature's messages were there to behold; but how were they to be internalized into the heart as the spirit of the soul?

Little did I know that an unexpected awakening lay in wait for me to opening . . . what (?) . . . my eyes, my heart. I could well have moved beyond my youth into maturity and old age and never felt the whisper of some sacred breath into the ear as a holy incantation, the sudden beating of the heart from a feeling of unannounced, ecstatic joy that momentarily fans us with wings of happiness, the hint of a shadow in the mind that suddenly turns to the consciousness of light that fills us with delight by the luminescence of its sheer presence. I could have gone on believing that certain doors would never be opened, that certain longings would remain forever unsatisfied, that certain questions and mysteries would continue to tempt and lure me out of myself; but would never give up their sweet nectar in the form of a revelation that would sweep aside all uncertainty and doubt, at least in principle, and open the heart onto a world of eternal discovery and a world without end.

I soon discovered that the Qur'an is a book like no other, a companion and friend that never grows old, a narrative tale of ancient and sacred history that never fades because of its universal appeal and symbolic significance, with powerful forces of energy and harmony, wisdom and blessing that overlay the mind and heart of the reader/reciter with a luminescent clarity and sense of sacredness that bring peace of mind and surety of heart to the faithful soul. It is a book that takes every Muslim on a journey through time whose ultimate destination is midway between eternity in the here and now; at the still point of the turning world, neither going nor coming, where past and future are gathered into the eternal moment of now. Every recitation and reading becomes a journey through the landscape of a strange and alien world whose essential knowledge identifies the true nature of everything within the creation. It is a journey that begins with the creation of the universe and the establishment of the sacred trust between the Divine and the human, and a journey that ends within the Paradise where rivers flow freely, and where the souls of the innocent and the just will reap in the "next world" what they have earned within the dimension of "this world".

The journey of the book takes us gingerly across the minefields of ignorance, human weakness and all the major vices that in the Western world are referred to as the seven deadly sins. Prominent among the forms of ignorance that plague our waking moments are hypocrisy and polytheism, hypocrisy being the veil of lies that we send forth as a psychological mask of pretending falsehoods in place of our true intentions that when unveiled would reveal us to be the venal, dishonest, and low-life individuals that we truly are, always seeking personal advantage and gain at the expense of others unless we work on ourselves in a manner that the Qur'an exhorts. "We created man in the best of forms; they we cast him down as the lowest of the low." (95:4) The hypocrites feature highly in the Qur'anic narrative, real-life people who lived at the time of the Prophet as representatives of the time, but who live in every time as models of falsehood and treachery. In point of fact, we know very well who the hypocrites are because we can see their very shade and color within ourselves if we look closely enough. It is hypocrisy that we have to fight within ourselves before we start making accusations of hypocrisy against those around us.

However, polytheism is an idea with great symbolic value shedding light on human nature in present times, in addition to being an ancient, historical phenomenon identified with the belief in multiple gods and deities. Polytheism actually lives within us as an artifact from an ancient time, a clear manifestation of our human nature to value that which is purely earthly and attached to the so-called "gods" of this world, a value and belief system that will actually lead us away from the spirit of our true nature which yearns to believe in a supreme Reality, an intelligent Creator and true Friend. What are the gods and deities of this era that fill our hearts of longing and desire, but the very artifacts of the modern world that provide us with our motivation and form the foundation and ground of our personal goals and desire to succeed.

What are the 21$^{st}$ century gods but the flourishing of the personal ego (we are our own gods), the desire for money at any price (even at the expense of our own integrity), and the pursuit of power and authority over others (even at the expense of the abuse of power). We want these things without fully knowing why; we think that satisfaction of the ego, the accumulation of money for its own sake, and the freedom that power and authority over others gives us are the three great keys to happiness and success in the modern world, only to realize that there is very little satisfaction in self-reliance and even less certainty as the vicissitudes of life force us to realize that we cause our own miseries in spite of ourselves, that with unlimited amounts of money we are still unhappy, and that power and authority over people leads to the dead end of injustice unless it is used in the name of supreme and universal principles that transcend the individual ego, the wealth of the world, and the power of individuals to rule over others for their own sake at the expense of the common good.

The journey of the book takes us through the modern-day wilderness of spiritual insight and holy experience. The human mind would constitute a wilderness of cognitive speculation, lost in the mystery of an unfathomable sense of origin, purpose and destiny within the human condition, if it were not for the intuitive yearning to meet the counterpart of the soul in the Spirit of God. The spirit of the Qur'anic journey takes us by the hand and leads us through the peaks and troughs of life with the piercing illumination of a light house perched like a pre-historic bird on a stormy promontory illuminating the obscure darkness of the mainland. The Muslim journey begins with the clarion proclamation of the one Reality and ends with a person's final accounting on the Day of Judgment, the balance of good and bad actions, and ultimately salvation of soul and fulfillment of the eternal condition in eternal repose within the embrace of the Supreme God, identified by name in the Qur'an as the Living, the Eternal.

Each encounter with the sacred words casts a spell of mystery and wonderment that bewitches the mind and heart with its sacred history, spiritual guidance and secrets of the natural order; we come to the book as to a fresh beginning or the dawn of a new day. Every time a Muslim picks up the book, he or she has entered a new world to be transported to another place and another time from the world we experience in the here and now. We can momentarily leave behind the myriad wonders and mysteries of this world, an informed touch that sends beautiful notes from the harp, shadow playing with sunlight on the river, clouds brushing mountain peaks with their evanescence, a silent bell waiting to be rung, the dust and ashes of forgotten dreams that will never become true. We sing songs of nostalgia and longing on our own, while centuries disappear, only to be reborn as the future's now when we pick up the book to read the words and verses of the revelation. In hearing our own voice, we hear the voice of the Prophet to whom the revelation came many centuries ago. To hear the Prophet's voice is to hear the voice of the Archangel Gabriel who appeared standing on the horizon in the aura of a white light amid a flutter of wings, intoning the majestic verses with the sound of thunder. To hear the voice of the Archangel Gabriel is to hear the very Voice of God resounding like the roar of waves on the shore of the mighty empyrean.

We invoke the traditional *bis mil-Llah*, which translates as the invocation "in the Name of God", for everything we begin anew is enshrouded within this formula of entreaty to the Sacred Name to hear our voice and recognize our efforts. Only when we put down the book and leave our prayer carpet is the captivating spell broken, as we come back down to earth and enter once again into the rigors of the world; no longer orphans and exiles, but as revitalized beings, new Muslims born again after every recitation into a world wrapped in blessing and promise, to live another day in the shadow of the Divinity, the day itself opening before us like the unraveling parchment of a sacred scroll. We respond to the summons of the book as an invitation and take with us the knowledge bestowed and the experience fully lived. If only we could remember throughout the day the sense of purpose and continue to feel the latent energy that accompanies Qur'anic recitation; indeed, the angels witness every reading of the Book after the dawn prayer (*al-fajr*). As such, as we move into the broad avenue of the morning, we have no need to fear life's outcome or feel unease about the forces of our destiny. They are meant to happen in the same way that God is Merciful (*al-Rahman*) and Generous (*al-Karim*).

As with a true friend with whom silence offers an easy familiarity, there is no need for words. A profound silence reigns within the book, within the room, within the heart, as we take up the book, sitting cross-legged on a prayer carpet. In our hands lies a jewel of incredible value ready to sparkle with the incandescence of heavenly light, if it weren't for the pre-dawn shadows, sitting in silence and darkness until the first sound is intoned on the tongue, within the mind, within the heart.

ALIF . . . LAM . . . MIM are the first sacred symbolic sounds of the reading, whose purpose and significance have been written about and speculated upon down through the ages. These are the sacred letters that open various verses of the Qur'an: ALIF is the vertical symbol, the vowelization of the aaahhhh of the Name Allah, a heavenly sigh as old and enduring as eternity, a visual symbol of vertical man standing erect among the other animals on the horizon of the animal kingdom, featuring *Homo sapiens* as the human *alif*.

*Lam* initiates the negative impulse so critical as the basis of our ethical behavior, and verbalizes into sound the primal impulse stated succinctly in the *shahadah* to deny multiple gods for the sake of the one God. *Mim* is one of the roots of the Arabic word to believe and recalls the believer (*mu'min*), the imam (*imam*), the mosque (*masjid*), all characterized by the beloved letter *mim*. The sacred sounds begin to emerge from the deep well of the soul which in turn links and moves outward in harmony toward the universal spirit that substantiates the essence of the creation.

Within seconds of commencing the recitation, we are transported for a brief moment back into the Cave of Light, in commemoration of the original command of the grand Archangel who recited the first revealed verse on behalf of the Divinity "Recite in the name of your Lord Who created, created humanity from a clay mixture." (96:1) Through the words, one transcends this body of flesh and bones to become like pure essence moving across the page, across the mind, across the soul. There is movement inside and outside the body in the form of sacred vibration and energy, looking up from below and looking down from above, indulging in what it means to be air, wind, spirit, infiltrating everything between the light and shadows of the room, between the leaves and branches outside the window, between the fingertips and the book they hold. There is no past or future, only the present moment conveying a sense of the eternal continuum of time. We can give ourselves up to the sweet embrace that lives within the world of the revelation through surrender to the Divinity that will give us back our true selves. The reading or recitation moves forward through precise sound like the elegant script of the letters across the page; but life is held in check for these moments of suspended time and we are reminded once again of what it means to be worthy of the Sacred Presence that invades the profane moment with its haunting aura of another world.

The core reason for it all—the words, the sound, the good intentions, the heart and spirit—lies in the knowledge, the consciousness, the serenity and the certainty encased within the calligraphic script and wrapped in the beauty of sound with ribbons of energy and light. Reading becomes a divine delight that has no comparison in this world. Everything about us becomes rewritten as a changed being as we sit cross-legged on the carpet. New things become possible and transformations are ready to take place that we would not otherwise experience on our own. It makes a person appreciate the obsession that the alchemists had for the transmutation of lead into gold. Through the reading, the human consciousness is lifted out of the doldrums of this world to a higher level of awareness, something has vanished of our former selves like the dead skin of a snake, and we are lost now amidst the stars and their luminescent ways. The experience lies beyond the human realm and we feel that we have awoken into another world, as though we are for a moment uncreated once again and lie within the "eye" of Allah as a promise with a name and a destiny still waiting to unfold.

Qur'anic recitation determines the very framework of the spiritual life of the soul. Muslims draw on the language of the Qur'an to give a spiritual frame to their hopes, fears, sorrows, regrets, and aspirations. They use the Qur'an as a means of withdrawing for a few moments during the course of the day, either in the early morning when the birds sing their own sacred verses, or after the sunset prayer when the calm of dusk merges into the stillness of night. The holy recitation relieves the mind, the psyche, and the soul of those who intone its verses from the gravitational pull of this world with its implicit imbalance, disharmony and lack of peace. When the Muslims arise in the morning at the call to prayer, they have available to them the sacred book that contains all they need to know and therefore they possess the means to realize that knowledge in their daily lives. Small wonder, then, that devout Muslims turn to the Holy Qur'an for sustenance and strength on a daily basis throughout the course of their lives, a turning that pre-empts doubt and despair and leads their inner being back to the center and ultimate source of their existence in surrender to the Divine Being who created them.

At the dawn prayer (*salat al-fajr*), the shadowy rays of a saffron moon float serenely across the window sill. In the pre-dawn darkness, the dark plate of the night sky shines forth the light of ancient stars with their message of eternity within time and infinity within space, before disappearing with the coming of the dawn. There is a hint of incense and musk in the air whose assault on the senses captures a feeling of sacredness that becomes a moving force within the mind and heart. Heavenly scents accompany the two angels who descend to witness the Qur'anic recitation that occurs in one place or another every morning across the crescent of the Islamic world. Having performed the ritual ablution and prayer ceremony, Muslims in various corners of the globe sit cross-legged on a prayer carpet and reach for the Noble, the Generous, the Holy Qur'an, an Illuminated Book (*al-kitab al-mubin*), a document that is "on a tablet well-preserved in heaven", as well as a printed book held in the hand. They kiss it out of profound respect, place it on forehead and heart, and then commence to recite the words and verses of the Holy Book. *Alif, Lam, Mim*, they chant sonorously the Arabic letters that commence the recitation and then recite the first verse: "This is the Book, of which there is no doubt, and guidance for those who fear God" (2: 1).

With the divine words of revelation, the Muslims forever repeat the task of planting in the ground of their soul the seeds of a divine knowledge that brings guidance and certainty to those who believe in God. They listen to His words and verses, and hold in reverence and awe the coming of the *Sakinah* or Holy Presence of the Divinity. When the mind becomes illuminated with divine knowledge, when the heart is on fire with desire, when the imagination paints dreams of mystery and beauty, and when the higher emotions are brimming with devotion and love, the seeds of the divine Mystery (*al-ghaib*) take root and grow, giving entrance into a realm beyond legends and myths where mystical power and self renewal far exceed anything we are capable of creating by ourselves. Dust settles on the furniture and the early dawn light creeps cautiously across the windowpane while the outsized autumn moon sinks heavily below the emerging horizon. As the words of revelation echo through the coming dawn, the aspiring soul becomes a staging ground of worship and praise that rises through levels of conscious awakening until it returns full circle to its origin and source in that universal consciousness radiating outward from the Mind of God.

Finally, reluctantly, the sublime recitation of verses from the Holy Book comes to a close and we take leave of our prayer carpet to attend to the duties of another day. The book lies there in silence once again, although the echoes of the recitation resonate their harmonies and energy across the coming hours of the day. We take with us a feeling as if some candle has been lit to illuminate the shadows of the mind. A velvet awakening and ribbons of blessing wrap around our ears and eyes, around our mind and heart, bringing the supreme knowledge of God down as the guiding principle of our lives. We begin to realize that something of ourselves has disappeared, in order to make room for the appearance of the Supreme Presence, as the soul of the book enters the soul of the person we wish to become.

Chapter Thirteen

The Book as Living Presence

_____

Devout Muslims live with the Qur'an not as a book on a shelf to be perused at random, but as a miraculous presence waiting to be encountered and experienced as a source of knowledge and as a form of worship. Their attitude calls to mind a statement of the American transcendental poet and essayist Ralph Waldo Emerson: "Other men are lenses through which we read our own minds." In the minds and hearts of Muslims, the verses of the Qur'an serve as reflecting lenses through which the Muslims can see themselves as a mirror reflection of the Truth of the Supreme Being. The words of the book are beacons of light connecting existential truths with celestial realities in the mind of the faithful. When Muslims read the Qur'an, the knowledge and light of a higher reality bursts in upon their ordinary consciousness, amounting to a an enlightening experience that is as unexpected as it is earth-shattering.

In previous chapters, I have endeavored to explain the mysterious value and significance of the Qur'an, which Muslims see as a revelation from another, unseen dimension of reality. In this chapter, I hope to portray the Qur'an not as pages of a book that only sit on a shelf collecting dust, but that serve as a living presence in the lives of the Muslims. Contrary to the sentiments of the modernite mentality with its rational and secular worldview and its inability to see beyond the physicality of this world to the spirituality of a higher "meta-physical" reality, the verses of the Qur'an present a picture of the true reality and therefore the only reality worth taking seriously when it comes to understanding the true nature of humanity. Coming to terms with the Qur'an and what it sets out to accomplish is crucial in understanding the spirit of the ambiance and culture of the Islamic world, along with the so-called Muslim mentality that is the logical extension of that world, steeped as it is in the spiritual culture of the Qur'an.

On a fundamental level, the Qur'an needs to be understood as a sacred revelation from a higher dimension of reality. The book and its verses must first be fully accepted in the abstract and in principle by the mind, then affirmed substantially by the heart with a faith that is ultimately based on the intuitive knowledge of God. In the previous chapter, we have explored the notion of the Qur'an as magical symbols strewn across a page or as oral sound that fill the air with sacred rhythms of the Divinity, symbols of knowledge that are accepted—indeed affirmed—by the mind and planted as seeds within the ground of the human soul. If that were enough, we could wrap it in velvet cloth and set it on the mantelpiece in our living room as the universal book of knowledge to be respected as the *prima facie* exemplar of universal truth.

However, contrary to what the modern secularist worldview would have us believe, we are not just the mind. Inclusive within the higher faculties of the mind, we have the discerning mirror of the intellect, the broad field of the imagination, the sacred niche of the heart, and the heat of the emotions and higher sentiments that give light to the intellect, wings to the imagination, mystery to a secret heart-knowledge, and burning embers to the higher sacred emotions that come together as the sublime experience of the Presence, the *sakinah* in traditional Islamic terminology. Like the words of revelation, the presence descends from above and settles upon the ground of the human soul from on high, representing none other than the ethereal presence of God Almighty, nurturing the seeds of the Qur'anic revelation within the ground of the human soul. In the spiritual state of consciousness aroused by a concentrated and devoted reading of the sacred Qur'anic text, the sound of a thousand thunders could not more effectively transform countless sacred syllables into a rhythmic force with the power to carry the human mind beyond the sorrows and tribulations of this world to an altogether higher plane of reality.

What did the Qur'an as a revelation from God mean to me forty years ago as a fledgling Muslim convert? The short answer must be "not much" in the initial stages of my conversion; because I had been sitting on the edge of our modern-day secular wilderness, although I had not yet fallen into the abyss of absolute forgetfulness concerning my true origins and ultimate destiny. Still, no one had to convince me about the importance, indeed the necessity, of a divine revelation in those days; I still retained some semblance of a fundamental belief in the existence of the Supreme Being and the need for some form of communication that could transcend the barriers that separate the Divine and human dimensions.

The idea of the Qur'an as a revelation from an Absolute Being to mortal humans captured my imagination and eventually seized the intellections—not to mention the reasoning and higher faculties—of my mind. Muslims would call it blessing (*baraka*) or mercy (*rahmah*); to my reckoning, it emerged out of nowhere, as though one day I had passed by a wintry bush shorn of any life-giving properties and saw reaching out to me from this bundle of dead vegetation a solitary bud closed tight and awaiting the process of self-awakening. If so, then the rest of my life has been a constant monitoring of that emerging bud, akin to watching the measured opening of a flower or the metamorphosis of a butterfly from a time-sequenced camera compacting eons of tedious observation into a breathtaking narrative of time-compressed seconds into a life lived in the shadow of the principle of unity (*tawhid*) that Islam heralds as the first law of a principled life.

I also firmly accepted the logic that if I had faith in a Supreme Being, and if that Supreme Being has spoken in words to a humanity in need of guidance and mercy, then I should find out not only what the Divinity has chosen to relate to His thinking creation, but also the manner in which this revelation has been delivered. What secrets lie sequestered within the letters, syllables, and words that make up the verses of the Holy Book? What mysteries of the unknown lie waiting for the human mind to experience and absorb?

Indeed, I was soon to find out that the Qur'an is much more than just a body of knowledge preserved within the covers of a book. It offers a resolution to the perennial mysteries concerning the origin of the universe, the origin of life, and the mystery of human consciousness, as well as providing a spiritual framework for the understanding of the human entity. In addition to being a Book, a Word, a Recitation, a Guidance, a Mercy, and a Light, the Qur'an is an experience of a unique and otherworldly Presence brought down into the world of humanity through letters, words, phrases, and verses that amount to the calligraphic signature and divine disclosure of a Supreme Being.

My love for the Qur'an finds its source in a tiny spark that must have flown off the burning embers of some cosmic hearth and fallen down to earth to find its way into the mind and heart of this then fledgling believer who found himself living in the remnants of a traditional civilization, grimly trying to stand firm during an era dominated by such mythologies and illusions as secular humanism and material progress. This initial spark re-ignited the smoldering ruins of an uninspired life with its affirmation of truth based upon the idea of unity at the heart of creation. Indeed, I had a willingness to believe, but where was I prepared to go with this impulse, I wondered, and where did I expect it to lead me?

I had been brought up as a devout Christian in an Irish Catholic community just outside of Boston, Massachusetts. I was well familiar with the idea of a created Word Incarnate. The image of Christ was imprinted on my developing mind as the human revelation *par excellence*. When I became Muslim,[58] I knew nothing of the Holy Qur'an, its contents, its history, and manner of delivery, or its role within the life of the Muslim; but I believed implicitly in the "idea" of revelation, namely that if a person accepts that a Supreme Being exists, then logic demands the acceptance of a revelation in which such a Supreme Being communicates the knowledge of His existence along with the means to respond to that knowledge in a meaningful and effective manner through effort and spiritual disciplines. That was one psychological hurdle I did not have to overcome, unlike many in the Western world today who have inherited no true understanding of the meaning of revelation and what it could mean to them and their lives. Only much later did I learn, not through knowledge but through experience, of the profound meaning of the *sakinah*, the blessed experience of the Presence of God that accompanies the experience of either reciting the Qur'anic verses by heart or reading the verses from the depths of the heart.

The Qur'an states that: "Wherever you turn, there is the Face of God." (2:115) Here the image of the "face" is symbolic of the all-pervasive and qualitative "personality"—for want of a better word—of the Divine Being in all His 99 qualities and attributes Who is subject neither to place, time, nor any other earthly condition. Humans, on the other hand, are subject to the logic of place and the continuum of time and live within dimensions where the true nature of reality is veiled from their direct view and must be understood symbolically and intuitively. The knowledge of God must be made available to us by virtue of our humanity; but once the revelatory knowledge has been made available, we alone are to blame for not abiding by His guidance. The experience of the Presence, however, is earned through spiritual discipline and sacred practices of worship whose effect is to lift the veil that separates the

---

[58] My conversion and the reasons why I became a Muslim are documented in an earlier book of mine entitled *The Seeker and the Way: Reflections of a Muslim Convert* (Kuala Lumpur, Malaysia: Noordeen Publications, 1999) and in the more recent *Wisdom's Journey: Living the Spirit of Islam in the Modern World,* Bloomington, Ind: World Wisdom Books, 2009.

human consciousness from the true face of the unseen Reality (*al-Ghaib*).

This question of the presence is crucial in understanding the true nature of Islamic worship and the spiritual disciplines, such as Qur'anic recitation, that together form the cornerstone of such worship. The words of the text are the sacred talismans of transmission. Muslims recognize that they have the words of God, words with which to speak and think and internalize the divine disclosure, words that reflect every virtue and every intimacy in life, words with which we can express sacred emotions and affinities that reside in the deepest well of our beings, words that relate of a primordial era when the story of the first man and woman began to unfold and that to this day remains a revelatory tale that captures the imagination of the receptive mind within every generation and civilization. By intoning the words and verses through rhythmic breathing and chanting and establishing a rhythm of sacred vibration that courses through the body in waves of sacred disclosure, the worshipper is able to call himself back to a more authentic mode of being that finds its source in the spiritual verities. Through rigorous discipline and an absolute adherence to the laws of recitation (*tajwid*), we are able to recapture a genuine sense of the divine presence that accompanies the verses of the divine disclosure.

Of course, I knew none of this sacred intimacy that could be made possible through the recitation and chanting of the sacred Qur'anic text. Armed with the primal impulses of an affirmative faith that expressed a readiness to believe and that made me a repository of hope to further nurture my experience of the spiritual world, I set myself as a new Muslim convert on a course to come to terms with the Qur'an and overcome any and all obstacles that may get in my way. Call it determination, decisiveness, short-sightedness, or possibly a kind of holy madness, but I remember a spiritual conviction to my attitudes which were tenacious and deep-rooted, although from whence they came, why they had arrived, and what form of expression they would take I had no clear idea.

Somehow, for I am a person who remembers the essence of an experience without necessarily remembering the details, I came in contact with a charming Kashmiri Indian while I was teaching at the University of Kuwait, whom I have referred to elsewhere as the "laughing Sufi." He was a merry fellow indeed, laughing his way through a minefield of philosophical speculation with a conviction and certitude that left me dizzy with desire, anxious to rise above myself and my own limitations, and hopeful of his promises to raise my consciousness to a level of awareness not previously experienced that would change my perception of self and my experience of the world. To me at that time, this sounded incredibly inviting. He explained at one point that he had a legendary aspiration to translate the Qur'an and he saw in me the perfect collaborator for such a project. Preposterous as it may sound, he made me a proposal that I could not easily refuse—namely to help him translate the Qur'an. He would orally transmit the meaning of the verses in English and I would later polish the language into a modern-day vernacular. As *tabula rasa* and virgin receptacle to the words of the Divine Pen, I could become the linguistic filter and wordsmith in this approximation of a translation from Arabic to English.[59]

It seemed to be the perfect opportunity of becoming acquainted, if not with the actual words of the sacred text, then its primordial knowledge and its sacred import. Its meaning would be delivered in the oral tradition out of which it was born. We embarked on this endeavor that ultimately took over one year to complete. Meanwhile, we had generated some interest in our "project" at the Saudi Embassy in Kuwait and were received by the Saudi ambassador amid all the pomp and splendor that comes to be associated with the princes and kings of such ruling elite classes in the Arab world. I was indeed astride the flying carpet of my childhood dreams and floating on a cloud of rarefied experience, half terrified and half in thrall of the visions of grandeur passing before me. When the project was completed after an unbelievable effort involving self-discipline and forbearance, we returned to the embassy and delivered the entire body of the work, all 600 pages or so bounded tightly together by a red ribbon squared in fours around the bundle of the manuscript. Sadly, the then reigning King Faisal of Saudi Arabia was murdered in his palace by a royal nephew who had ostensibly come to greet the king and offer his *salaams*. Official Saudi interest in our project died with the king's unexpected passing, or else the pages have frayed and the ribbon faded that wrapped the manuscript as it sits neglected on some shelf in a ministry file. The experience itself, however, is not forgotten and led to my further investigation into the true experience of the Qur'an in the lives of the Muslims.

That was my first introduction to the meaning of the Qur'an in English, personally delivered to me by my "laughing Sufi" whose love of the text and whose faithfulness and devotion to its meaning and import passed into me with the words of his translation. As I suggested in Part One, in explaining the meaning of the Qur'anic text, his was the voice of the Prophet, the voice of those companions who first repeated the blessed word, the voice of the

---

[59] Of course, the Muslims say that technically speaking, it is impossible to translate the Qur'an in the same way that a work of literature may be translated. Because the essence of the Qur'an relies upon the literal Arabic letters as the formal representation of the revelation, the liturgical value of the text is lost in translation.

archangel and ultimately the Supreme Voice of Allah. My faithful friend, my earthly master and beloved spiritual guide, has since passed beyond the known horizon at the hem of this world; but I will always remember the image of his chubby, mirthful face as he delivered to me, if not the sacred words of the original text—for that privilege would come much later once I was able to read the Arabic script—then the translated meaning of the Noble Qur'an, verses and stories and a body of knowledge as from father to son, as from the messenger to his companions, as from the great archangel Gabriel to the mind and consciousness of our beloved Prophet, words and verses that sparkle like sunlight on the bay and illuminate the great cave of the heart like the flickering light of a camp fire on a clear dark night. This was a rare and unique introduction, if not to the Qur'an itself and its very words, then to its meaning and import, amounting to being a very important first step for a non-Arabic speaking new Muslim in coming to terms with the Holy Book.

## Chapter Fourteen

## Mastering Qur'anic Arabic

---

And recite the Qur'an with measured recitation. (73:4)

It is the holy month of Ramadhan once again and the blazing heat of the desert sun makes its impact felt on the tongue as hunger and thirst and on the mind as a commitment of "will" to follow the rigorous code of the Ramadhan fast. I hear the sweet voice of numerous children reciting the Qur'an in a melody of sound that echoes and mimics the bird chatter one hears in the trees at sunset. The Qur'an tutor sits with the eight children of the Pathan family I have adopted on the outside porch under the mimosa tree, pacing the pronunciation and rhythms of the sacred verses with his dry stick as an extension of his withered hand. The children love their tutoring sessions of Qur'an recitation and run to their places around the table at the sound of the imam's bicycle bell, the children clutching their Qurans that are wrapped and tied respectfully in cloth. Muhammad Raouf, the 8 year old, has just finished one full reading of the Qur'an and his face is beaming with pride. A sheep will be slaughtered and the meat will be distributed to the poor in the surrounding neighborhood. Thus continues the cycle of learning to recite the Qur'an that has occurred in the same traditional manner across the Islamic crescent down through the centuries since the time of the Prophet.

Through a *madrasah Qur'aniyah* system of education in all traditional Islamic cultures, the study of the Qur'an begins in early childhood at the age of reason, concentrating on the correct recitation of the Arabic letters, sounds, words, phrases, and finally full verses in all Arabic-speaking countries, and also most notably in Islamic countries where Arabic is not the native tongue. Because the verses of the Qur'an are considered to be the absolute word of God, it is imperative that young children gain mastery of the fundamentals of Qur'anic recitation in Arabic at an early age, no matter what their mother tongue is, a skill they will carry with them for the rest of their lives., not to mention the countless blessings that come with Qur'anic recitation in its original Arabic, just as it was delivered to the Prophet himself.

The tradition of the Qur'anic *madrasah* began with the first *madrasah* in the mosque of the Prophet Muhammad (PBUH) where the "Companions of the Bench" devoted themselves to the study of the Qur'an from the Prophet himself, in itself a privilege and blessing that one can only imagine and pretend to appreciate. It is hard to recreate the thrill it would be of actually learning verses of the Qur'an from the Prophet himself. Many of his companions, the original first Muslims, then traveled far and wide in the propagation of the newly emerging religion, reciting Qur'anic verses to people they met as they travelled to countries beyond Arabia. They established mosques and settled in distant lands to the Maghreb in the West and as far as China in the East, where they started to teach Qur'an and Hadith to students seeking knowledge of Islam using its original sources. Thus, they initiated and perpetuated the tradition of the *madrasah* by carrying on the *isnad* or chain of transmission from the beloved Prophet himself.

I recently asked my faithful Pathan friend Farman Ullah about his *madrasah* experience as a child, wishing to hear firsthand the native impressions of a devoted, traditional, and conservative Muslim. "We study morning and evening at mosque after prayer and sit in a circle with imam," he says with bravado. I asked him what he remembers learning. "We first learn the graded books that introduce the system of Arabic letters and their correct pronunciation." Coincidentally, these innocent exercise books are called *al-qaeda*, which in Arabic means "base" or "basic," a term that is now universally recognized as the name associated with Osama bin Laden's terrorist organization. "Did you know what you were reading," I asked my friend tentatively, not wishing to offend. "Of course," the Pathan shouts with good-humored indignation. "We know and love our holy book. What you thinking?

We prepare ourselves to make reading with *wudhu.*[60] I doesn't touch book otherwise. We very respect Qur'an at that age and every time." And I think that his love of the Qur'an has its roots in a holy instinct that was born early in childhood as he studied with vigilance the letters, words, and phrases of his *qaeda* reader that to his young, innocent mind comprised the very words of Allah. There is no compromise when it comes to the Qur'an; devotion is instinctive and a matter of personal honor among devout Muslims to maintain a close and respectful relationship with the Holy Book of Islam.

I came to Islam as a grown man who had embraced the religion as a matter of decision and active choice, but this was only the first step on a long road of realization of the doctrine and practices, together with acclimatization that was required in coming to terms with the true Islamic culture, a spiritual culture that identifies what it means to be a practicing Muslim—and what it means to me—an effort of self-discovery and consciousness-raising that is personal and unique to each individual. "For every soul," according to one well known tradition, "there is an individual path to follow." As such, I knew that I had to learn and be able to read the Holy Qur'an in its original Arabic, if not then when I first became Muslim, then eventually over time, the Noble Book being the alpha and omega of all Islamic spirituality, its source material and its means of expression and worship. The religion began with its first descent into the mind of the Prophet in the Cave of Light in Makkah, and will come to fruition through the sincere expression of each individual Muslim life faithful to its dictates and guidance.

In my childhood, I attended catechism class regularly and had religious teaching in the Catholic grammar school that I attended. I initially knew nothing about a traditional Qur'anic *madrasah* because I was not born Muslim and converted to Islam later in life when I first went to work at a university in the Middle East over forty years ago. I have documented the story of my conversion in one of my earlier books.[61] However, like all serious devotees of the religion, I very soon set about learning the intricacies of Qur'anic recitation, without which Islamic worship in the form of prayer, which uses Qur'anic verses as part of its ritual or Qur'anic recitation, would be impossible.

While my initiation in the mysteries of Qur'anic recitation as a Muslim convert was quite different from the traditional one of the madrasah for young native born Muslims, I have traveled extensively throughout the Islamic

---

[60] This is the Arabic term for the ritual ablution in Islam that not only precedes the prayer, but also Qur'an reading. Muslims cannot touch the Book unless they have ritually purified themselves, and this injunction is strictly adhered to by the faithful.
[61] *Wisdom's Journey: Living the Spirit of Islam in the Modern World*, Bloomington, Ind: World Wisdom Books, 2009.

crescent and visited a number of traditional Qur'anic madrasah along the way. Recently, I took the opportunity of accepting an invitation from a friend who had two young sons to visit their madrasah in Abu Dhabi where I lived at the time. Various classrooms fanned off a corridor adjacent to the mosque. After a brief introduction to the director, a pleasant and indeed surprised Bengali Muslim who graciously allowed me visit the madrasah, I entered a room filled with a number of children in various stages of recitation. Was the Western-style classroom with its awkward little desks and chairs a concession to what is considered a modern academic setting? It didn't seem to matter to the children whose ages ranged from about 7, the "age of reason" in Western parlance to about 12, the age of approaching puberty, who hovered over their graded readers (*qaeda*) in various stages of absorption to the task at hand. One little fellow had taken the luxury of falling into an innocent sleep with hishead on the desk. Happily, there was a normal cross-section of children representing humanity and not the fanatic, gargoyle-like urchins from the abode of the jinn and the *shayateen* (devils), the so-called "jihad machines" that Western writers would have people believe take up residence in a Pakistani-style madrasah. A number of children sat in their chairs cross-legged almost in instinctive defiance of the schoolroom setting, as if the cultural ambiance of traditional Islam had found its way into the double helix of their DNA in spite of the imposition of the modernistic rather than the traditional setting when worshippers and students would sit on carpets on the floor.

As images of seer-eyed young extremists and radical youths with twisted faces roamed in the backdrop of my mind like a desert mirage, I gazed reflectively upon the young children gathered in front of me. In truth as I looked upon the pure faces and miniature bodies of these young boys and as they briefly looked back into my own eyes as if placing the open book of their souls at my disposal, all I saw was a group of young boys earnestly attempting to come to terms with the rigors of the Qur'anic text. They looked as if they had been touched by the wand of heaven, leaving behind in its wake the sweet aura of innocence that settled over the children like early morning dew. These innocent waifs called to mind the poetic words of Ralph Waldo Emerson:

> The hyacinthine boy, for whom
> Morn well might break and April bloom,
> The gracious boy, who did adorn
> The world whereinto he was born
> And by his countenance repay
> The favor of the loving Day.[62]

---

[62] *The Portable Emerson*, Mark van Doren (ed.), New York: The Viking Press, p. 333-334.

Was I left with images of young jihad machines slavishly, indeed robotically, absorbing the essence of a fanatical code bent on the destruction of all worlds alien to their dogmatic beliefs or was the sober but determined effort of these young children to come to terms their Holy Book enough for me? The answer lies embedded in the original intent and purpose of the traditional madrasah. What takes place there—and in countless traditional madrasah across the Islamic crescent—remembers and recreates the sacred sensibilities of earlier times when the youth of a well-defined traditional culture such as Islam adopted the early markings of a spiritual discipline that will awaken in them a feeling for the otherworldly as they make their way through "this world". The message of Islam is the message of interface between two concurrent worlds, where the simple, uncorrupted mentality of a young boy can walk from one world into the next and back again without noticing any border and without anyone else asking awkward questions or even taking notice.

The inner connection to another world makes the story of the traditional madrasah a unique one that may be difficult to comprehend in today's modern, secular world. This invisible door to a higher reality dispels the erroneous conception of the contemporary madrasah as an institution of propaganda and indoctrination and as an outmoded form of education based solely on memorization and rote learning. What we have attempted to portray here is the ambience that lies at the heart of the traditional madrasah, where the sacred resonance of the Qur'anic text and the calligraphic art of the Arabic language is reflected in the mind and heart of those for whom "the dawn breaks" and "the flowers bloom"

♠ ♠ ♠

Once I had familiarized myself with the meaning of the Qur'an in translation with the aid of my Sufi friend Haneef, I set myself the task of learning the basics of the Arabic script. Of course as a Westerner, even though I had a focused interest in other languages as an English teacher and spoke French and German with ease having lived and worked in Belgium and Germany before coming to the Middle East, I had great difficulty initially with the Arabic letters. Yet there was an appealing magic to the formation of the letters that radiated a whimsical quality of arabesques and changing profiles that seemed to spread across the page like untied knots leaving behind initially a bold air of incoherent mystery. Once thoroughly familiar with the alien letters and their related sounds, however, I set about reading and repeating the words and phrases of the sacred text, just as children do in the Qur'anic madrasah.

A point of interest worth mentioning in this regard is the fact that Arabic is still a pure language, that is to say, a phonetic language in which every letter of the alphabet has a specified sound and there are no exceptions to this rule. This is in counterpoint to English, for example, or worse French, where there are many individual letters and combinations of letters that either produce no sound (as in French) in the speaker or produce a sound that is not in keeping with the original sound associated with a given letter (as in English), no doubt a merciful coincidence for many. The phonetic characteristics of Arabic allow a non-native speaker to read Arabic with ease without making mistakes, once they have accurately mastered the alphabet and its related symbolic sounds.

Eventually, I felt comfortable enough with the letters to enable me to begin mouthing the sacred speech with reasonable accuracy. It is one thing to be a child and undergo the demanding rigors of learning the basics of one's mother language letter for letter and sound for sound as though playing a game and quite another to be a grown adult in the throes of an alien wilderness of symbols and sounds patched together with an exact science of pronunciation (*tajwid*) with fixed rules and regulations that require the intonation of a chanted psalmody as a natural rhythm of sound emergent from within the sacred text and given life by the human voice. How was I to learn this on my own? I couldn't very well sit myself down next to the seven-year-olds of a Qur'anic *madrasah*; at least my state of development at the time would not have permitted such recourse. Nor could I sit myself down amid the faithful who often gather after the early morning *fajr* prayer in many mosques across the Islamic crescent to fine-tune their Qur'anic recitation skills, a difficult and exacting feat even for native-speaking Arabs. Any genuine attempt to read the Qur'an at that stage in front of Arab speakers would have proved most embarrassing if not downright scandalous. Somehow, I needed to develop a reasonable amount of skill and accuracy before gathering the courage to join the circle of worshippers after the dawn or sunset prayer.

The next phase in this process of familiarization with the physical demands of the text in terms of pronunciation, intonation, and the rhythmic tonal qualities implicit in correct psalmody led me to the convenience of a newly developed technology at that time in the mid-70s, the walkman tape player. While nowadays our smart phones would make us laugh at this cumbersome device and its countless tapes (30 all told), it was a remarkable device at the time that was not only convenient but very fashionable, particularly with joggers and bicycle riders. In this age of pre-internet, the Qur'an was conveniently available in its entirety on a series of tapes; some of the traditional Egyptian and Syrian sheikhs who are adept at the fine art of Qur'anic recitation are legendary. There are of course different styles of psalmody; I followed the advice of a Muslim friend and purchased the entire

Qur'an recited by an Egyptian sheikh known for the quality of his "sound" and the perfection, accuracy, and clarity of his pronunciation. The entire Qur'an came to thirty different tapes that coincided with the thirty equal parts (juz) that the Qur'an is divided into.[63]

After the maghreb prayer at sunset, I would set aside a half hour's time and listen to the tape while reading aloud and meticulously following the progress of the text. In this way, I was able to detect whether I was making a mistake or not, and I read along while simultaneously listening to the sheikh's pronunciation through earphones. The tonal clarity and the vibratory resonance of the sound of the human voice intoning the sacred verses rang through my head with the clarity of a resounding bell, echoing the famous comment of the Prophet when he told his wife Khadijah that when he heard the first verses of the revelation being recited to him by the Archangel Gabriel, they had the clarity of a clarion bell, and later he was to say: "It was as though the words were written on my heart." I spent about a year in this process of becoming more familiar with the text until I felt that the words were somehow written on my mind as resonant echoes from some distant, higher plane; but they were yet to be written on my heart.

One lesson had already come clear to my novitiate mind: the Qur'an is by name a recitation rather than a reading per se, meaning predominantly an oral tradition in commemoration of earlier revelations delivered to peoples of other time periods and recalling the universal quality of legends and myths whose knowledge and meaning conveyed truths delivered orally and that were intended to be transmitted orally. As such, the Qur'an is yet another manifestation in a long history of oral traditions that have been passed down through time as sacred forms of communication that are direct and immediate between people, rather than being relegated only to some fixed place on a page, lying closed in and sequestered within the covers of a book. The symbolic value of an oral text conveys meaning effectively and economically to the mind without necessarily having the intermediary of a formal script whose practical value now serves us well, but that does not supersede or enhance the

---

[63] According to the tradition of Qur'an recitation, the verses of the Qur'an are divided into various sections and parts and are usually read in accordance with one of these divisions. The thirty equal parts remain the traditional and standard length for a routine recitation because it coincides with the length of a single month. Devout Muslims make efforts to read a juz a day as a matter of routine and inculcate this habit into their daily life. Reading the entire Qur'an during the holy month of Ramadan is considered standard practice by all Muslims. Other divisions of the text are three, seven, and ten parts, but these take considerably more time to perform and are sometimes attempted as part of a night vigil or during the holy month of Ramadan.

intuitive directness that takes place orally between people. The written page contains nostalgia for the time when the words on a page were spoken as oral poetry or solar speech; the meaning transcends dimensions as well as distance. These oral revelations were as intangible and invisible as the Spirit the words convey and as eternal as the Cosmic Mind from which they were born.

I was yet another recipient vessel among generations of humanity poured full of knowledge and blessing, but I still couldn't claim to have gotten inside the words of God any more than they have gotten inside me. In truth, as a vessel of the Divine Spirit, I felt as hard and brittle as glass, ready to be broken and shattered into pieces at the slightest whim of destiny and at the merest contingency of this world. How I needed these words of revelation to fill me up and cast me to the spirit of the wind that "bloweth where it listeth." I was gradually becoming more familiar with the formalities of the text; but its inimitable spirit and the higher consciousness made available through the intonation of the text still eluded me. Where was the "holy presence," the descent of the *sakinah*, I had read about in all the traditional books that I so eagerly devoured? Where was the beloved presence that creates within the human mind a sparkling consciousness cracking open with fresh awareness like the report of river ice in a raw winter dawn? Was I only a dense and tightly woven sieve leaving the thick film of sweet nectar behind at the doorstep of my being? I continued to search for the living reality of the book that would not come easy and without care, and I continued to work at the process of internalization of its knowledge and blessing that would hopefully set me truly on the quickest and surest path of return to God until reaching the spiritual station of no return, even if it took a lifetime of effort.

Only when I felt sufficiently comfortable with listening to the tape-recorded text did I consider myself qualified to enter, not a *madrasah Qur'aniyah* as such, but a Qur'anic circle of the type held after the early morning (*fajr*) or evening (*maghreb*) prayer in many mosques throughout the Islamic crescent for reasons that have hopefully been made clear. For one full year, I sat in a small group of Muslims with the imam of a mosque who guided us through the intricacies of learning the "science of *tajwid*" mentioned earlier to facilitate correct Qur'anic reading. It is a complicated reading discipline designed to enhance and stylize the forward movement of the text with well defined rules that involve correct pronunciation of each letter, the elongation of certain vowels, the use of ellipses, indications to pause and stop in the reading to facilitate breathing and to enhance meaning, to name only a few of the ritual complexities required in order to achieve correct recitation. This is not even to mention the psalmodic chanting that the voice eventually assumes, a skill that comes with practice and time. It takes diligent effort to become adept at Qur'anic recitation, but having once passed through the rigors of this well-specified discipline, it becomes an aspect of sacred ritual that every Muslim takes very seriously, not wishing to misread and distort the sacred flow of the text. Any interruption in the flow of the text and any misreading or mispronunciation is immediately repeated correctly to preserve the integrity of the meaning and out of deference and respect to the integrity of the sacred text.

I feared that this kind of public Qur'anic recitation would take on the character of a trial by fire that I was not prepared for. As a foreigner and non-Arab, I would obviously be subject to rigorous attention, a novice subject to close scrutiny among a den of wolves. This, however proved to be pure fantasy on my part and had no place in the reality of the experience. The Sheikh exhibited infinite patience as well as an infinite rigor appropriate to the demands of the task. One did not make mistakes in reading and reciting the text without strict censure, as even the slightest errors of pronunciation, intonation, and rhythm were not overlooked. Certain Arabic letters such as "ayn" (ع), "ghayn" (غ), "sad" (ص), and "dhad" ض do not exist in the Western alphabet and are extremely difficult to pronounce like a native speaker; but with practice, I soon learned that anything is possible.

I discovered to my surprise that Arabs themselves have difficulty reading the Qur'an without making errors of some kind. Either a lack of habit in routinely reciting the text or perhaps occasional over-familiarity with the Arabic language and a tendency to resort to colloquial pronunciations sometimes hindered an accurate delivery. In fact, my slavish devotion to the literal text and my conscious effort at the correct reading of letter for letter gave me an edge over those native-speaking Arabs who felt lulled into a false familiarity with the classical Arabic of the text that they had not truly mastered. I took nothing for granted and worked hard at becoming adept at recreating every letter and sound with precision and accuracy.

Had I arrived at the "holy gate" of some cosmic experience that could propel the mind and heart across eternities of cosmic awareness and infinitudes of cosmic space? The answer must be a resounding "no!" One does not approach the book with the intention of shattering cosmic barriers and arriving on the shores of some vast enlightenment. It was enough for me not to make too many mistakes, taking care not to betray the integrity of the sacred speech and to fulfill the mandate of its ritualistic discipline and worship. I just wanted to get the text right; the rest of the experience I would leave to the discretion of God.

At some point within this time frame—it must have been nearly a decade into my experience as a Muslim living in the Islamic world—I decided it was time to carve the words of some of the verses onto the encasement of my stone heart. I still did not feel the softening of the heart that I had read about in some of the mystic literature of the Islamic traditions, and still less the expansion of some higher awareness raising my consciousness above the mundane level of my own immediate concerns. Where was the burning desire to transcend my limitations; when would the melting of the heart take place before it could flow through some alchemical metamorphosis into the realms of the higher sentiments and spiritual emotions? When would I experience the "gift of tears" that I had read about or smell the heavenly perfumes that betoken higher levels of spirituality? I decided to learn some of the *ayat*(s) (verses) and *surah*(s) (chapters) so that I could recite them from memory. I wanted to learn some of the Qur'an by heart, as the idiom goes. In other words like the Prophet, I wanted to learn the verses to the extent that they were "written on my heart."

There is a well known and enduring tradition in Islam of committing large portions of the Qur'an—if not the entire Qur'an—to memory, a tradition that goes back to the Prophet himself and most of his original companions. To become *hafez al-Qur'an*—preserver in memory of the Qur'an—remains a deep aspiration for many devout Muslims. We can only imagine the incredible intensity of the people of that time, not only living in close proximity to the Prophet himself, but also listening firsthand from his holy person to the very words of Allah as they were revealed to him. It is small wonder to imagine the fire and the determination to internalize these words in whatever manner possible, not the least being their full memorization. The tradition has lasted down through the centuries to this day, when young children still learn large portions of the Qur'an by heart. It is an on-going commitment that must be maintained through a systematic process of daily repetition and review, a process that amounts to continually living in the presence of the Noble Book.

Once I had committed my mind to the task and set myself on the road of memorization of certain of the shorter "Makkan" chapters of the Qur'an that traditionally come in the last several parts (*juz*) of the book, I began the slow and meticulous process of committing to memory verse by verse of one, then a second and a third chapter, until I had finally accumulated a goodly number of *surahs* within easy reach of my mind. I had set myself the task of learning the verses "by heart" and ended up learning them "with the heart." It is interesting that in the Islamic perspective, Muslims refer to the heart when explaining such matters rather than the mind. Indeed, the heart is the "seat" of the intelligence according to Islamic scholars, the place where the fusion of knowledge and sacred emotion takes place in order to bring about the full realization of the truth that lies embedded within every aspect of existence. As the symbolic pulse of the human entity, it is knowledge of the heart that will lead us out of ourselves on the road to union with the Supreme Being.

The process of learning something by heart implies first of all the realization of how true learning takes place. Wanting to understand and have some knowledge internalized within one's being as an applied wisdom is not enough. Before truly understanding a thing as an internalized reality, the simplicity of true learning is required. Using the senses, first the eyes are engaged in reading the letters and words, then the tongue is engaged to give voice to the words as they were intended to be heard and whose resonance moves out into the atmosphere like ripples on a placid sea. Repetition is the key: The fervent and continuous perfecting of the sacred words through the repetition of the syllables, far from eroding the language and wearing it down into platitude, actually energizes and revives the words, making them real on the tongue and then sacred within the heart. I repeated syllable by syllable, phoneme by phoneme, word by word, phrase by phrase, verse by verse, both visually and verbally, until I felt that they were committed to memory. The next day, I would review what I had learned to make sure it was still a part of me and if it wasn't, I repeated the process until it was firmly embedded in my mind. There were of course advances and retreats, peaks and valleys, slow conquests and persistent failures, until the moment arrives when the verses are engraved on the heart. To this day, there are verses written on my heart in indelible ink that I memorized thirty years ago. They are with me now forever as part of my permanent record.

In truth, what happens is that the mind falls down into the well of this learning process; one feels awash in the sacred text partly because it opens onto a world of transcendence and enlightenment and partly because of the harmonious effect the vibratory sound has on the physical body. Oftentimes, you will see Muslims in the mosque swaying from side to side during a Qur'anic reading, a habit that I found myself falling into as well, if for no other reason than that the entire body seemed to want to take part in this sacred adventure in worship and praise of the Divinity. The end result is that the doctrine is not learned mentally as we are accustomed to learning things in the West, imposing so many facts onto the plate of the mind. The living experience of the Qur'an is engraved on the heart as a prelude to becoming a part of the person's entire being, internalized as it were as part of the fabric that makes a person what they truly are in their essence, the verses ready to be drawn upon for guidance and support during the course of a person's life, as the need arises in making decisions and going about the business of living. Being able to summon the words of revelation and draw them out of the well of one's inner being without the aid of a book gathers together the spirit and the voice from what a person has internalized rather than calling upon some reasoned or intellectualized meaning from the mind alone.

The art of memorization has been lost in the Western world. Even as a child over half a century ago, I used to memorize portions of the catechism and learn poems and nursery rhymes by heart. Being able to recite them at will was considered a high accomplishment, representing a kind of internalization of the poetic ambiance and mind of the poet himself and in this way the creative process he went through remains a living reality through the force of the words imprinted on the memory. Children seem to understand and take delight in certain things of the natural order that adults only make fun of and laugh.

People in the West have nearly forgotten the value of reciting sacred verses from memory in the tradition of Qur'anic recitation or as in the Hindu tradition of repeating sutras in the Vedic scriptures. In their need for mobility, speed, and continual change, the idea of repeating a sacred scripture, a consecrated mantra, or one of the Names of God seems tedious, repetitious, and without value. We have lost the realization that through such repetition of the sacred Name and/or memorization of revelatory verses of scripture, a person comes to identify him or herself with the divine name and consequently with God Himself.

According to Ramakrishna, "God and His Name are identical." In Christianity, the Hesychastic "Prayer of the Heart" continues the Brahman tradition of repetition of the Name by repeating the name of Jesus over and over again until it becomes "second nature." The verses of the Qur'an, the names of God, the sacred epithets incorporated into the language even are all there as reminders of "the one thing needful." Their repetition are exercises in concentration and application of principial knowledge that brings about an appeasement of the mind and a strengthening of the spirit. Who could ask for anything more?

## Chapter Fifteen

## Mastering the Written Text

---

I still asked myself what else I could do to take leave of the borderland of an ego-entrenched psyche and climb inside the text, wrap it around my heart like a warm woolen cloak, and attain the proximity as well as the abiding love of its sacred presence. How could I give up the familiarity of my own human voice for the grandiloquence of the single sovereign voice of the sacred text whose power knows no bounds and whose energy contains modes of transcendence? How could I capture the spirit of a voice of a thousand years, the voice of power and wonder, the voice of eloquent silence that resounds within the cave of the heart in search of a suitable resting place?

After much contemplation, I resolved to leave behind temporarily the vocalizations and verbalism of the original form and turn to the written script of the text whose calligraphic splendor and alien majesty as a sacred Islamic art calls upon the intuitive sense of sight. I hoped that the engagement of all the senses of the body would allow them to serve their rightful function as effective instruments to facilitate the internalization and realization of the spirit of the text within the mind if not the higher consciousness of my wandering, modern-day soul.

The gifted writer and story-teller Somerset Maugham recounted in his revealing work entitled *The Writer's Notebook* that he taught himself how to write by sitting down and copying out classical essays and sections from the great works of literature "by hand." He theorized that by using his eyes and hands and body, by touching the paper, copying the letters and words sentence by sentence, and by using as many of his senses as possible, since they are the very portals of experience, he could get under the skin of the text and venture forth into the mind of the writer. He wished to recreate for himself the act and experience of creation and what it means to capture in words the essence of a meaning that originates in the mind but that must be translated from abstract thought to concrete words that convincingly convey a meaning as they lie upon the page. Of course nowadays, people do not write with feathered plumes and indigo ink, preferring instead the speed and facility of the word processor; but that did not preclude my taking Maugham's advice to approach on a more intimate level the actual mind of the writer and the creative process involved in the writing. In the case of a sacred revelation, I wondered where this would lead me.

As a prototype of language, the Qur'an itself is the product of both an oral and written tradition. The Qur'an is primarily a recitation and the Prophet himself was instructed by the archangel Gabriel to "recite in the name of your Lord," this verse being the very first verse revealed to the Prophet of Islam. However, the *sakinah* or spiritual presence is to be found in the written as well as the recited Qur'an. According to a Holy Tradition, God wrote with a Mystic Pen that symbolizes the Universal Intellect, the inner reality of all things that is preserved on the Guarded Tablet before the creation of the world.[64] The Supreme Pen (*al-Qalam al-a'la*) has traditionally been identified with the Universal Intellect, while the ink is the reflection of All-Possibility and results in the possibility of the manifestation of the creation, recalling the Qur'anic verse: "And if all the trees on earth were pens and the sea—with seven seas added—[were ink] yet the words of Allah could not be exhausted" (31:27). The Pen, therefore, has important significance as a universal symbol of the creation of the Word, the Logos, and the revelation, while the Guarded Tablet

---

[64] "The first of the things Allah created is the Pen (*Qalam*) which He created of Light (*Nur*), and which is made of white pearl; its length is equal to the distance between the sky and the earth. Then He created the Tablet (*Lawh*, or *Lawh al-mahfuz*, the 'guarded tablet'), and it is made of white pearl and its surfaces are of red rubies; its length is equal to the distance between the sky and the earth and its width stretches from the East to the West."

"preserved in Paradise" maintains the record of universal manifestation[65] and sets the precedent for the significance of the written word.

Needless to say, the Qur'an as book and written document (*al-kitab*) for future generations needed to be written down. The act of writing the text of the Qur'an ultimately became the sacred art of calligraphy which is central to the mystique of Islamic art and spirituality. Oral Qur'anic recitation as a sacred sonoral art of chanted psalmody found its counterpart within the written tradition as the sacred art of Qur'anic calligraphy. According to 'Ali ibn abu Talib: "The beauty of writing is the tongue of the hand and the elegance of thought." The imagined, spoken, and written word complemented the essential meaning through different mediums of expression. This was the origin of the tradition that I then turned to in my endeavor to wrestle with the complexities of the Qur'an and more fully come to terms with all its sublime aspects.

It is one thing to passively regard the written word on the page and quite another to actively engage oneself in the writing of a particular text.[66] The experience becomes a challenge when the letters, words, and phrases are derived from an alien alphabet that needs to be scripted and learned as a child learns to write its native alphabet. Having set myself the task, I bought a special notebook and pen to use as my calamus and blessed reed, in order to faithfully execute my sacred endeavor. I began with the 7-verse opening statement of the initial *surah* appropriately entitled *al-Fatihah*, the Opening. I did not concern myself with the length, scope, and breadth of this challenging task; had I done so, I might have developed a fear that I was not up to the challenge. When dealing with the Qur'an, what counts is the effort of worship and the quality of concentration, and not the amount of verses that one reads or writes. Like a true friend, the book does not count the hours and days; it is enough to be there, together and entwined in a holy relationship that becomes a continuum of the ever-present eternal moment striking a vertical sword across the horizontal axis of earthly time. The ethereal and timeless power of the text is persistent and will not freely and easily give up its secrets. If a person is fortunate enough to partake of the sacred blessing (*baraka*), it reaches inside to touch the pulse of the heart and one must decide one way or

---

[65] Another tradition, reported by Ibn Abbas, says that "Allah created the Pen before He created the Creation." Also, "the Pen burst open and the Ink flows from it until the Day of the Resurrection."

[66] There are 6,234 verses in the entire Qur'an. Copying 12 verses a day on average would produce a completed manuscript in about a year and a half. It took me roughly 2 years of periodic work on the project to complete the task, one that I am happy to have accomplished.

another what it means and what to do about it.

Whenever I could find the time, but preferably at least once a day in my established routine, I sat myself down in a state of ritual ablution to copy the sacred text in the humble tradition, if not the accomplished style, of the traditional Qur'anic calligraphers and illuminationists. Over time, the quality of my written script improved dramatically, the words and verses multiplied upon the page, pages multiplied upon pages, as I worked my sacred reed through the contours and curves that make up the physical formation of the Arabic letters. The formation of the Roman alphabet relies predominantly on its straight and angular lines and has a forward movement from left to right down the page that we are all familiar with. The letters of the English alphabet seem to have clearness and efficiency as their primary focus, but they do not inspire as do Chinese pictograms or the gracefully arabesque and fluid style of the Arabic script. In the traditional Islamic setting, everything commences from the right: People leave elevators from the right side first, circumambulation around the Ka'aba in Makkah is from right to left, greetings and salutations occur from the right and hand-writing has a forward movement from right to left down the page. Within the world of the Roman alphabet, one would look in vain for the flexible, complex, and gently ornate quality offered by the flowing letters *noon, sheen,* and *lam* (ن، ش، ل) of the Arabic alphabet. While Western landscape art is full of space and light, the sonorous and calligraphic arts in Islam are full of echoing sound and undulating stroke.

Consider the bold, vertical line of the Arabic letter *alif,* statuesque and statesmanlike as if in commemoration of the distinctive vertical stance of *Homo sapiens.* The letters *noon, ba, ta,* and *tha*—differentiated by mere dots resting either above or below the form of the letter—contain all the suggestive, symbolic, and sensuous curvature of a cup ready to contain the nectar of some sublime meaning. Like shapely crescent moons and spiraling galaxy clusters that harbor within their sublime forms the darkness of night and the silence of the universe, the letters spread out across the page as silent sentinels to the underlying sense of mystery that pervades all of existence, just as the trees and texture of a solemn forest create a sense of the sacred through the ambiance that emanates from their presence. It is almost as if the symbolic images of the letters contain metaphors of meaning even before they constitute the totality of a word. In writing stroke for stroke and letter for letter, the traditional calligrapher virtually stepped inside the written text and wrapped himself around them as in a holy cocoon, creating within himself the sense of a larger presence beyond the very horizon of the self.

You enter a revelatory text through the medium of copy writing as you might enter into the lost valley of Shangri-la. In doing so, you enter a realm that transcends the limits of the individual self, taking you far beyond snow-capped mountains and the puffed elegance of the cumulus clouds that gather at their summit. It takes you beyond the trite sensibilities of the human mind, beyond the horizon of one's limited cognitive world, indeed beyond the contoured and shapely elegance of the Arabic script and the florid manner in which the words and verses of the Qur'anic text are written, beyond and into a world where the great mystery becomes a part of us by virtue of our symbolic participation in the actual writing of the sacred words of God.

Imagine for a moment walking to the very edge of the horizon. You sit yourself down with legs dangling into the void and examine the broad illusion before you, revealing the vast meeting ground of Heaven and Earth that makes the horizon what it is. Before your eyes and beyond your wildest dreams, there is spread out before you a wilderness landscape seemingly beyond the continuum of time and space in which the primordial spirit hovers amid stately millennium trees and divinely sculptured rock formations. There is a primitive aspect to the shape of the Arabic letters that seems wild and unruly to the uninitiated; their emergence as words takes on a primordial quality that weaves arabesques of symbols and shapes that actually trace a kind of spiritual presence onto the terrain of the blank white page, a page that by filling up with verse after verse of the sacred discourse becomes a calligraphic map whose terrain veils in secrecy an actual spiritual presence, the very same presence that looms beyond the horizon of the known world.

The experience of copying the Qur'an created a spiritual discipline within me that spilled over into untold areas in the experience of my daily life. You cannot spend days of your life writing down the words of revelation without becoming touched by some indelible sense of the sacred permeating other aspects of one's daily routine. Emotions become raw and facts become bold. There is a truth and a reality to every created thing, from the atom with its elemental building particles to the spiraling galaxies with their uncounted billions of stars. Everything takes on symbolic value and therefore everything has meaning and significance, creating a kind of vibratory confluence of power and energy that makes itself known through sounding rhythms and symbolic strokes of the Arabic alphabet, through letters and words that are mere symbols for a far greater reality. Reciting the text or writing down its verses becomes an intimate private encounter with the sounds and symbols that reveal the meaning of the universe. The personal ego fades away and what takes its place is the sublime experience of the truth of the Noble Book before you, with its message of the oneness and unity of Reality, the very message and summative height of the entire religion, contained within the primordial point that commences the formation of any written word.

To step into the text you become a part of it and it becomes a part of you. In participating in the sound, the memorized texture and hand-scripted formation of the letters and words, the text then touches you with its energy and power. You and the text are one and the same for those moments that you take up the book in hand, recite the sacred verses, or copy them down and fill a blank page with their extravagant beauty. A written script that was once nothing more than nonsensical and incomprehensible scribbling on a page had now become for me artful and sacred calligraphy that unlocks the secrets of the universe. The largeness of the revelation, which encompasses all mystery that is to be resolved and all knowledge worth knowing, allows a person to come to an understanding of reality that would not otherwise be accessible in daily existence. When that knowledge is put into practice, it creates a manner of living that is in direct reflection of the meaning and spirit of the Holy Quran.

The experience of worship that accompanies Qur'anic recitation is so haunting and so elevating, indeed so entrancing an experience, that it makes the reciter cry sometimes in spite of our sensible, rational, and modern mentality and in spite of the hard shell that surrounds the viewfinder that filters the perceptions of our minds and shapes our conscious world. There is an archaic affinity to the experience that is so strange and beautiful it also makes a person feel afraid of being unable to live up to the moment once it passes. When The Muslims take leave of the Book, just as when they take leave of their prayer carpet and re-enter the contingencies of daily life, they take the experience with them because it has become a part of their being by virtue of the participation in the sacred discipline.

In this way, and over the course of over forty years as a Muslim, I have attempted to come to terms with the generous, the holy, the noble Qur'an. Have I succeeded in this endeavor to become fully versed in its mysteries? It is not for me to speculate on such matters, and who can measure such things? It is enough to know that I have grown to love the Qur'an as I have grown to love the Prophet Muhammad (PBUH) who delivered it to humanity and can no longer conceive of living without it any more than I can conceive of living without the beat of my heart or the breath of my life. When I sit down after the dawn prayer after many years of practice in coming to terms with the Arabic script, I now read and recite the verses with familiarity and ease, to the extent that coming to the Book and reciting its verses feels like coming home. When I close the book and walk away from a session, I feel refreshed and complete, like having visited some far distant country whose vistas put things in perspective and whose language gives voice to knowledge beyond the distant stars with their swirling galaxies making their way through infinity.

I have filled multiple notebooks over the years with my hand-written verses, perennially adding to and complementing the first primer that initiated my child-like attempts to get closer to the Divine Revelation by copying down the verses letter for letter and word for word. I realize now that it is not the having done but the doing that fills me with joy. In keeping with my namesake, the Prophet Yahya[67], I have followed the guidance he was given when one of the verses of the Qur'an admonishes him to: "Seize the Book with (conviction and) strength." (19:12) I have been living all these years in the presence of a revelation whose truth and light fills my advancing years with the same Truth and Light that has filled the universe since time immemorial. In remembrance of that Truth and Light, I hope to continue to "seize the Book" until the end of my days.

---

[67] Yahya is the Arabic name for John.

Chapter Sixteen

## The Book as Knowledge and Worship

For several reasons, the true value of the Qur'an as it is understood in the mind of the Muslim escapes the understanding and appreciation of non-Muslims, especially the Euro-American Western community. This applies firstly to the Qur'an as a means of worship, and secondly to the language of the Qur'an as the absolute speech of God and how the worshipper relates to the literal and inner content of the words and phrases on multiple levels of understanding and accepts the fact that they may never know the final significance of the revelation in absolute terms. It is enough that they meet the book on their own terms and at their own level of understanding, provided it is done in good faith and with trust in God.

In the Islamic tradition, Qur'anic recitation is a form of worship on a par with prayer and the other spiritual disciplines, such as *zakat*, prayer and fasting for the full month of Ramadhan. In Islam, every person performs a sacerdotal role as the celebrant of the sacred rites of worship. Even the birds in the air and the lilies in the field perform worship and praise the Divinity in their own capacity and according to their own true nature. The human and the Divine, however, come together in a sacred, indeed unique, encounter that is direct and ultra-personal. Reading the Qur'an provides the perfect means for such a direct and intimate encounter with the Divinity, who according to a well known verse "is nearer to him [mankind] than his jugular vein." (50:16) Islamic practice encourages Qur'anic recitation in the morning after the dawn prayer (*salat al-fajr*), when keeping vigil at night, and upon the completion of the ritual prayer during the prescribed times. "Establish regular prayers, at the sun's decline till the darkness of the night, and also (reading) the Qur'an after the morning prayer: indeed the recitation of dawn is ever witnessed (and carries its own testimony)." (17:78)

The true value of the Qur'anic recitation as a form of worship is borne out by the fact that millions of non-Arabic speaking Muslims read and recite the Qur'an without necessarily understanding the literal meaning of the words. Yet, they approach the Book with a conscious reverence and a fundamental desire to worship God that transcends the literal meaning of the text. That said, most devout non-native-speaking Muslims attempt to learn as much Qur'anic Arabic as possible to facilitate at least a rudimentary understanding of the literal text. In addition, it is possible that God may bless the sincere heart and intention of a devout Muslim with a realized knowledge of the doctrine without having to necessarily pass through the gate of a literal knowledge.

There is even a serious danger that could arise from either complacency from habitual reading or an over-familiarity with the text. Native speakers of Arabic who may know the linguistic nuances of the text may fall short of a realized knowledge for one reason or another, such as lack of intent or sincerity of purpose. In other words, a literal knowledge of the language carries with it no guarantee of an assimilated knowledge of the text or of the many and varied levels of knowledge and meaning that are lodged within the verses as mysteries. On the other hand, non Arabic-speaking readers who struggle through a careful recitation of the text may well approximate a better and more accurate reading then a native-speaking Arab who through habit and routine may rush through a well-known portion of the text and lace the reading with multiple errors. Only intention, effort, and an underlying sincerity can define the parameters of Muslim worship and not a specific race or language type. Needless to say, it goes without saying that translations of the Qur'an into other languages for the purpose of conveying its essential knowledge have no liturgical significance for the purpose of worship.

The Qur'an is a miraculous blend of meaning and sound. Obviously the Qur'an conveys a meaning upon those who understand the literal words, while intuitive meaning can be conveyed directly to the non-Arabic speaker, depending on the intentions of the person reciting the verses together with the mercy and blessing of God. However, there is no doubting the miraculous effect that the sacred sounds and word combinations have on the faithful generally, Arab and non-Arab Muslims alike. In addition to the words, phrases, meanings, aphorisms, stories, and symbolic images, the sacred text is replete with rhythms, cadences, intonations, elisions, ellipses, and sacred sound vibrations that, together, add up to a glorious psalmody having a powerful, cumulative effect on the reader, who makes every effort to chant sonorously, clearly, slowly, and above all correctly the holy verses.[68] "It exercises its effect not only upon the mind but on the very substance of the believer, although it can do this only in its integral character, that is to say, as the Arabic Qur'an."[69] No doubt, the words and their associations have echoes and reverberations in the ear and mind of the faithful with a power that can melt hearts and stir souls. The Prophet once told his companions that "hearts become rusty just as iron does when water gets at it." When asked how this rust could be removed, he replied: "By frequent remembrance of death and frequent recitation of the Qur'an."

If during the course of a Qur'anic reading, tears come to the eyes and there is a welling of emotion from some unknown source, one should not be concerned because not all tears bear the mark of leave-taking and sorrow. Some tears wash the soul of its residue of evil and evoke feelings of bliss in the heart of the faithful soul. These are tears that untie the knots of the heart, that unravel the complexities of the world. It is not uncommon during Qur'anic recitation for a Muslim to weep for no apparent reason other than the subliminal and cumulative effect that the recitation has on the mind and heart of the reciter. This phenomenon is commonly called the "gift of tears." These tears are symbolic of the profound emotion present within the person at that time, while the emotion itself serves as a purification and release of repressed feelings and attitudes that often reside unconsciously within us.

The sacred words of the Divinity represent a great complexity of sound that fills the quivering air with their sonorous, sacred rhythms. It is as if one has never heard the singing of birds before or the roar of the ocean, never seen a sunset, never wept like this before. Muslims often feel spiritually refreshed after a session of Qur'anic recitation, uplifted and ready to meet the forces and challenges that they may be confronted with during the course of their day. The mind, heart, and soul have been washed clean and a sense of mental and spiritual refreshment hovers like the scent of fresh soap from an early morning bath. Another uncommon manifestation that sometimes takes place during a

---

[68] In quantum terms, everything vibrates, even the human body as the physical manifestation of the soul.

[69] Charles Le Gai Eaton, *Islam and the Destiny of Man*, Cambridge, UK: The Islamic Texts Society, 1985, p. 78.

holy recitation has to do with another one of the senses, this time the sense of smell. Certain smells are known for their capacity to capture the essence of a thing. In the case of Qur'anic recitation, the physical book has been known to emanate waves of heavenly scent that intoxicate the reciter with a sense of the eternal and infinite as one enters into close proximity with the words of God.

The Qur'an exudes a mysterious and in a sense miraculous power. Ibn 'Arabi (*Risalat al-Quds*) quotes the case of Sufis who spend their whole life reading or ceaselessly reciting the Qur'an. This would be inconceivable if not impossible to sustain were there not, behind the words of the literal text, a concrete and active spiritual presence that goes beyond the words and the actively conscious mind of the reciter. Moreover, it is by virtue of the miraculous power of the Qur'an that certain verses can expel evils and heal illnesses in many circumstances. Christians familiar with the exorcism of devils from the body will not be surprised that Muslims also use the Qur'an to cast demons and evil *jinn* from the body of human beings that they have taken possession of. Similarly, Qur'anic phrases are used in traditional massage and other healing techniques, such as energy projection through breathing in which physical methods work together with spiritual aspiration to cure the person of his or her disease. One sees that the Qur'an is truly "a cure and a mercy" (17:82) for the faithful.

A Muslim's relationship with the Qur'an involves something more than establishing the facts or acquiring the knowledge it contains. It goes far beyond an acquiring of the Arabic language or appreciating the aesthetic quality and visual impact that Islamic calligraphy has on the mind. There is a harmony and a rhythmic flow to the words and verses that virtually defy a close or literal analysis. Non-Muslims who are unfamiliar with the Arabic language liken its mysterious rhythm to poetry, but it is not poetry in the normal sense of the word since its rhythms follow no poetic rules and contain a power that goes far beyond the realm of any earthly poetry. "The eloquence does not reside so much in the ordering of the words into powerful poetic utterance as in the degree of the inspiration as a result of which every sentence, every word, and every letter scintillate with a spiritual presence and are like light congealed in tangible form."[70] The rhythms themselves are subtle and mysterious and cannot be compared with what is found within the great works of literature that have been written down through the ages.

In addition, rhythmic patterns flow out of the Qur'anic images and symbols into the very soul and have the power to create feelings of primordial bliss. These images and symbols are not classical or literary, rather they are

---

[70] *Ibid*, p. 5

archetypal in their character and universal in their message. They are of two kinds, the macrocosmic and microcosmic. The macrocosmic symbols recall the great and harmonious rhythms of the natural order that include the passage of night and day, the movement of sun, moon, and stars, the magnitude of the zodiacal heavens, the phases of the moon, and the spiral movement of galaxies all ponderously swirling around a central metacosmic core.[71] These are symbolic images expressive of a rhythm and movement that touch the very soul of those reciting the verses as they sit with the book and intone the sacred words and phrases. "The Qur'an . . . engenders, in whoever hears its words and experiences its sonorous magic, both plenitude and poverty. It gives and it takes, it enlarges the soul by lending it wings, then lays it low and strips it bare; it is comforting and purifying at one and the same time, like a storm; human art can scarcely be said to have this virtue."[72] We touch the Book, take it to hand, read it, aspire to absorb its meaning and internalize its holy essence; in return we are touched by the very words of God.

Similarly, there are the microcosmic images and symbols that relate directly to our human nature. The heart, for instance, stands out as the archetypal seal of all knowledge and feeling. It is the "seal" of the intelligence in the Islamic perspective as well as the sacred cave or niche of all higher emotion and noble sentiments. We refer here not to the physical heart of course, but the spiritual heart of each individual that serves as the central spiritual faculty and therefore must reside behind the physical projection of the pulsating heart pump. Allah knows what is in the human heart and He knows what lies at the heart of the cosmic universe. There are other powerful symbols that relate to the human body such as the Hand, Eye, and Face of God. "Allah's hand is over their hands;" (48:10) "Allah is the All-Seeing; wherever you turn, there is the Face of God." (2:115) These microcosmic symbols are powerful channels of insight that can lift the veil and cross the unbreachable isthmus (barzakh) that exists between the physical and spiritual planes of existence.

Finally, we should not overlook the fact that the phrases and verses of the Qur'an enter the daily life of the Muslims to the extent that the rhythm and texture of life itself becomes interwoven with prayers, epithets, litanies, and invocations that are derived expressly from the sacred text. "It is easy to understand the capital part played in the life of the Moslem by those sublime

---

[71] "Truly, the creation of the heavens and the earth is greater than the creation of man" (40:57).
[72] Titus Burckhardt, *Mirror of the Intellect* (Cambridge, UK: Quinta Essentia, 1987), pp. 244-245.

words which are the verses of the Qur'an; they are not merely sentences which transmit thoughts, but are in a way beings, powers, or talismans. The soul of the Moslem is as it were woven of sacred formulas; in these he works, in these he rests, in these he lives, and in these he dies."[73] The Qur'an is an integral part of a Muslim life, permeating every aspect of daily routine, shaping its parameters, providing its coloration, motivation, and ultimate goal. It is the first sound that is whispered into a newborn's ear, and, if one is blessed with a so-called "happy death," the final sound that is uttered as one takes leave of this world, becoming a verbal bridge into another dimension.

Beyond these key moments of intonation, however, there is the language we use in our daily lives that is punctuated linguistically with Qur'anic epithets. Every formal action, such as beginning a work project or setting out on a journey, commences with the phrase "In the Name of God, the Compassionate, the Merciful." When a person sneezes, asks how another person is, or even finishes a meal, he praises God by way of thanks. When a disaster overtakes the Muslims, they immediately say that "there is no power except in God"; but when a thing of beauty presents itself, they are quick to say "glory be to God." When Muslims express the intention to accomplish something and has a future wish, they immediately invoke the will of Allah as the guiding principle to their every desire. They wish a thing to happen only if God wishes it.

Such epithets have their origins in the sacred Qur'anic text and become, through the use of everyday speech, expressions of sacred sentiments that are embedded within the very soul of the Muslim and emerge to the surface in the form of daily linguistic usage no matter what may be the mother tongue of the person. Turkomans, Iranians, Malays, Pakistanis, Bangladeshis, and Mongolian Muslims all employ these Qur'anic phrases in their Arabic formulation within their own mother languages, wherein these phrases function "as is," unchanged and original, Qur'anic at source and fully comprehensible as a form of communication. In return, these languages are sometimes referred to as Islamic languages.

Qur'anic recitation also determines the very framework of a Muslim's spiritual life. Muslims draw on the legendary language of the Qur'an to give a spiritual frame to their hopes, fears, sorrows, regrets, and aspirations. They use the Qur'an as a means of withdrawing for a few moments during the course of the day, whether it be in the early morning when the birds sing their own sacred verses, or after the sunset prayer when the calm of dusk merges

---

[73] Frithjof Schuon, *Understanding Islam* (Bloomington, IN: World Wisdom Books, 1994), p. 60.

into the stillness of night. The holy recitation relieves the mind, the psyche, and the soul of the reciter from the gravitational pull of this world with its implicit imbalance, disharmony, and lack of peace. When Muslims arise in the morning at the call to prayer, they have available the sacred book that contains all they need to know; they therefore possess the means to realize that knowledge in their daily lives. Small wonder then that devout Muslims turn to the Holy Qur'an for sustenance and strength on a daily basis throughout the course of their lives, a turning that pre-empts doubt and despair and leads them back to the center and source of their existence within the Divine Being.

At the dawn prayer (*salat al-fajr*), the shadowy rays of the saffron moon flow across the window sill. In the pre-dawn darkness, the night sky shines forth the light of ancient stars with its message of an eternity within time and an infinity within space, before disappearing with the coming of the dawn. There is a hint of incense in the air whose assault on the senses captures a feeling of sacrality that becomes a moving force within the mind and heart. Heavenly scents accompany the two angels who descend to witness the Qur'anic recitations that occur every morning across the crescent of the Islamic world. Having performed the ritual ablution and prayer, Muslims in various corners of the globe sit cross-legged on prayer carpets and reach for the Noble Qur'an, the Illuminated Book, (*al-Kitab al-Mubin*) a document that is "on a tablet well-preserved in Heaven," as well as a printed book held in hand. They kiss it out of profound respect, place it on forehead and heart, and then commence to recite verses from the Holy Book. *Alif, Lam, Mim*, they chant sonorously the Arabic letters that commence the Qur'an's second chapter: "This is the Book, of which there is no doubt, and guidance for those who fear God" (2:1).

With the divine words of revelation, Muslims forever repeat the task of planting in the ground of their souls the seeds of a divine knowledge that brings guidance and certainty into their agitated lives. When the mind becomes illuminated with knowledge, when the heart is on fire with desire, when the imagination paints dreams of mystery and beauty, and when the higher emotions are brimming with devotion and love, then do the seeds of the divine Mystery that have been planted in the human soul take root and grow. The early dawn light creeps cautiously across the windowpane while the outsized autumn moon sinks heavily below the emerging horizon. As the words of revelation echo through the emerging dawn, the aspiring soul becomes a staging ground of worship that rises through lower levels of conscious awareness in order to return to its origin in the universal consciousness radiating eternally from the Mind of God.

Chapter Seventeen

The Names of the Book

---

Another rarefied aspect of the Qur'an for the Muslim community lies in the "presence"—for want of a better term—that accompanies the physical appearance of the book in a mosque or home. The true presence of the Qur'an lies not in the pages and binding as with other books, but rather in its resonant splendor and its calligraphic majesty. Muslims read the Qur'an for the clear knowledge, guidance, and truth implicit in the words and verses; but they also read the verses because they contain a "spiritual presence" through the recitation and intonation of the divine speech that remembers the beloved personality of the Prophet of Islam (PBUH) before literally bringing them into the Presence of God.

As sacred sound, the letters, syllables, words, and verses of the revelation call forth the inner voice of the self, the voice of the prophet, the voice of the archangel, and the Voice of the Supreme Being[74] who has chosen to reveal a knowledge of Himself and speak in words of the knowledge of

---

[74] According to a *hadith qudsi*, which is a saying of the Prophet that quotes the direct speech of the Divine Being, a regular reciter of the Qur'an is he "who reads the Qur'an is as if he were talking to Me and I were talking to Him."

Creation and Origins, thus recalling the primordial man within each of us through the power of sound. When a Muslim recites the verses, he hears his own voice reciting the words first of all in the here and now. Then as a kind of echo beyond the voice of the individual lies the voice of the Prophet Muhammad (PBUH). Through the voice of the Prophet passed the divine revelation of God to humanity, whereby he became the instrument and intermediary through whom the world of the Spirit was able to enter and influence the spirit of the world. Beyond the voice of the individual self and the voice of the Prophet lies the voice of the Archangel Gabriel who as intermediary of the Divinity delivered the verses to the Prophet. Finally, all these voices are earthly echoes of the Voice of God Who communicates through these revelatory words to the soul of every human being a profound sense of wonderment for the numinous and the other-worldly. Through words, the Divine Being is able to pluck the violin strings of a person's inner being to sound a cord of the timeless Reality whose echo reverberates throughout the human entity in all its physical, mental, psychic, and spiritual aspects.

The sounds of these primordial, revelatory words of God emanate a feeling of proximity to the Divine Presence, and once spoken aloud or whispered inwardly they reverberate deeply within the cave of the heart and take root in the ground of the soul. Muslims who read the sacred verses over and over on a daily basis can experience within their minds and hearts a pulsating ripple of energy caused by the sacred auditory rhythms embedded within the letters and words of the text itself. The words of the Qur'an create an inner harmony that in the eloquent words of Seyyed Hossein Nasr produce "an echo in the minds and world of the men who read it, and returns them to a state in which they participate in its paradisal joy and beauty. Herein lies its alchemical effect."[75]

The Qur'an cannot be translated without seriously diminishing the spiritual presence that emanates from its sacred letters and sounds. There is a majestic projection of sound that is primordial, central, and eternal; primordial in that the sound and meaning evoke within the heart of the reciter feelings for the mythic dimension of primal origins; central because it brings the Muslims immediately back from the periphery of their earthly existence to the very center of their being; eternal because it lifts the reciter out of the march of a lateral, advancing time to the eternal now, the sacred present, that transcends and extinguishes time with its window into eternity.

There is also the perennial question of the language of a text that fundamentally cannot be translated because of its otherworldly texture and its

---

[75] *Ibid.*, p. 77.

inherent sublimity. Non-Muslims justifiably wonder what it is about the text that renders it untranslatable any more than another text. The answer is first and foremost that the text is the word of God; to alter the text in any way, especially through the expression and form of another language is to withdraw the Presence by taking away the very words that make the text sacred, noble, and holy. In both its meaning and form, the text is sacred in character: the written word as calligraphy, the sounds of the recited text as chanted psalmody, the physical presence of the book, and the message itself are sacred and liturgically important as a vehicle of blessing and grace. The very form of the book is treated with reverence by all Muslims in their homes. It cannot be touched unless a person is in a state of ritual cleanliness. When Muslims sit down to read and recite the Qur'an, they go through the ritual washing just as they do in preparation for the ritual prayer. Also, the book itself holds a special place within the household, set aside in an elevated place and never below the level of other books within a room.

Revelation brings a doctrine that conveys a meaning, a morality that establishes a purpose, and spiritual sensibilities that lead to a virtuous life. The depth and profundity of this doctrine containing the Truth of the One Reality, given its supreme luminescence and spiritual consequences for humanity, cannot be fully understood and internalized without the descent of a supernatural communication whose divinely inspired text neutralizes all mystery and whose theurgic radiation suffuses the mind, heart, and soul with its radiance (*al-nur*) and blessing (*al-baraka*).

The Qur'an has variously been described as a recitation (*al-qur'an*), a discernment (*al-furqan*), the mother of all books (*umm al-kitab*), the essential guidance (*al-huda*), the perennial wisdom (*hikmah*), and the ultimate remembrance (*dhikr*). Its very name "recitation" (*Qur'an*) recalls the manner in which it was delivered, the way it was received and remembered, and the means with which it is treasured and preserved, for the Qur'an is a reading and a recitation first and foremost, a compilation of verses and the word of God on the tongues of the faithful. As a criterion and discernment, it establishes once and for all time the true nature of the Real as opposed to the unreal, the light of truth as opposed to the darkness of falsehood and ignorance. The Qur'anic guidance shapes all personal and ethical conduct and gives definition to the actions of the believers who would not always know otherwise how to behave given the sometimes conflicting nature of their hidden desires; while its wisdom becomes an internalized knowledge within the heart and ultimately manifests within the world community as virtuous behavior.

As Divine Remembrance, however, the Qur'an contains the ultimate sacred psychology, leading the human soul[76] back from the periphery to the Center and establishing the doctrinal knowledge and the sacred sentiments necessary for the soul's journey of return to the Divine Fold. The Qur'an is identified as the *dhikr Allah* which is also one of the names of the Prophet and recalls the Qur'anic verse: "Nothing is greater than the remembrance of God" (29:45). Its vital presence, with all the crystalline quality of a sparkling diamond within the mind, focuses the human consciousness on "the one thing needful" and recreates the ambiance of primordial beatitude that constituted the consciousness of Adam before the fall from Paradise.

The interaction of human consciousness and Divine Remembrance is subtle and intricate. The very *raison d'être* of human consciousness is to realize within the individual self the knowledge of the Universal Self. Remembrance, then, whether it be through the Profession of Faith (the *shahadah*), through the repetition of the Name of God, through the ceremony of prayer, or through the recitation of the holy Qur'an, activates the human consciousness with the living presence of the Divinity. To enjoy a consciousness of the individual self without a connection to the Supreme Self constitutes a desire to roam on the periphery rather than to be at the center, to live in an evanescent rather than in a transcending world, and to recognize a fundamental mystery at the heart of existence, while refusing to explore its true origin and source.

The Qur'an, as Divine Discourse and Revelatory Word, remains the ultimate source of all essential knowledge, the well-spring of all morality and ethics, and the means of spiritual worship that permits the faithful to transcend their limitations and approach the true knowledge of the Reality as Truth and as Presence. Like the earth with its arctic and tropic zones, its seacoasts and mountain ranges, its plains and valleys, its deserts and woodlands, the Qur'an has a broad range of topical representation, including poetic heights and legalistic depths, dogmatic theology as well as mystic aphorisms, lists and litanies, prayers of supplication and praise. Every letter,

---

[76] "The more traditional mentality believed in the concept of the soul as the ultimate locus of man's individuality; the soul was the ground upon which people invest in a principle that is not rooted exclusively within themselves but that transcends their physical limitations. Behind the intuition of higher truth, behind all the emotive experience that colors and shapes man's inner world, behind all the sacred sentiments and virtues that can result from the rich texture of a human life, behind the free will and the wisdom that adds to the qualitative uniqueness of the human being, behind all the seeing and hearing of our senses and deeper than the deepest thought lies the human soul as the source of the individual being" (John Herlihy, *Borderlands of the Spirit: Reflections on a Sacred Science of Mind* [Bloomington, IN: World Wisdom, 2005], p. 118).

word, and verse is packed with layers of symbolic meaning that reach the human mind according to the receptiveness of the recipient.

The Book can be summarized in three distinct ways. Firstly, it represents a doctrine containing the metaphysical knowledge of God and science of reality concerning the ultimate nature of things. Secondly, it presents an ethical code of conduct as the basis of an Islamic law (*shari'ah*). After all, one of the purposes of revelation is to ground the morality of humanity within the precinct of a sacred knowledge that has the power to deliver a truth that is absolute and that finds its source and efficacy beyond the whims of the human mentality. As such, it provides an objective, moral foundation that transcends the subjectivity of humanity and finds its root in the authority and judgment of a Supreme Being. Thirdly, the Word of God narrates a history that transcends linear time by appealing to the sensitivities of the human soul, a sacred history of the soul that casts in cameo the great personages of Biblical and Qur'anic history, from messengers and prophets to pharaohs, conquerors, and kings. In recounting the strengths and limitations of the great figures of sacred history, the Qur'an teaches mankind a wide range of moral and spiritual principles. These sacred narratives appeal directly to the human soul wherein the battle ultimately is fought between the forces of good and evil. To become aware of the currents of a sacred history is to become aware of the history of one's own soul, for humankind was made from "one soul" and enjoys a unique human nature that is as changeless as it is enduring.

The descent of the knowledge of God in the form of a metaphysical doctrine, a moral law, and a sacred chronicle of the soul remains the one true source we still have available for an absolute expression of an Absolute Truth. The ascent of humanity through spiritual aspiration and experience based on the knowledge of God remains the one true means we still have available to transcend our limitations and perfect ourselves. Knowledge descends as sacred speech because Allah is the Living, the Knowing, and the Omniscient. Consequently, humans can make their journey of ascent and return to God because these divine attributes are reflected within their theomorphic nature as Life, Knowledge, and the power implicit in Free Will.

We can live as wise beings (*Homo sapiens*) who have full access to the essential knowledge, who choose what we wish to believe, and who must put our beliefs into practice through the force of an inner power that actualizes this knowledge. Finally, through the worship implicit in the Qur'anic recitation, the Muslims have the means to actualize the encounter of the human with the Divine and thereby to counterbalance the sacred encounter of the Divine with the human made possible through the descent of the revelation.

## Chapter Eighteen

## Key Symbols of the Qur'an

---

The earth is full of signs evidencing the work of Allah.
They are perceived by those who are certain of the truth (51: 20)

The Archangel Gabriel delivered the 6234 verses of the Qur'an to the Prophet Muhammad (PBUH) during a time span of 23 years. Young Muslims begin the learning process of coming to terms with the intricacies of reading and chanting Qur'anic Arabic when they reach the age of reason, and the Muslim majority spend an entire lifetime of ritual and heart-felt recitation of the Holy Book as a means of worship and as a way of informing themselves about the essential knowledge of God as guidance in the way they conduct their lives. It is a never-ending task to unfold the broad tapestry of the Qur'an whose rich texture of nuance and meaning overlays the human soul with a willingness to address and deal with whatever circumstance destiny may require of them in life. The revelation meets individual Muslims at their own level of perception and within their own ability to understand the verses in such a way that they can absorb the meaning into their lives as relevant truths, whatever their background, mentality and stage of development.

Scholarly translations have been attempted down through the centuries until modern times in order to shed light on its verses in a wide variety of foreign languages, and extensive commentaries (*tafasir*) have been written by erudite sheikhs that enlighten the faithful of many generations through a wide variety of interpretations and schools of thought to shed light across a broad spectrum of interpretations on what the verses of the Qur'an mean on multiple levels. The commentaries, as a documented record of Qur'anic interpretation, have well served succeeding generations in coming to terms with the meaning and significance of the individual verses. As such, it is not possible or perhaps necessary within the confines of this short treatise to delve in depth into the actual meaning of the Qur'an, a daunting endeavor that most Muslims accept as a life-long challenge as part of their pursuit of a life of spirituality in this world.

For our purposes in this work, it may be useful and informative to give the reader "a taste" of the intellectual and spiritual insights the book contains by highlighting certain key Qur'anic words, phrases, and symbolic images that contain layers of meaning that well serve to open and satisfy an inquiring mind, especially those who may be unfamiliar with the broad scope and intent of the holy book. Many people have often asked me about the Qur'an and expressed an interest in having a copy in translation; but I could always sense a certain reluctance and feeling of being overwhelmed with the daunting prospect of attempting to come to terms with the Qur'an on their own. With its selective use of key terminology, the Qur'an has the power to revitalize the symbolist spirit of the traditional person within the mind of modern readers as a means of integrating the phenomena within nature with an intuitive understanding of the higher realities that the natural order reflects.

Perhaps it is time to refresh our memories and recall the latent forces of perception that the human mind has the capacity to envision and contain. It is time once again to read the messages that abound within the created universe and that are highlighted in verses of the Qur'an as signs and symbols of remembers of "the one thing needful". It is time to remember that we still have the capacity to observe and understand the inner messages that are conveyed to us through the sacred symbols and substances within the natural order. It is time once again to open our eyes, to release the forces of our inner psyche, to activate the broad reasoning powers of the human mind, and to draw upon our spiritual intuitions and sympathies in order to understand the sacred knowledge that lies within the symbolic forms that exist within the creation.

The time has come to liberate the well of sacred emotions within the heart that has traditionally been considered the "seat" of the intelligence as well as the source of all sacred sentiment in Islam. It is time to make ready the ground of the soul, in order to raise our consciousness to higher levels of the spirit and activate a living awareness of universal truth that hovers in the background of our lives like the mystery of the night hovers behind the clarity of the day. We need to realize once again and remember that the truth, the reality and the spirit that we seek clothes itself within our world as manifested forms. Symbols help us understand and eloquently express something meaningful about the hidden reality that hovers below the surface of the manifested world like a promise awaiting fulfillment, leading us into a virgin world as remote as a star and as thrilling as snow crystals falling from the night sky.

Because of the generosity and spirit of the Qur'an that is available to Muslims today in its original and unaltered form, the Muslim mentality[77] still remains steeped in awareness of the value and significance of traditional symbols, and had still preserved something of the symbolist spirit that traditional peoples instinctively exhibited. One reason for this lies in the fact that the Qur'an, taken in its totality, is the most direct symbol of the spiritual world, both in its totality and in its multiple fragments of letters, words and sounds, all of which constitute a sacred "science" of symbolism. In addition to its implicit symbolic value, the Qur'an repeatedly entreats the faithful to observe the signs (*ayat*) that are everywhere visible. "It is He Who has sent among the unlettered a messenger from among themselves, to rehearse to them His Signs, to sanctify them, and to instruct them in Scripture and Wisdom." (62: 2)

Muslims have traditionally been deeply interested in the relationship between the outward manifestation of the world through Mother Nature, the primal origin of the human being as a creation from nothing (*ex nihilo*), and the existence of a Divine Being as the Creator and Sustainer of the universe and everything therein. For Muslims, everything serves in their own way as a sign and symbol of God. Nature is the macrocosmic revelation awaiting discovery and humans are the microcosmic revelation awaiting fulfillment through the life process. On both levels of manifestation, a Muslim has the opportunity of acquiring knowledge of God and of the true nature of Reality if he/she recognizes the signs that are available both on the horizon, within the natural order and above all within themselves. Everything is significant and has

---

[77] We refer to the Muslim mentality as we might refer to the traditional or the modern mentality. Certain characteristics and features of mind stand out within the majority of the Islamic community, the collective Islamic *ummah*, traits such as hospitality, charity, and a kind of resigned detachment that accompanies belief in a God of absolute power whose Mercy, according to a well known Holy Tradition, precedes His Wrath. Certainly the universal acceptance of the symbolic nature of the universe within the Islamic community also aptly characterizes the Muslim mind as symbolist.

meaning within the creation; nothing is insignificant and subject only to chance occurrence as is believed by many people in today's modern world. "Everything We have created and prescribed for it its measure, its character and destiny." (54: 49) "No creature creeps on earth but Allah provides for it its sustenance. He knows its purpose and destiny. For it is He Who prescribed them in His eternal order." (11: 6)

As microcosmic symbol of a higher reality, nearly every aspect of the human body serves as a specific symbol[78] with a particular mandate that ultimately leads back to the Divinity. For example, the heart (*qalb*) and breast (*sadr*) of humanity are mentioned repeatedly in the Qur'an as symbols of spiritual intelligence and emotion. The *sadr*, the inner chest and heart enclosure, has traditional been associated with the act of surrender to the Divinity which in Islam is the initiation into the religion and the very meaning of the word *islam*. "Is one whose breast [*sadr*] is open to Islam, so that he has received enlightenment from Allah [no better than one hard-hearted]?" (39: 22) On a literal level, the *sadr* of humanity is the encasement of the lungs and heart cavity, but on a figurative level it suggests the expansion and the contraction, the aspiration and the expiration, indeed the very breathing of the human spirit. The human breast as the sacred chamber of expansion and contraction recalls the names of God, the Expander (*al-Basit*) and the Contractor (*al-Qabidh*) of His inner spirit, highlighted in the Qur'an as essential qualities of the Divinity.

The human heart (*qalb*), on the other hand, has traditionally been considered the "seat" of the intelligence[79] and the repository of human faith (*imam*) in Islam. "Allah has endeared faith to you, and has made it beautiful in your hearts, and he has made hateful to you unbelief, wickedness and rebellion." (49: 7) The heart combines the knowledge of God together with the spiritual emotions, both of which interact in order to create the longing for the Divinity and the certitude that accompanies a person's faith. Within the inner chamber of the heart lies the *fu'ad*, or inner heart, and this is activated for high ranking prophets and saints (*awliya*) who are able to apprehend and experience the intuitive knowledge of spiritual truth directly. This is the seat of the *ma'rifa*, or the intuitive, gnostic knowledge that the Holy Prophet

---

[78] "Have We not created for men their eyes, their tongues and lips? Have we not granted them their senses of orientation?" (90: 8-10)

[79] This may come as a surprise to the modern mentality that associates all intelligence with the cerebral mind. Intelligence in the traditional view is not mind but rather an interaction of mind, intellect, and heart and is firstly and directly associated with the knowledge of God. To be intelligent is to know God; to be wise is to act upon that knowledge.

Muhammad (PBUH) received from Allah (53:11) and another person, unidentified in the Qur'an[80] but referred to only as one of Our servants, "on whom We had bestowed mercy from ourselves and whom We had taught knowledge from Our own presence." (18: 65)

The human heart establishes its signature and utters its truest word by being the symbol of spiritual center of the human being and the vertical axis upon which all knowledge and human affection ascend heavenward. As the symbolic image of the true human center, the physical heart lends its physiological meaning to the totality of the person, but the force of its symbolic presence draws upon far deeper reserves within the vital essence of the human being. As such, the heart is the center not only of the bodily individuality, but also the center of the integral individuality, or the human being known and realized on both physical and spiritual modes of expression. When a person is referred to as having "all heart", he or she expresses their inmost knowledge and feelings in such a way that the external world can witness the full range of their intelligence and heart sensibility, like sunlight over meadows, like night over snow.

Ironically in today's world, the heart that we now identify and remember as the seat of affection and sentimentality is actually the heart that forgets, while the other heart, the forgotten one, is actually the heart that remembers. The "heart that forgets" implies the absence of the knowledge and light that integrates the independent fragments of humanity into a synthesis of the Whole that is based on the unity and oneness of the Reality and the Supreme Identity projected into the universe by the Divinity. The other heart, "the heart that remembers", implies the presence of the knowledge and light that illuminates the totality of human beings with the remembrance of their forgotten origins in the primordial garden, when they walked with God, spoke with God, and knew God directly with a heart knowledge that experienced the truth directly without any barriers or veils.

The human heart is not the only organ mentioned in the Qur'an that has symbolic value and properties that extend far beyond its physical image and functions within the corporeal system. The eyes, nose, ears, mouth and hands are all instruments of the senses as well as symbolic images that lead to an inward knowledge. Space and thematic constraints do not permit us to

---

[80] The traditions suggest that this refers to Khidr, who knowledge was "special" since it came directly from the Presence. Khidr is a mysterious being who was sought out because allegedly he had the secrets for the paradoxes of life which ordinary people do not understand. St. Paul writes about him in one of his epistles to the Hebrews (v. 6-10; vii. 1-10): "He was without father, without mother, without descent, having neither beginning of days nor end of life."

elaborate too extensively concerning specific symbols and their related meanings. The Qur'an itself stands as the eternal reference to the sights, sounds, images and symbols that reflect the higher realities. It is enough perhaps to make mention of the fact that virtually every major aspect of the human body, from the fingertips to the feet, is mentioned symbolically in the Qur'an in order to suggest a meaning or a specific emotion relating to the content of the symbol. The jugular vein is well remembered because of its proximity to the life force and more importantly because the Divine Being has said: "We are nearer to him than (his) jugular vein." (50: 16) The heart itself is referred to innumerable times in multiple verses and different contexts: hearts are open (39: 22), locked (47: 24), and sealed (30: 59). Hearts sigh and express regret (3: 156); others are filled with disgust and horror (39: 45). They whisper (114: 5) and they repent (64: 4). Some hearts are deceased (47: 29; 2: 10), other hearts conceal what they know (40: 19). Some unfortunate hearts rise up into the throat (40: 18). Finally, hearts are referred to as strengthened in faith (58: 22), devoted (50: 33), and ultimately pure[81] (*salim*) (37: 84). Ultimately, the heart "finds satisfaction in the remembrance of Allah, for without doubt in the remembrance of Allah do hearts find satisfaction." (13: 28)

The Hand of God is a universal symbol of power, creativity, skill, and sensitivity. The human hand expresses all these attributes by way of inference; it does not mean on some literal level that God has a hand. Concerning the Divinity, the Qur'an tells us that "In Your Hand is all goodness" (3: 26) and "the Hand of Allah is over their hands." (48: 10) In addition, hands are the symbol for deeds accomplished. (78: 40) While bounty is in the hand (3: 73), hands are also used to kill (5: 28), destroy (59: 2) and bring misfortune (42: 30). Ultimately, human hands have earned what they have done (30: 41) and will send forth (30: 36) in front of them that which they have accomplished in this life in order to be weighed on the scales of justice.

Two symbolic images that feature highly in the Qur'an and are embedded within the mind, heart, soul and thus the mentality of every Muslim are the image of the home and the image of the way. The image of the home has been immortalized in the well known expression, the *dar-as-salaam*, the home of peace. The concept of home has traditionally been associated with both origins and final ends and always summons feelings of safety, security, familiarity, comfort and secludedness from the contingencies of the outside world. In addition to the *dar as salaam*, or the home of peace, the Qur'an also

---

[81] Most notably, Abraham is identified as having a heart that was pure (*salim*) and unaffected by the diseases that afflict others. Abraham is called *Haneef*, the True One (2: 135).

makes reference to the home in the hereafter (28: 77). This is none other than the final abode and it is described as the home that will endure (35: 35), the eternal home (41: 28) and the permanent home (40: 39). Finally, there is also the home of misery (40: 52), and those who dwell there will not be able to escape, since it is the home of utter desolation and damnation.

The symbol of the way is none other than the familiar straight path (*sirat al-mustaqim*) mentioned in the opening *surah* of the Qur'an and repeated by the Muslims during the recitation of the prayers. "And unto Allah leads straight the Way, but there are ways that turn aside." (16: 9) The Qur'an mentions a number of different roads, paths and by-ways in order to give emphasis to the concept of the journey of return that the faithful are embarked upon during the course of their lives, a journey that will ultimately bring them to their origins and source in union with the Divinity. Similarly, we should not forget to mention the *sirat* or "bridge" spanning across the flames of hell that, according to tradition, everyone must cross before entering the Paradise. During the prayer ritual, the Muslims entreat the Divinity to guide them on the straight path, and the Qur'an itself has come down as the truth "that guides to the path of the Exalted (in might), Worthy of all praise." (34: 6) There are two highways that people have been shown on the earth; one is the steep and difficult path of virtue, and the other is the easy path of vice and the rejection of God, "but he hath made no haste on the path that is steep." (90: 10) In addition, the Muslims are encouraged to follow the path of righteousness. (40: 10) The earth is described as a carpet with roads (43: 10) through which the faithful may find guidance. The Qur'an advises the faithful to follow the middle course (35: 32), even though humanity is inclined "to follow divergent paths." (72: 11) Some people take the path that is identified as the *sabeil Allah* (61:4) or the causeway of Allah (His way and His cause combined into a single image); others take the way to the fire (*sirat al-jaheem*) (37: 23), a human choice with grave and lasting consequences.

In terms of symbolic imagery, perhaps we are most familiar with the images of eschatology catalogued with graphic clarity in the Qur'an. These images include the scales, which will be set up so that "not a soul will be dealt with unjustly in the least, even if there be (no more than) the height of a mustard seed," (21: 47) the earthly balance which is universally understood as a symbol of justice and equilibrium. The bridge suggests the dangerously narrow passage that leads over the fire into the sublimity of the Paradise. The Qur'an refers indirectly to this bridge in *surah* 19, verse 71, when it states "not one of you but will pass over it," in referring to those who are "most worthy of being burned" in the fire. Then there is the familiar eschatological instrumentalia most directly represented by the searing fire that burns but does not consume, the boiling oil, the revolting drinks and the putrid smells that will assail the damned are well known and should be understood not in their literal sense, but in the fundamental spiritual reality behind the symbol that suggests a just recompense for one's evil actions. The graphic images speak directly to us from our own experience. We know them for what they are and they cast no doubt as to their implications and consequences.

Certain individuals and objects are associated with the prophets and other named individuals in the Qur'an who serve as identifying symbols. Jacob's ladder immediately comes to mind within the Biblical context, but the Qur'an abounds with references to particular and specified objects or even members of family that Muslims immediate associate with any number of messengers and prophets. Adam of course is mentioned as the first man,[82] the one tested, the one fallen, yet he is referred to in the traditions as *safi Allah*, the pure one of God. Sacrifice is always associated with Abraham and the son of Abraham always calls to mind implicit and unwavering faith, in counterpoint to the father of Abraham (6: 76) who represents infidelity and faithlessness. Hagar, the wife of Abraham and the mother of Ismael, is well remembered for her stamina and endurance during in her frantic search for water between the Makkan hills of Safa and Marwa. The wife of Pharaoh,[83] (66: 11) represents the triumph of faith, humility and righteousness over faithlessness, arrogance and injustice. The wife of Zachary (*Zakariya*) represents a triumph of another kind, when he cried to his Lord: "How shall I have a son, seeing I am very old and my wife is barren? "Thus," was the answer, "Allah accomplishes what He wills." (3: 40) The wife of Zachary reminds us that nothing is impossible with the Divinity, the source of all justice and mercy; we are His instruments and vehicles; their son, the Prophet Yahya, proves this. The wife of Noah and the Wife of Lut are also specifically mentioned in the Qur'an as powerful human symbols of rejection and faithlessness. They are both identified with the wicked worlds Noah and Lut departed from and left behind as they followed their way of return to God.

Similarly, certain objects associated with the prophets have symbolic value. Muslims remember the white hand of Moses, shining as with a divine light. The Qur'an also speaks of the foot of Job (38: 42), the sandals of Moses (20:12), the strength of David (38: 17), who could make iron soft and pliable (34: 10), and his gift of music (38: 18), for David is the prophet wrote the Psalms

---

[82] Eve is not directly mentioned in the Qur'an by name.

[83] Traditionally known as Asiyah, she is considered one of the four perfect women, the other three being Mary, the mother of Jesus, Khadijah, the wife of the Holy Prophet, and Fatimah, his daughter. Asiyah is thought to be the same woman who saved the life of the infant Moses. (28: 9)

which are considered to be some of the most beautiful of the Biblical verses. The Qur'anic revelation reminds us of the wind and staff of Solomon (34:12) as well as the mirrored floors of his palace. Jacob is remembered for his patience: "patience is beautiful against that which you (Joseph's brothers) assert." (12: 18) Joseph himself is remembered for his shirt, firstly because it was smeared by his brothers with false blood, secondly because his shirt ripped from behind proving his innocence against the advances of the noblewoman of the Pharaonic court, and thirdly because his scented shirt signaled for his father Jacob the presence of his beloved son Joseph. Zakariya is remembered for his silence as a symbol of patience,[84] Yahya is remembered for the Book that he held fast to.[85] Jesus serves humanity as the prophetic incarnation of the word (4:171) and he was a sign (43: 61) for the people, both then and now.

Traditional symbols have the power of "remembrance" embedded within the sacred form of the human body even, symbols that can trigger within the mind of humanity a sacred memory of the Divinity and spiritual experience of the highest order. The human body itself participates in the language of symbols. There is not a limb or major organ that doesn't in some way convey a meaning and make an impression for a specific spiritual purpose. For example, the sense of taste features highly in the Qur'anic terminology.[86] Humanity will eventually "taste" a broad range of experiences that vary from sublime rewards to loathsome punishments. It is repeatedly mentioned in the Qur'an that the believers will "taste" the blessing and mercy of the Divinity. (30: 46) The unbelievers, on the other hand, shall taste "a boiling fluid, and a fluid dark, murky and intensely cold." (38: 57) Above all, believers and unbelievers alike will taste the fruits of their deeds, tasting in some cases humiliation (39: 26), eternal punishment (32: 14), and the corruption they have earned (30: 41). Ultimately, "every soul shall have a taste of death." (3: 185) Death comes to all living creatures as the ultimate experience of a finite life.

Human minds witness and have faith. Human wills surrender and act upon their beliefs. The human face is set steadily and with true piety in the direction of the pure religion. (10: 105) The five senses will all bear witness, including the eyes for what they see, the ears for what they hear, the mouth

---

[84] "He said: 'O my Lord? Give me a sign?' Thy sign shall be that thou shalt speak to no man for three days but with signals." (3: 41)

[85] (To his [Zakariya's] son came the command) "O Yahya! Take hold of the Book with power; and We gave him wisdom even as a youth. (19: 12)

[86] The Sufis, or Islamic mystics, have traditionally referred to the experience of *dhawq*, which literally means "taste" but has come in higher religious circles to mean the experience of the Divine through a taste of knowledge, an intuition, and thus an experience.

for what it says, and the skins for what they feel. (41: 20) Bellies will be filled with the fruit of a tree "that springs out of the bottom of the Hellfire, the shoots of its fruit-stalks are like the heads of devils." (37: 65) Yokes will be put on the necks of the unbelievers (34: 33) "up to their chins so that their heads are forced up (and they cannot see)." (36: 8)[87] The knee is the focus of kneeling and prostration (45: 28), while in the traditions the beard has been called the "light of God". In addition, there is a "sign" in the variety of colors [races] (30: 22) and in the multitude of languages (tongues). The image of the tongue is the universal symbol for language, the mother tongue being one's native and original language learned from one's mother. The Qur'an itself has been delivered in the "tongue" of the Arabs (44: 58). The twist of the tongue can become an instrument of slander (4: 46). The tongue of the prophets David and Jesus pronounced curses on those who had disobeyed and persisted in committing excesses among the children of Israel (5: 78).

Similarly, the revelation refers to the hypocrites as those who say with their lips what was not in their hearts" (3: 167), and those of the unbelievers who say "We believe" with their lips but whose hearts have no faith (5: 41). The mouth can be the instrument of enmity and evil. In speaking of those who corrupt others, the revelation says: "They desire only your ruin: rank hatred has already appeared from their mouths: What their hearts conceal is far worse." (3: 118) Humanity is actually powerless in the shadow of the Divinity and this is no more fittingly symbolized than through the human forelock, which is as it were the crown of man's beauty, which Allah has firmly in his grasp (11: 56) like a trainer with his horse. Sinners, who are well known by their "marks", will be "seized by their forelocks and their feet and dragged into hell." (55: 41) The skins of those in the hellfire will roast and as often as their skins are roasted through, We shall change them for fresh skins that they may "taste the penalty." (4: 56)

On the other hand, "the skins of those who fear their Lord tremble thereat; then their skins and their hearts do soften to the celebration of Allah's praises." (39: 23) Stomachs will be "filled with the fruit of the Tree of Zaqqum", which is identified in the Qur'an (17: 60) as a cursed tree; while "the bowels of the unbelievers will be cut into pieces by a disgusting drink of boiling water." (47: 15) "Fingers are thrust into ears by those who want to block out the knowledge of the true reality" (71: 7) or they will "bite off the very tips of their fingers in their rage." (3: 119) Feet are mentioned many times through the revelation, for they are traditionally the symbol of firmness, stability, and

---

[87] The wife of Abu Lahab will have a twisted rope of palm leaf fiber around her neck (111: 5).

deep-rootedness, all aspects that are usually associated with a sincere faith and a strong determination. Feet are actually referred to as firmly planted (47: 7) for those who follow the way (sabeil) of Allah, while the believers will only ask their Lord to forgive them their transgressions and establish their feet firmly on the ground. (3: 147) Finally, in a symbolic picture of the agony of death, the soul will reach to the collarbone (in its exit) (75: 26) as it takes its reluctant leave from the body.

♠ ♠ ♠

In addition to the anthropomorphic symbols related in the Qur'an, there is also a geometry of symbolization that is significant, meaningful and immediately recognizable. The dot, the diacritical point under the Arabic letter *ba*, is conducive to visualizing both summary and center. It is the primordial and absolute point, source and final end, first drop of the Cosmic Pen and end point of the cosmic narrative. It summarizes both the microscopic and macrocosmic realms with a center and cosmic core, heart, kernel and ultimately the ever mysterious essence. The straight line emerges out of the primordial point, commencing all movement, direction and destination. The straight line is none other than the straight path of scripture, the most direct avenue between two points. The line that is crooked moves off the mark and represents in a single image all that is errant and devious. The inner line of every individual reflects purpose and intent; to follow the inner line is to remember the Divinity. The absolute point becomes the infinite circle, a circle that can remembers "the circle of evil" (48: 6) and the circle of knowledge, of which the Divinity encompasses all.

Then there are the elements and substances of nature, how they have developed and grown within certain optimal conditions that were conducive to their order and design. Is this pattern of development an accident, a chance happening, some form of necessity as many modern scientists would have us believe, or are we dealing once again with the miracle of the creation symbolized by the Hand of the Divinity. We only need to think of the great substances of nature such as diamonds, gold, silver and other natural elements, how beautiful and desirable they have always been. Think of the qualities of such precious stones as the transparent crystalinity of diamonds, the bold indigenous colors of emeralds, sapphires and rubies, the perfection of pearls, and the solidity and smoothness of marble. Even the varieties of wood that characterize certain trees make broad statements that extend far beyond the literal constitution of the tree. We are thinking here, for example, of the majesty of the oak, the dignity (and scent) of pine, the verticality of the poplar, and the ethereality of the willow.

All these objects within nature are natural and pure, without artifice or pretense. They express integrity and completeness, and they speak a message to all those who appreciate their natural beauty, a message of remote dignity far from the turmoil of our human world coming as they do from the depths of the earth and expressed most eloquently through the voice of silence. Precious stones in particular are known to have a unique resonance whose sympathetic vibration can have a soothing, even healing, effect on a person. Ivory has traditionally been used for carving exquisite statuettes and other handicrafts because of its unusual color and pliability; while marble has provided the source material for ancient monuments and world renown sculptures because of the implicit beauty of its configuration, its integrity of stone, and its simplicity. Wood has traditionally been associated with the sense of smell or taste. Pine is remembered for its exquisitely odoriferous scent evoking the mysterious lure of the woodland forest; frankincense is the solidified sap of a tree found especially in Oman; maple syrup is the drawn sap of the maple tree and let us not forget the valuable drippings of the rubber tree.

The sense of smell plays a major role among the faithful in Islamic countries as an aid in the remembrance of God when performing their religious duties. Oftentimes, the Muslims experience waves of an exquisite, otherworldly aroma emanating from the holy book as they sit and read the Qur'an after prayer, for recitation of the Qur'an in Islam is a form of worship in Islam in the same way that prayer is a form of worship. This is perhaps not that surprising when the traditional sources themselves suggest that the Qur'an in some mysterious manner contains the perfume of the soul of the person through whom it was revealed. Since the revelation literally passed through the mind and soul of the beloved Prophet, it is small wonder that the book itself may sometimes give off a beatific scent that remembers the Prophet who delivered the divine revelation to humanity. It is not uncommon for Muslims to sit down on their prayer carpets either before or after the early morning prayer to read and recite the Holy Qur'an.

The image of the heavens has always presented an immediate image of the cosmic universe and its seven heavens have always conjured up the idea of the multiple layers of reality that are manifested both within and beyond the human plane. The Divine Throne prevalent within the Christian and Islamic traditions and mentioned explicitly in the Qur'an[88] summons to mind the cosmic power, authority and dominion of the Divinity, as the renown Throne Verse (2: 255) in the Qur'an attests: "His throne extends over the heavens and

---

[88] At the base of the Throne (*al-arsh*) of Allah lies the sublime and seemingly comforting verse: "My mercy precedes my wrath."

the earth." The sun universally exhibits centrality and luminosity and is understood among the various traditions to represent the Universal Intellect, while the moon has traditionally been associated with the beauty of the beloved because of its pale, reflective light. The sacred Tree of Life is a concept that goes back to ancient times, rooted to the earth but reaching for the heavens. It features in both the Christian and Islamic traditions as the pivotal image of knowledge and life. Adam was tempted with the Tree of Eternal Life and because of his fatal choice, it became for him the Tree of Knowledge between Good and Evil.

One of the greatest symbols of all time, widely recognized because of its comprehensiveness and universality is the symbol of the veil which, as *maya* in Hinduism and as *al-hijab* in Islam, plays an important role in Middle-Eastern as well as in Oriental metaphysics. Human beings are veiled from the immediate and direct perception of the spiritual realities through a formal and manifested world that is in itself a veil, a veil that is increasingly opaque during this time period because the modern mentality exhibits a narrow understanding of reality as embodied within the framework of modern science, a science that refuses to recognize the transparency of the world and settles instead for the literal interpretation of the world as a reality unto itself.

The veil has been traditionally understood as being two-edged in its meaning and implication. On the one hand, the veil acts as a firm barrier to further insight in which no penetration into the true nature of things is possible, such as we find during these times. The veil of knowledge protects itself from the uninitiated, the unwilling, and the unfaithful. On the other hand, the veil also serves as an open door, such as we find in the science of symbolism and within the symbolist spirit, and becomes transparent so that a human intuition and an appreciation for the higher realities can become possible for the human mentality that is willing to life the veil. Thus, the veil of knowledge within the traditional framework both protects and reveals, and the veil of the world both hides and manifests the true nature of reality.[89] In Islam, one of the Holy Traditions states: "God has seventy thousand veils of light and darkness; were He to draw their curtain, then would the splendours of His Face

---

[89] "In a symbol, there is concealment and yet revelation: here therefore, by silence and by speech acting together, comes a double significance. . . . In the symbol proper, what we can call a symbol, there is ever, more or less distinctly and directly, some embodiment and revelation of the Infinite; the Infinite is made to blend itself with the Finite, to stand visible, and as it were, attainable there. By symbols, accordingly, is man guided and commanded, made happy, made wretched." Thomas Carlyle, a Scottish essayist of the 19th century, in his *Sator Resartus*, Book 3, chapter 3, as quoted in *The Columbia Dictionary of Quotations*, New York: Columbia University Press, 1995.

(*wajh*) surely consume everyone who apprehended Him with his sight." Also, the archangel Gabriel has said: "Between me and Him are seventy thousand veils of light." In the ancient Egyptian traditions, it is written that no one shall lift the veil of Isis. Isis is "all that has been, all that is and all that shall be;" and "no one hath ever lifted my veil."

By attempting to lift the veil that separates the known world from the unseen reality, faithful Muslims can empower themselves to become their own symbol and thus their own revelation. By reading the verses of the Qur'an and seeking to understand their inner message, they can reflect the qualities and attributes of their Creator Who is both Reality and Truth (*al-Haqq*). By witnessing the world of forms as symbols of a higher reality and as mirrors of a higher knowledge, modern individuals can once again see eternity in time, the absolute in the relative, spirit in form, and thus transform the temporal shapes of natural phenomena into the timeless symbols of reality.

The ultimate beauty of the Qur'an lies in its ability to lift the human soul beyond its station in life, to guide it along the way of return, and to offer direction and fulfillment to the rational mind as a complement to the aspiring soul. It is the journey of a book that begins in the cave of the human heart and finds its ultimate fulfillment in a heightened awareness of the universe of the one true Reality, where Light (*an-Nur*) illuminates the darkness of the night and the Spirit (*ar-Ruh*) fills the void of the universe with the knowledge of the one Reality, one Truth, one God.

Epilogue

# Challenge and Promise

---

In reviewing the concluding comments of the final chapter, some lingering thoughts continue to hover in the background ready to find their rightful place within these pages, like stray cats arching their backs to draw someone's attention, hoping to ingratiate themselves with a merciful master. Even in this modern age of secular philosophies, advanced science and new age technologies, the Muslims across the globe are still routinely drawn back to the captivating spirit of their holy book, its universal themes, its sound guidance, and its clarifying doctrines and articles of faith in spite of their human weaknesses and limitations, or perhaps because of them. Similarly, in digging deep within my own experience in attempting to write an intimate portrait of the Qur'an and having spent several years on this endeavor, I am reluctant to take my leave of the project without a few final words about a book that addresses individual readers as if its perfection and light has come down to earth for them alone. Without the book's comforting intonations, we are watching and waiting, listening in vain for sounds that will make us whole.

A faithful Muslim can never have enough of the Qur'an and its solemn verses are never very far from mind, unlike other books that you read from cover to cover and then give away to friends or store on your bookshelves to create a certain ambiance perhaps in your home surroundings. Finishing a Qur'anic recitation and closing the book is not an ending, but a beginning like a newly born star. The Qur'an is always there in some prominent place in the home or mosque waiting to be opened. When the recitation is finished, the book is closed and put away for safe-keeping, with the promise to return to its pages, today, tomorrow, whenever the memory stirs of ancient mysteries, whenever the desire arises for a taste of the otherworldly and the sacred, whenever life's challenges need to be placed in a context that makes sense and whenever life's miseries call for the comfort of its reassuring verses that all is not lost, that there is a faithful Friend who listens and gives guidance.

The call for the first of the five prayers that mark the key meridians of the day, *the Salat al-Fajr*, commences at first light before the coming of the dawn, the hour of awakening and wild imaginings. It is a world, an hour, a moment created for meditation and solitude when a person can feel the presence of their own soul. Worshippers often take the Holy Book in hand after the prayer ritual, open its pages, and begin to intone through rhythmic chanting the sacred verses in Arabic as a matter of habit, to call forth the presence of the Spirit, to re-establish one's center and sense of balance, unhinged during the nocturnal hours by the netherworld of sleep, and to call down from celestial ramparts the *sakinah* or holy peace we mentioned earlier that hides mysteriously behind the vibrations of sound that miraculously come together to form the verses of light.

A person sits in the presence of the mystery of the Unseen (*al-ghaib*) and recites the sacred verses in the original Arabic as it was delivered by the Archangel, an act of worship that, according to the Qur'an (17:78),[90] is witnessed by the angels. It is the time when night has fallen back into obscurity, the sun has begun to climb back out of its haystack to rejuvenate the earth with its luminescence and warmth, and the human mind lies receptive and willing to draw upon the spiritual energies and blessings that will guide it though the day. Candles sputter their dying flames within an inch of their wick's life and light illuminates the room; the sounds of the dying night sent forth their solemn echoes, sending hypnotic melodies that swell the silence of the mind with their plaintive call before moving across the rooftops into the sky. This is the Qur'an; sound and light from deep wells and open skies for those ready and willing to open the pages of the book.

The Religion of Islam, and the Holy Qur'an that forms the inspiration and

---

[90] "You shall observe the prayer at the *duluk* (the decline from the highest point) of the sun until the darkness of the night, and the Qur'an at dawn. (Reciting) the Qur'an at dawn is witnessed." (17:78)

source material of the religion, was always intended to be a beckoning invitation as well as a call to action. The challenge of the Qur'an lies in finally uncovering layer by layer, like a fresh onion waiting to be pealed, and word by word like an enigmatic hieroglyph that needs deciphering, the inner meaning of its verses and their significance in giving shape and coloration to the way we live our lives. This is what the Muslims endeavor to do whenever they take the Qur'an down from the shelf, kiss the cover and open its pages in sweet anticipation. The Muslims lay their foundation of faith on the principles of knowledge whose origin and source take root in a divine revelation that originates within the all-encompassing knowledge of a Supreme Being. This knowledge forms the parameters, the substance, indeed the very heart of an essential knowledge that is identified as the Truth and that represents the true nature of Reality. It is no wonder that the Muslims always sit in reverence and awe when they hold the calligraphic script of verses in their hands as they intone the Words of God.

As we have already mentioned, the revelation puts into perspective the knowledge of the Absolute, a Self-Disclosure from God to humanity that recalls the primordial revelation first delivered to Adam that has come down through time, as an eternal legacy of the Divinity, as individual revelations and scriptures that substantiate the various world religions with their profound, universal insights. Revelation views the physical world as the consequence of actions initiated by the Creator and it offers the study of Nature as a virtual science of signs and symbols that reflect the order, pattern and levels of higher reality that ultimately arrive at the Throne (al-arsh) of the Supreme Intelligence. It sets forth an understanding of human beings as thinking beings made in the image of the Divine Being, not literally of course but figuratively, symbolically, with a consciousness that reflects Truth and that connects humans with this higher order of Reality. Thus, the Truth has been made known to the human mentality in an absolute and unequivocal manner. In return, humans are at liberty and enjoy free will to accept, turn to and surrender their minds and hearts to this Supreme Intelligence and this Absolute Being. Human intelligence, with the support of the faculty of reason and the intuitions of the intellect, makes its own conclusions and lives out the consequences of its choice.

The promise of the Qur'an lies encoded within its letters and sounds of an ancient script, a revelation of divine origin, that knows no fear, that fills one's cup of inquiry with inspiration and insight, that unravels psychological knots of the psyche to become the "rope of Allah", that opens closed doors of the mind to enriching vistas of spiritual imagination where dreams are born and hope comes to rest as a permanent promise, and where redemption is not far behind. Because we are born with souls, we have everything to lose and possibly nothing to gain unless we open ourselves to the mysteries of revelation and the unraveling of our true selves, like a ball of yarn, through recitation of its verses. Our aspirations rise like autumn smoke from the burning leaves of what we accomplish in this world; but the soul's fullest expression and its ultimate fulfillment begin with a willingness to fall into the comforting embrace of the unknown and unseen, by heeding the knowledge and guidance from an otherworldly source such as the Qur'an, whose verses sparkle with the light of clear water as they slowly penetrate and then illuminate the shadowy caverns of the mind with their luminous intensity.

What does the human soul desire most; what does it reflect deep within the mind and heart as the fundamental human aspiration? What is humanity required to do in response to the plenitude of this divine offering of the revelation? The human soul will respond by natural inclination to the focus of its ultimate desire, namely an intimate and all-inclusive relationship with God Who according to the Qur'an is the one true Companion and Friend (al-Wali). The great themes of the Qur'an address the broad expanse of all human endeavor and enlighten humanity on all the mysteries of the human condition from the origin of the universe and of life itself, to the purpose of one's living and our ultimate destination after we slip through the trap-door of death and enter the other side of reality.

The profound doctrinal themes, the great ethical questions, the inspirational tales of the trials and suffering of the prophets, and the sacred sentiments to follow the straight path and strive for perfection all reflect the fundamental elements that constitute the human framework of spirituality which must take account of the knowledge (doctrine), the behavior (ethical morality) and the potential virtue (the sentiments) of humanity. The trials and insecurities of life are counterbalanced by the serenity and peace that is the promise of a person's *islam* (surrender). The uncertainty reflected in the perennial mystery of life is counterbalanced by the absolute quality and the certainty that is the lodestone of the Word of God. The imbalance and disequilibrium of the human soul is offset by the balance and equilibrium implicit in the knowledge of the one Reality. The forgetfulness of our true identity is compensated by the consciousness of the Greater Self. The gravity of the earthly environment and the heaviness of the mundane is offset by the ethereal quality of the mystic and the spiritual. The linear quality of the strictly horizontal perception is elevated by the incisive quality of the vertical perception. Finally, the endless diversity and multiplicity of "this world" are resolved by the unity of the Transcendent Center. Reading the verses is like passing through an enchanted mirror whose reverse side opens onto some mystical reality that knows no bounds.

In our quest for the essence of a truth that we can weave within the fabric of our being as a golden thread connecting us with the unity of the universe, it may come as a surprise for some people in today's world to learn that Truth speaks to humanity in one of our own human languages, in this case the consecrated language of Arabic. A sublime revelation has descended from Heaven setting forth the actual words of God that gather together all human experience into a single purpose, none other than the unity (*tawhid*) that the Qur'an has come to proclaim. With the challenge comes a harvest worthy to be gained, a promise waiting to be claimed by the aspiring soul.

These seed words of the Qur'an contain a knowledge, a blessing and a presence both in their physical representation as meaningful words and as supreme guidance for humanity: Knowledge because the universal mystery that underlies all of existence must offer a resolution to the enigma at the heart of the human condition, blessing because, especially in today's world, people need divine compassion to offset the intrinsic drag and weightiness of "this world", and presence because the human mind, heart and soul represent their own unique presence and find satisfaction and peace through an intimacy that is born through the intimate friendship of the Creator with His human creation. When planted in the ground of the human soul, these seed words of God take root and grow, inspiring the human entity in unexpected ways and leading toward a destiny that finds its fulfillment in living the open book of one's own being by reciting the revealed book of the Supreme Being.

## ACKNOWLEDGEMENTS

By asking many probing questions about the origin and true nature of the Quran, many people have contributed to the development of this book and provided me with the motivation to pursue its writing as an inside portrait of what the Qur'an means to Muslims as a source of inspiration for their day-to-day life of spirituality. Not the least among them is my brother-in-law who once asked me so many questions about the Qur'an that I finally decided that it was time for me to set down in words some of the answers to his earnest questions. I figured that if he wanted to know more about the holy book that shapes the lives of Muslims in the world, there would be others also interested who should have their curiosity satisfied with some heart-felt answers.

## BIOGRAPHICAL NOTES

JOHN HERLIHY was born into an Irish-American family in Boston, Massachusetts and educated at Boston University and Columbia University in New York City. He converted to Islam in 1974 when he was a lecturer in Academic Writing at a Middle Eastern university. In addition to writing for such traditional journals as *Sacred Web* and *Sophia*, he has written a number of original works, including *Borderlands of the Spirit* and *Wisdom's Journey*, published by World Wisdom Books. His recent book, *Wisdom of the Senses*, has been published by Sophia Perennis in 2011. He currently works as a Visiting Academic at Qatar University and serves as a Director for Accrid International, an educational consultancy firm located in the United Arab Emirates.

www.ingramcontent.com/pod-product-compliance
Lightning Source LLC
Chambersburg PA
CBHW031255090426
42742CB00007B/469